SOUL, BODY, AND SURVIVAL

Soul, Body, and Survival

Essays on the Metaphysics of Human Persons

Edited by

KEVIN CORCORAN

CORNELL UNIVERSITY PRESS

Ithaca and London

First published 2001 by Cornell University Press
First printing, Cornell Paperbacks, 2001

Printed in the United States of America

Library of Congress Cataloging-in-Publication Data

Soul, body, and survival : essays on the metaphysics of human persons / edited by Kevin Corcoran.
p. cm.
Includes bibliographical references and index.
ISBN 978-0-8014-3829-5 (cloth : alk. paper)
ISBN 978-0-8014-8684-5 (pbk. : alk. paper)
1. Philosophical anthropology. 2. Man (Christian theology) 3. Christianity—Philosophy. 4. Metaphysics. I. Corcoran, Kevin, 1964–
BD450 .S635 2001
128—dc21 00-012503

Cornell University Press strives to use environmentally responsible suppliers and materials to the fullest extent possible in the publishing of its books. Such materials include vegetable-based, low-VOC inks and acid-free papers that are recycled, totally chlorine-free, or partly composed of nonwood fibers. For further information, visit our website at www.cornellpress.cornell.edu.

Cloth printing 10 9 8 7 6 5 4 3 2 1
Paperback printing 10 9 8 7 6 5 4 3 2

Contents

II Alternatives to Cartesian Dualism

III Does Life after Death Require Dualism?

Acknowledgments

I wish to thank the following individuals for their role in the production of this volume. First I owe a debt of thanks to Ted Warfield and Dean Zimmerman for their 1998 Notre Dame conference, "Varieties of Dualism." The contributions by Foster, Leftow, Kim, and O'Connor are all versions of papers presented at that conference. Warfield and Zimmerman were kind enough to steer these papers in my direction. I should also like to thank all the contributors for their interminable patience in the gestation and completion of this volume. Special thanks to Eric Olson, who suggested the title (after the volume labored under a very unattractive title for quite some time), and Roger Haydon of Cornell University Press for all his help in bringing this book to print. I also must thank the student assistant than which none greater is possible, Jamie Dillon, for her extraordinary help in preparing this volume for publication. Thanks are also due George Lanning for helping with graphics, Laura Pohler for help creating the index, and The Council for Christian Colleges and Universities for making it possible to enlist the help of several fine students in the production of this volume. Finally, I owe the greatest debt of thanks to three people who enrich my embodied existence more than words of mine can ever hope to express: my wife, Dorothy, and our two children, Shannon and Rowan.

KEVIN CORCORAN

Calvin College

SOUL, BODY, AND SURVIVAL

Introduction: Soul or Body?

Aristotle said that philosophy begins in wonder. Reflection on facts such as that you and I are *persons*—thinking, feeling, intending, relational, moral beings—is sufficient to inspire such wonder. We are, in fact, *human* persons—beings at the very least *contingently* bound up with biological bodies through which we sense and act on the world. But are we nothing more than extremely complex physical organisms, as many contemporary Anglo-analytic philosophers are inclined to think? Or are we instead *essentially* immaterial beings and so *only* contingently embodied, as Plato and Descartes seem to have thought? Are there alternatives to Cartesian dualism and reductionistic versions of physicalism? And what of the relationship between particular metaphysical views of persons and the belief in postmortem survival. Must some version or other of dualism be true if we human beings are to have any reasonable hope of surviving death? As the essays in this volume amply demonstrate, these questions are not the relics of some bygone era of scholastic speculation. Contemporary analytic philosophers are exploring these issues afresh with renewed rigor and offering provocative and sometimes even surprising answers.

Twenty years or so ago Daniel Dennett assessed the then current state of research into the nature of human beings and the philosophy of mind, offering us a glimpse into the shape of future research.[1] Dennett said then two things that are especially noteworthy. First, he summarily dismissed dualism as "not a serious view to contend with." And second, he forecast that the lines of research into the nature of mind would converge on some

[1] See his "Current Issues in the Philosophy of Mind," *APQ* 15 (1978): 249–61.

physicalistic version of functionalism, a consensus that would be only short lived and soon enough replaced by other physicalist doctrines.

Within two years, Saul Kripke published *Naming and Necessity.* In one of the lectures that make up that book, Kripke had this to say about research into philosophy of mind and the nature of human persons: "I regard the mind-body problem as wide open and extremely confusing."[2] Kripke accurately describes how things presently stand with respect to research into the metaphysics of persons. Not only are there now a myriad of physicalist alternatives to functionalism, with no particular one being the *terminus ad quem* of a convergence, but dualism is making a come back. In fact (perhaps to Dennett's surprise) there are today a *variety* of dualisms to choose from. And there are also many views on the person-body relation that attempt to steer a path between physicalism and dualism, views that attempt to incorporate the insights of each without giving into the excesses of either. In short, the so-called mind-body problem is presently "wide open" if not also "extremely confusing."

I. Cartesian Dualism

The first part of this volume contains a discussion of what is standardly called Cartesian dualism.[3] According to Cartesian dualism, properties can be divided into those that are mental (for example, being in pain, desiring an ice-cream cone, or believing some proposition) and those that are physical (for example, having a certain weight, shape, and mass). That is dualism about *properties.* Cartesian dualism, however, is a dualism about *substance* also. Cartesian dualism follows from accepting property dualism together with the claim that a single thing can have properties of only *one* sort. Hence, the Cartesian dualist claims that there are *two* fundamental kinds of substance with fundamentally distinct natures—unextended thinking substance (soul) and unthinking, extended substance (body). The appropriate bearers of mental properties are thus unextended, thinking substances (souls or minds), and the appropriate bearers of physical properties are unthinking, extended substances (bodies). Descartes

[2] See Kripke, *Naming and Necessity* (Oxford: Blackwell, 1980), 155 n. 77.

[3] Whether or not Descartes himself actually held the view I am about to describe, or how consistently he did, is not my concern here. The view I mean to pick out with the name 'Cartesian Dualism' is a view very frequently associated with Descartes, whether or not he actually held it. In point of fact, in the course of the sixth meditation, Descartes speaks both of the *real distinction* between soul (or mind) and body and also of his being *intermingled with* his body, soul and body forming a *single unit.* For more on this point, see Eric Olson's essay in this anthology.

famously argued that he is essentially a thinking thing. And if that is so, then Descartes is a soul.[4]

On the Cartesian dualist view, the relation between a soul and its body is analogous to the relation between a room and a thermostat. A rise of temperature in the room causes changes in the thermostat, whereas changes in the thermostat affect the room, raising or lowering its temperature. Souls and bodies are thus *causally* related. But also on the Cartesian dualist view, although it is true that I am now in some sense inextricably bound up with this particular body, my existence does not depend on my possessing either this or any other body; that is, I can exist without having any body at all.

John Foster opens the first part of this volume with "A Brief Defense of the Cartesian View." On the basis of certain introspective or subjective aspects of experience, Foster argues against psychophysical identity by arguing that *mentality* is both sui generis and fundamental. The truth of this claim alone, however, is not sufficient to secure *substance* dualism. So Foster goes further. Against the claim made by David Hume that mental items are ontologically autonomous, being had by no underlying substance, Foster provides reasons for believing that mental items are to be represented as elements in the biographies of mental *subjects,* entities that are nonphysical *substances* in that they lack both extension and material composition.

This final claim of Foster's, of course, qualifies his view as Cartesian. And it is precisely this claim, and Foster's move to it from the first two claims, that creates difficulties. The first difficulty is a familiar one and it concerns whether or not it is at all intelligible to hold that entities lacking both extension and material composition can *causally* interact with entities that are both extended and characterized by material components.

In "Lonely Souls," Jaegwon Kim takes up just this worry. He examines several arguments against Cartesian dualism which are based on the criticism that Cartesian dualism cannot plausibly explain just how two things so utterly different as unextended souls and extended bodies can causally interact. Kim suggests that one way to flesh out the insight of such criticisms is in terms of a pairing relation that is excluded by the essential *nonspatiality* of souls and the essential *spatiality* of bodies. Kim argues that given the essential natures of souls and bodies, and given the nature of causality, Cartesian dualism is unintelligible.

The other difficulty associated with Foster's argument concerns his move from (i) Mental items are neither identical with nor reducible to

[4] But see note 3.

physical items and (ii) Mental items require a subject, to (iii) This subject is unextended and simple. Isn't there room in conceptual space for a view according to which (iii) is false even if (i) and (ii) are true? Isn't this precisely what views that are monist with respect to substance but dualist with respect to properties claim?

In "Causality, Mind, and Free Will," Timothy O'Connor offers an interesting version of just such a view. O'Connor first provides a nonspatial framework for understanding causal interaction among objects, one which he believes, contra Kim, renders mind-body (and even mind-mind) causal interaction intelligible. He then elaborates a Cartesian-inspired view according to which mind and body constitute a unified natural *system,* and not independent objects that somehow continually find one another in the crowd of similar such objects. On O'Connor's "weak" dualistic view, token mental events are ontologically emergent and sui generis, distinct from any complex token physical state yet without there being any substance distinct from the body which is the direct bearer of those events. O'Connor shows further how this sort of "property or capacity-emergent dualism" is consistent with the kind of freedom of the will embraced by many more traditional Cartesian dualists.

According to property dualists like O'Connor there are some mental properties (states, events, activities, etc.) that are not identical with physical properties (states, events, activities, etc.). On such a view, although the ache of a headache is inextricably bound up with and caused by certain brain processes, it is not the very same thing as a brain process. This kind of view has been defended by many others. According to Charles Taliaferro, however, property dualism faces several formidable problems. First, it faces the problem of accounting for the emergence of conscious states from physical states and processes. As Colin McGinn has so aptly put it, just "how can technicolour phenomenology arise from soggy grey matter?" Second, insofar as property dualists hold that the mental and physical are not identical, there is a gap between the two that is very difficult to bridge. A further difficulty facing property dualism, according to Taliaferro, is the apparent contingency of the mind-body relation. It is very difficult to understand how it is that the mind and body are necessarily (i.e., causally) so related in the face of their apparent contingency. In his essay "Emergentism and Consciousness," Taliaferro seeks to account for the appeal of property dualism and to offer a reply to some forceful objections to substance dualism advanced by Colin McGinn. Taliaferro argues that substance dualism can be supported by a comprehensive metaphysic, theism, which has greater credibility than naturalists like McGinn usually recognize.

Some readers of Descartes are inclined to believe that he takes human beings to be neither immaterial souls nor material bodies, but rather objects having two parts: a soul-part and a body-part.[5] On such an interpretation, a human being *thinks* because her *soul* thinks, and a human being *weighs* thus and such because her *body* weighs thus and such. Eric Olson calls this view "compound dualism," and he argues in "A Compound of Two Substances" that compound dualism faces serious ontological problems that have nothing to do with the usual (causal) criticisms of dualism and that do not apply to construals of dualism according to which human persons *are* immaterial souls. After carefully surveying several of the ontological problems that accompany compound dualism, Olson argues that if you are going to be a dualist about persons you should adopt a "pure dualism," the view that persons like you and I are identical with immaterial souls.

In the final essay of this first part, Stewart Goetz considers modal arguments for substance dualism. Modal arguments for dualism take as their point of departure a claim of the form 'possibly, I exist but no bodies exist'. Underlying such arguments is the conviction that *conceivability* is a reliable guide to *possibility*. In "Modal Dualism: A Critique" Goetz claims that arguments for Cartesian dualism from the ability to conceive or imagine one's disembodiment are epistemically circular. They are circular, Goetz argues, because one must already be aware of one's distinctness from one's physical body (which is the conclusion of the argument) in order to be able to conceive of one's possible disembodiment. Goetz suggests that in order for one to be *genuinely* aware of being distinct from one's body, one must be aware of the properties of being simple and being complex, which are exemplified by oneself and one's physical body respectively.

Goetz, Kim, O'Connor, and Olson discuss some of the important challenges facing Cartesian-inspired arguments for dualism. As Foster and Taliaferro amply demonstrate, however, Cartesian dualism is not without the theoretical resources to mount a defense. Cartesian dualism is not, contrary to Dennett's judgment, a view that can be dismissed with a mere wave of the hand. Nevertheless, even those who approach the Cartesian view with the seriousness and respect it deserves often feel moved to propose alternatives. The essays that comprise the second part of this book discuss some of those alternatives. Although these views differ in important respects from Cartesian dualism, as we will see, they are still dualist in spirit.

[5] See Richard Swinburne, *The Evolution of the Soul* (Oxford: Oxford University Press, 1997), esp. 145–61.

II. Alternatives to Cartesian Dualism

Cartesian dualism holds, inter alia, that souls (or minds) are capable of disembodied existence. Why? According to Descartes, the fundamentally dissimilar natures of souls and bodies accounts for this. Descartes notes that nothing in the nature of soul requires for its existence the existence of a body. Nor is there anything in the nature of body that requires for its existence the existence of a soul or mind. To be a soul is to be simple, unextended, and thinking. To be a body is to be complex, unthinking, and extended. Thus Descartes reckoned it *possible* for each kind of substance to exist without the other.

Emergentism like that advanced by O'Connor is an alternative to Cartesian dualism that is not obviously compatible with Descartes's disembodiment thesis. But O'Connor's emergentism is only one species of a more a general view. The more general view makes two claims. First, all emergentists claim that consciousness and mentality do not appear until physical systems reach a sufficiently high level of configurational complexity. Just as *liquidity* and *solidity* are features that require matter to be suitably arranged before they are manifested, so too does the mental. According to emergentism in the philosophy of mind, mentality causally depends for its existence on a physical system of appropriate complexity. Emergentists want to claim more, however. The second claim made by all emergentists is that mentality is in some important sense *irreducible.* It is with respect to this irreducibility that mentality is unlike liquidity and solidity. For the latter are nothing *over and above* organizational / causal features of matter. But the mental is said by emergentists to be a *novel* feature of the world, something that in a very important sense *cannot be* reduced to the neurobiological processes that cause it. In what sense is consciousness and the mental irreducible? Well, one important sense in which the mental is said to be irreducible is simply the sense in which it is true to say that a complete neurobiological account of consciousness would fail to capture its first-person, subjective, qualitative features. Take a toothache, for example. Knowing all of the neurobiological facts about toothache is not to know the *ache* of toothache. The ache *hurts* and that *pain* would not get captured in a complete neurobiological account of toothache.

In "Persons as Emergent Substances" William Hasker argues for what might be called "ambitious emergent dualism." For according to Hasker, not only is it the case that novel *properties* or capacities emerge at certain complex levels of physical organization (à la O'Connor), but sometimes whole new *substances* emerge. Hasker contends that human souls or minds are just such emergent substances and that they stand to human brains as [say] an electromagnetic field stands to its generating source. A magnetic field, for example, is an emergent *individual*; it normally occupies an area larger than that of its generating magnet and enters into causal commerce with it. So too with human persons. Human persons emerge when biological systems reach the complex level of organization we normally associate with mature human brains in mature human bodies. One of the things that makes Hasker's emergent dualism especially ambitious is the suggestion that it is at least logically *possible* for human souls to outlive their source of generation and thus at least logically *possible* for a human person to survive into an afterlife.

There are still other alternatives to Cartesian dualism. For example, one could argue not for the emergent, soul-body dualism of Hasker, but for the soul-*matter* dualism of Aquinas. According to Aquinas, the body is not a *substance* with which the soul interacts, but rather it is the soul that makes some body a *human* body. Aquinas's view of human nature is notorious, however, for seemingly equivocating on the term "soul," using it sometimes to mean the "form" or kind of "state" a body is in and sometimes to mean a particular *thing* or individual. There is also the problem of understanding just how human beings can be material things on Aquinas's view when neither human souls nor human bodies (as apart from their souls) are. In "Souls Dipped in Dust" Brian Leftow offers a fascinating reading of Aquinas which attempts to resolve these puzzles. He also seeks to advance Aquinas's claim that souls are directly created by God against views like Hasker's which view souls as emerging directly from their bodies.

Each of the alternatives to Cartesian dualism so far discussed are still dualist in spirit. What about alternatives to dualism that are, on the contrary, *materialist* in spirit?

Let us suppose, for example, if only for the sake of discussion, that *all* persons are embodied as a matter of natural or metaphysical necessity. Would it follow that *human* persons are *identical with* physical organisms? In "Identity, Composition, and the Simplicity of the Self" E. J. Lowe answers no. He claims that human persons cannot be identified with their bodies because human persons and human bodies have different persistence conditions. There are also reasons of a more Cartesian flavor for denying that persons are bodies. For example, Lowe believes that there are compelling reasons for believing that persons are *simple* rather than composite substances. What is so surprising about Lowe's alternative to Cartesian dualism is just that he refuses to draw the conclusion that persons are unextended Cartesian egos, somehow mysteriously attached to their physical bodies. Instead, he argues for the provocative claim that the noncomposite or simple nature of persons is consistent with their possessing such physical characteristics as shape and weight. And, what is more surprising, Lowe argues that it is at least conceptually possible for persons to survive disembodiment.

A relatively new view to appear in the philosophical literature is one according to which human persons are wholly physical, nonsimple entities that are neither identical with nor reducible to physical organisms. The view's most eloquent defender, Lynne Baker, argues in "Materialism with a Human Face" that what makes an entity a human *person* is its possessing a "first-person perspective." What makes an entity a *human* person is its being "constituted by" a human organism. Baker argues that a thing *x* "constitutes" a thing *y* just in case *x* and *y* are co-located and stand in a genuine relation of unity. Persons and bodies, Baker argues, stand in the constitution relation. What is perhaps most interesting is that according to Baker's constitution view a person could start out as a *human* person and survive through changes which would render him or her *non*human. Although this last claim appears to make way for the possibility of a human person surviving the death of his or her body it also entails that human persons are not *essentially* human. Many will regard that as a high price to pay for the view. Moreover, the view seems to leave such a cleavage between human persons and the human bodies that "constitute" them that it warrants the charge of being a version of dualism after all. And this brings us to the final part of the volume.

III. Does Life after Death Require Dualism?

The question concerning the prospect of personal survival into an afterlife is a vexing one. Much about our lives leaves the unmistakable impression that we are physical beings, not in Baker's sense of being merely contingently constituted by a human body, but in the much more seemingly problematic sense that we are, if not strictly and literally human animals, then at least essentially constituted by the human bodies that do constitute us. From this perspective it might seem that the possibility of survival sinks or swims with dualism. For it might seem that if dualism (in all of its permutations) should turn out to be false, then human beings have no reasonable hope for survival. After all, experience seems to teach us that human bodies at some time or another cease to exist. So if I am a human body, and not simply contingently constituted by one, then one day *I* shall cease to exist. And if I will one day cease to exist, how is it possible that *I* shall live again?

In "How to Live Forever without Saving Your Soul" Trenton Merricks responds to worries about how a wholly and purely physical person, a human animal, who utterly ceased to exist could possibly come back into existence at a later date. After criticizing the two most familiar responses—the reassembly of material parts response and the personal identity grounded in psychological continuity response—Merricks develops his own bold response. Merricks believes that objections to the possibility of survival by way of resurrection rely either on the assumption that there are criteria of personal identity over time which rule out the possibility of temporal gaps in a person's existence or on the notion that temporal gaps of the sort required for resurrection are just impossible.

As to the latter, it has seemed self-evident to some philosophers that identity supposes continuous, *uninterrupted* existence. Gaps in the existence of a thing would entail that a thing can exist before it begins to exist, which is absurd. But Merricks makes a plea for metaphysical modesty when it comes to the fruits of modal intuition. He thus dismisses claims of the form "temporal gaps of the sort implied by resurrection are simply impossible" as the product of an overweening confidence in one's modal intuition. Modesty is more becoming.

As for the former assumption, building on his previous work on criteria of identity over time, Merricks claims that there are *no* criteria of personal identity over time. So all criterion-based worries and arguments against the possibility of resurrection dissipate. In the end Merricks offers reasons of his own for believing in the possibility of resurrection for wholly physical persons, frankly admitting that if resurrection occurs, it's going to take a miracle.

In my essay, "Physical Persons and Postmortem Survival without Temporal Gaps," I assume that human persons are wholly physical and that human bodies *cannot* enjoy temporally gappy existence. I then offer a view of postmortem survival that is consistent with *both* of these theses, a view that does not require one to deny the plausible assumption that if x is a physical object x is *essentially* a physical object. The view I offer does not come without a price tag, however. One who embraces it must be prepared to deny some commonsense intuitions about human beings (that they die and cease to exist, for example) and embrace some pretty radical claims (that the physical simples that compose human bodies have a capacity for fissioning, for example). Still, I contend that it is a logically coherent view and that it, or something very much like it, might even turn out to be true.

The problem of survival has been discussed so far only as regards its logical compatibility with certain controversial philosophical claims about the metaphysical nature of persons. But the notion of survival, especially when discussed in explicitly "resurrectionist" terms, has its home in the domain of religious and theological tradition. An important question is this: Despite the *logical* compatibility or incompatibility of survival and a metaphysics of materialism with respect to human persons, to what extent do the theological sources suggest a metaphysics of persons? Do the Hebrew and Christian Scriptures, for example, present a view of human persons that is more or less compatible with materialism or dualism? In "Biblical Anthropology and the Body-Soul Relation," John Cooper argues that the best reading of the Hebrew and Christian Scriptures yields the teaching that human persons continue to exist, probably consciously, between death and a final, general resurrection. Cooper believes that this doctrine entails that human persons are so constituted that they can exist temporarily without a body. And this, of course, would seem to entail that some variety of dualism is true.

In the final essay, "Physicalism and Resurrection," Stephen Davis provides an assessment of both the philosophical and theological discussion of the nature of human persons and the prospect of survival. He disagrees with the claim made by Merricks that a rejection of "criterialism" declaws a major class of objections to resurrection. Davis argues that criterion-based objections can be reformulated in *non*-criterion-based ways. If so, then according to Davis, Merricks's rejection of criterialism does not advance the debate about the possibility of resurrection at all.

Davis also argues against a claim I make in my essay. I argue that there are plausible reasons a theist might have for believing that it is *impossible* for there ever to be multiple candidates for identity with oneself in the afterlife. Davis disagrees. At the same time, however, he wants to maintain what seems to contradict this, namely, the plausible assertion that identity is a relation that each thing *necessarily* stands in to itself. Davis makes a valiant attempt to reconcile two seemingly contradictory claims, and it is left to the reader to judge whether or not Davis succeeds. In the end Davis contends that although he himself has given up physicalism about persons in favor of dualism, physicalism about persons and the doctrine of resurrection are compatible.

What are we? We are human beings, of course, embodied entities with aims, dreams, and aspirations, *persons*. But what are we essentially? Are human persons immaterial or material? And if they are material, then are they identical with their bodies? And what is the connection between our answer to the question, What are we? and the possibility that we survive the death of our bodies? The essays in this volume probe these questions.

Is there a convergence of answers on the horizon? It would appear not. For there are at present many answers and not all fall neatly into the two mutually exclusive views commonly discussed: Cartesian dualism and reductionistic physicalism. Nor is it obvious, despite what we may have been inclined to think, that physicalism with respect to human persons is incompatible with the doctrine of postmortem survival. If anything is clear after reading the essays in this volume, it is this: the mind-body problem remains wide open.

PART I

Cartesian Dualism

JOHN FOSTER

A Brief Defense of the Cartesian View

I. The Three Cartesian Claims

Insofar as it concerns the nature of the mind, substance dualism—or *Cartesian* dualism as I prefer to call it—makes three claims.[1]

The first claim is an endorsement of a dualist view of mentality. This involves a denial of any form of psychophysical identity (the identity of mental phenomena with physical phenomena). And it also involves denying that psychological facts can be in any way reduced to nonpsychological facts, or to facts whose canonical formulation is in exclusively nonpsychological terms. In short, this first claim amounts to the assertion that mentality is something sui generis and fundamental.

The second claim is concerned with the ontological structure of the mind. Let us speak of the various instances and episodes of mentality which form the concrete ingredients of the mind as 'mental items'. So such things as sensations, thoughts, emotions, and desires, as concrete mental phenomena, qualify as mental items in this sense. Then what the Cartesian claims is that, in the philosophically fundamental account, mental items are to be represented as elements in the biographies of mental subjects—that, for any occurrence of such an item, the fundamental situation is that of a subject's being in a certain psychological state or performing a certain psychological act or engaging in a certain psychological activity.

This is a slightly revised version of a paper which I delivered at a conference on dualism at the University of Notre Dame, March 1998.

[1] Cartesian dualism also makes claims about the nature of the physical world. But it is only the claims about the mind that concern me here.

This contrasts with the Humean view that mental items should be ultimately thought of as ontologically autonomous, and that if we recognize the existence of mental subjects at all, we should think of them as logically created by the unifying relations in which mental items stand to one another, either directly or via their causal attachment to bodies.

The third claim is concerned with the nature of the relevant mental subjects. In our ordinary system of thought, the entities which we primarily think of as the subjects of mentality are things with corporeal natures—things which, whatever else, have shape, size, and material composition. But, according to the Cartesian, the things which fundamentally qualify as subjects—the *basic* subjects as I shall call them—are wholly nonphysical: they are entities without extension or material composition, and even without location in physical space. In this way, the Cartesian extends his dualist view of mentality (Claim 1) to cover the whole mental realm—including, crucially, the category of mental subjects which he takes (under Claim 2) to be the primary ontological ingredient of that realm.

My aim, in this essay, is to present a case for the Cartesian view in all three aspects. Given the amount of ground to be covered—the three separate areas in which the view has to be vindicated—I shall not be able to set out this case with anything approaching the thoroughness it deserves. In effect—though with one significant exception—all I have space to do here is provide an outline of the arguments which I elaborated in detail in my book *The Immaterial Self*.[2] But, with this disclaimer, I hope that the discussion will at least serve to bring out some of the main issues in the relevant areas, and perhaps succeed in showing that, contrary to what is now normally assumed, the Cartesian view has to be taken seriously.

I shall begin by considering the issue of ontological structure, where the case for accepting the Cartesian position (Claim 2) is particularly clear and straightforward.

II. The Ontological Structure of the Mind

Certainly, from the standpoint of our initial intuitions, it is hard to see how, on this issue, we can make sense of anything other than the Cartesian view. Whatever points of controversy there may be about the nature of mentality and the nature of the mental subject, it seems plainly incoherent to suggest that mental items are capable of occurring without a

[2] London: Routledge, 1991. The exception I refer to occurs in section 4, where I distinguish two versions of the view that basic subjects have corporeal natures.

subject, or that the presence of the subject is not a fundamental aspect of the situation. The basic problem with such suggestions is not (as is sometimes thought) that, without a subject to 'own' them, there would be nothing to group mental items into minds. In fact, I think that there are ways (in terms of the overlap of successive total experiences in the same stream, and the potential of streams in the same mind to join if suitably extended) in which such grouping can be defined without reference to a subject.[3] But what makes the Humean approach prima facie unintelligible is that our very conception of the mental seems to be the conception of how things stand with a subject. Just as we cannot understand what it would be for there to be an instance of motion except in the form of something which moves, or an instance of death except in the form of something which dies, so likewise, on the face of it, we cannot understand what it would be for there to be concrete instances of pain, thought, or perception, except in the form of something which is *in* pain, or which *does* the thinking or perceiving.

It is sometimes said that this intuition merely reflects an aspect of our ordinary linguistic practice: we are taught to record the facts of mentality in subject-involving terms (the recognition of an ontology of subjects being a convenient device for covering the fact that mental items are genuinely grouped into minds), and this misleads us into supposing that the subject-recognizing account is what captures the fundamental nature of the situation. But this response would only have some plausibility if, taking account of the putative point it is making, we were able to adjust our thinking accordingly, and thereby achieve an understanding of mentality in an explicitly subjectless form. We do not, after all, have any difficulty in accepting that the phenomenon we ordinarily describe as 'sunrise' is really to do with the rotation of the earth rather than the motion of the sun. But the fact is that, whatever effort we make to try to see things in a different way, we cannot rid ourselves of the commonsense perspective, in which mental items are conceived as elements in the biographies of subjects. The notion of pain without a sufferer, thought without a thinker, or perception without a perceiver, remains, to the eye of intuition, stubbornly unintelligible. That so many philosophers have nevertheless tried to develop non-Cartesian accounts of the structure of the mind is because they are driven by some other theoretical concern (for example, they think there is no satisfactory account of the nature of a mental subject), not because they can achieve an intuitive understanding of the situation—of fundamentally subjectless mentality—which they postulate.

[3] Thus see my account in *The Immaterial Self*, chap. 8, section 2.

It seems to me, then, that, on the issue of ontological structure, the Cartesian is on strong ground.

III. The Nature of Mentality

In comparison with this issue, the situation with respect to the dualist view of mentality is much more complicated, because of the variety of ways in which the view can be opposed. But here too it seems to me that, when we focus directly on the various opposing theories, our intuitions support the Cartesian position.

The dualist view, that mentality is something sui generis and fundamental, involves the rejection of two basic approaches. One approach is that of the *psychophysical identity thesis,* which claims that mental phenomena are to be identified with physical phenomena. The other is that of *mental reductionism,* which claims that psychological facts can be reduced to nonpsychological facts, or to facts whose canonical formulation is in nonpsychological terms. We need, then, to consider these two nondualist approaches in turn.

With respect to the first approach, we must start by noting that the thesis of psychophysical identity can itself be advanced in two forms. Thus, on the one hand, it can be advanced in a strong, *type-type,* form, where types of mental item (as universals) are identified with types of physical item (as universals). For example, it might be claimed that *pain* (the mental universal) is the same as *C-fiber firing* (the physical universal). On the other hand, the thesis can be advanced in a weaker, *token-token,* form, where only the mental items themselves—the concrete tokens of the mental types—are identified with something physical. For example, it might be claimed that, for any subject S and time *t*, if S is in pain at *t*, then there is some neurophysiological state E such that the concrete event of S's being in pain at *t* is the same as the concrete event of S's being in E at *t*. It is obvious why the token-identity thesis is weaker than the type-identity thesis. The claim that a certain mental type is identical with a certain physical type logically entails that each token of the mental type is identical with a token of the physical type. But the claim that each token of a certain mental type is identical with something physical does not entail that the type itself is identical with something physical, or that the physical items with which its various tokens are identical are themselves tokens of a common physical type.

It is now generally acknowledged that, even when it is relativized to a zoological species, the type-identity thesis is very implausible. There are, I assume, reasonable grounds for supposing that, in the case of something like pain, the neurophysiological processes underlying its occurrence in different members of the same species will exemplify some common type; and indeed, this may even, to some extent, apply across species. But there seems to be no reason to expect this kind of uniformity in the case of mental states *with conceptual content*. For example, given the variety of ways in which it can be acquired, and the different networks of interdependent beliefs of which it can form an element, there seems to be no reason to expect that a single type of belief will be associated with a single neurophysiological state in all human subjects. Indeed, given the constant changes in a subject's overall belief system over time, it would not be surprising if a single type of belief was associated with different neurophysiological states in the same subject at different times. In any case, even if a given type of mental phenomenon does happen to be always associated with the same neurophysiological type in the actual world, it is still very difficult to think of this association as holding constant through all possible worlds. And, as Saul Kripke has shown, such constancy is required for genuine identity.[4]

The only remotely plausible form of identity thesis is the token-token form, which allows the same type of mental item to be realized in radically different physical ways in different subjects and on different occasions. But, even with this weaker thesis, there is a challenge which has to be met before we can take it seriously. For we have to be able to understand *how* items of such apparently different kinds can be numerically the same. On a particular occasion, Jones is in pain. And, on that same occasion, and in some kind of association, the neurons in a certain part of his brain are firing in a certain way. On the face of it, these events, however close their causal association, are of quite different sorts—the nature of the neuronal event being entirely physical, the nature of the pain event being entirely mental. Before we can take seriously the suggestion that the events are really identical, we need to be given some way of understanding how a neuronal event is able to have the character of a pain (how a pain event is able to have the character of neuronal firing). And there is a further twist to this. Even if we entertain the possibility that the neuronal event has the character of a pain, we are strongly inclined to say that it possesses this character at best *contingently*. For surely we can envisage a possible world in which this very same event—identified by its physical properties, its physical setting, and its causal origins—occurs without any associated sensation of pain. But we are also strongly inclined to say that the pain event

[4] See S. Kripke, *Naming and Necessity* (Oxford: Blackwell, 1980), lecture 3.

possesses its painful character *essentially*—that there is no possible world in which it occurs without being an instance of pain. And if these twin intuitions are correct, then, as a matter of logic, the neuronal events and pain-events cannot be identical since they differ in their modal properties.[5]

It seems to me that the only way in which we can hope to make sense of token-identity is by combining it with a *reductive* account of mental facts. For, by suitably altering our ordinary conception of the nature of mentality, such an account could leave it unproblematic as to how a neurophysiological item is able to have a psychological character. This then brings us to the second area of investigation, concerning the possibility of mental reductionism. We are interested in this possibility, of course, for its own sake, and not just for its bearing on the issue of token-identity. For, as we have made clear, it is something which the dualist account independently excludes.

The most obvious and familiar way of pursuing the reductive approach is as a thesis of *analytical* reduction. Here, what is claimed is that, by subjecting them to a process of conceptual analysis—a process of unpacking what is implicit in their content—propositions about mentality can be re-construed as propositions with a quite different subject matter. So we have, for example, the thesis of *analytical behaviorism,* which claims that propositions about mentality are to be construed, on analysis, as propositions about the subject's behavior and behavioral dispositions. And we have the thesis of *analytical functionalism,* which claims that propositions about mentality are to be construed, on analysis, as propositions about the subject's functional condition—propositions which represent the subject as in some state which has a certain kind of functional role with respect to sensory (environment-monitoring) input, behavioral output, and the realization of other central states. This functionalist thesis is nowadays the most fashionable version of analytical reductionism. It is also a version which, in a very straightforward way, facilitates the acceptance of token-identity. For if the psychological character of a mental item turns out to be specifiable in purely functional terms, there is no difficulty in supposing that what possesses this character is a purely physical item, whose physical nature and physical setting equip it to play the appropriate functional role.

Analytical reductionism has been a popular approach to mentality among philosophers in the twentieth century, with the behaviorist version dominating the scene in the earlier period, and functionalism coming to the fore more recently. But it also faces a number of difficulties. Perhaps the most obvious difficulty is that it is hard to see how any analytically re-

[5] Cf. ibid., 146–47.

ductive account can do justice to the *subjective* aspects of mentality. Thus it is hard to see how any set of propositions about behavior, functional organization, physiological makeup, environmental circumstances, or anything else that might feature in the chosen reductive analysis, could suffice to specify *how it feels to the subject* to be in pain, or to be having a certain type of sensory experience, or to be in the grip of a certain type of emotion, or to be in any other mental state of an experiential kind. One way of bringing out this point (one among many) is by employing the so-called 'knowledge-argument'. Thus envisage someone who is congenitally deaf, and, being thus, has no introspective knowledge of what it is subjectively like to hear. Despite his deafness, such a person could become a world expert on the physics of sound, the physiology of the auditory system, the functional role of hearing in the behavioral life of the normal subject, and anything else which the reductionist might think relevant, and which is capable of being fully specified in nonpsychological terms. But could such knowledge supply the information which he cannot acquire through introspection? Could it reveal to him what hearing is like *subjectively,* so that he comes to know what it feels like to the normal subject to have an auditory experience, as much as he knows what it feels like in his own case to see or taste or smell? It is surely clear that it could not. But why not, if analytical reductionism is true? For if such reductionism is true, then the content of all propositions about mentality, including what the hearing subject introspectively knows about the character of auditory experience, is to be analyzed in terms of the very factors about which this deaf scientist is fully informed. And so there should be a deductive route from the facts he knows to the subjective facts of which he is ignorant—a route that may be complicated, but would in principle suffice to impart the relevant knowledge.[6]

In the light of this, and other related objections to an *analytically* reductive approach, I think that the only hope for the reductionist is to adopt what we might speak of as *metaphysical* mental reductionism. Here, it is conceded that psychological propositions are not amenable to reductive analysis: the facts they express are sui generis, and cannot be reformulated in nonpsychological terms. But it is still insisted that each such fact is, as we may put it, 'constituted by' facts of a different (nonpsychological) kind. That is, it is insisted that, for each such fact F, there is a set of wholly

[6] For a detailed presentation of an argument along these lines, see *The Immaterial Self,* chap. 3, section 4. For earlier versions of the knowledge argument, though ones that relate to a slightly different issue, see H. Robinson, *Matter and Sense* (Cambridge: Cambridge University Press, 1982), chap. 1; and F. Jackson, "Epiphenomenal Qualia," *Philosophical Quarterly* 32, no. 127 (1982): 127–36.

nonpsychological facts N, such that F obtains in virtue of the obtaining of the facts in N, and the obtaining of F is nothing over and above the obtaining of the facts in N. In a sense, this is a *weaker* form of reductive claim than that of analytical reductionism. It does not imply that we can dispense with our psychological language and system of thought and still be in a position to say and think everything that we might want to say and think. Indeed, it explicitly concedes that mental facts cannot be expressed in any but psychological terms. What it implies, reductively, is merely that, where mental facts obtain, with their irreducibly psychological character, this obtaining is entirely due to, and wholly covered by, the obtaining of certain other (nonpsychological) facts—for example, facts about the physical world. It takes the mental facts to be additional facts, but sees their obtaining as something logically secured by the obtaining of these other (metaphysically more fundamental) facts.

Adopting this metaphysically reductive approach improves the position of mental reductionism in certain respects. In particular, the kind of knowledge-argument which I directed against its analytical form is no longer applicable, since, if propositions about mentality are not amenable to reductive analysis, there is no reason to expect that a knowledge of the nonpsychological facts which are taken as constitutively basic would suffice for a knowledge of the psychological facts which they supposedly sustain. But the trouble is that, by protecting itself from that kind of objection, metaphysical reductionism becomes vulnerable at a different point. For, without the backing of a reductive analysis, there seems to be no way of understanding *how* psychological facts could turn out to be constitutively sustained in the envisaged way—*how* they could obtain in virtue of, and their obtaining be nothing over and above, the obtaining of nonpsychological facts. There are, I think, other areas—not concerned with the constitution of *mental* facts—where we can understand how a metaphysically reductive account is supposed to work. But these are all cases in which facts about mentality crucially feature in the constitutive base. For they are all cases where what underlies the constitutional claim is the thought that the facts which are alleged to be constituted are ones whose obtaining is, in some way, *relative to the viewpoint of human mentality*. For example, it might be claimed that, while propositions about physical color cannot be analytically reduced to propositions about something else, the facts they express are constituted by the dispositions of physical objects to have certain forms of color-appearance to the human observer. Or it might be claimed that, while propositions about moral duty cannot be analytically reduced to propositions about something else, the facts they express are constituted by facts about human evaluative attitudes. Or it might be claimed that, while propositions about the physical world cannot be reduced to propositions about something else, physical facts are constituted by facts about the themes and regularities in human sensory experience. All these claims of constitution are controversial; and some will no doubt strike us as very implausible. But, in each case, we can at least make sense of what is envisaged; for we can see that what lies behind the constitutional claim is the thought that the one set of facts constitutively sustains the other set of facts by determining how things require to be characterized *from the human experiential viewpoint.* But obviously these ways of pursuing a metaphysically reductive approach have no relevance in the present context, where it is mentality itself which is the target of the reduction, and so where psychological facts are automatically excluded from the constitutive base. And, with this exclusion, I do not see how the reduction is supposed to work. I cannot discern a 'mechanism' of constitution by reference to which we could understand how the nonpsychological facts suffice for the obtaining of the psychological facts.

It seems to me, then, that mental reductionism fails in both its analytical and its metaphysical forms. And since the *type*-identity thesis is unacceptable from any standpoint, and the *token*-identity thesis can only be made intelligible in the framework of a reductive account, I conclude that there is no viable nondualist theory of mentality at all. In other words, I conclude that the dualist conception of mentality, as something sui generis and fundamental, is correct. It is true, of course, that a number of arguments have been advanced from the other direction—arguments which try to show that the dualist view itself faces insuperable difficulties. For example, it is often argued that the dualist cannot provide an intelligible account of psychophysical causation, since there is no way of understanding how the nonphysical mind and the physical body could come into causal contact. Or again, it is often argued that, even if the dualist's version of psychophysical causation is intelligible, it is scientifically implausible. These, and other objections, are ones which the dualist needs to address; and indeed, I have tried to address them in *The Immaterial Self*.[7] But I do not have the space to deal with them, even in a cursory fashion, here.[8]

IV. The Nature of Basic Subjects

I have tried to present, in outline, a case for accepting each of the first two claims of the Cartesian view—concerning the nature of mentality and the

[7] See in particular chap. 6.

[8] But see the contributions of Jaegwon Kim and Timothy O'Connor in this volume for a sustained discussion of the relevant issues. *Ed.*

ontological structure of the mind. We must now turn to the third claim, that the basic subjects of mentality (the entities which are to be represented as subjects in the philosophically fundamental account) are wholly nonphysical. And here we immediately notice a difference in the initial dialectical situation. In the first two cases, the Cartesian view is in harmony with our ordinary, commonsense outlook. Thus, in our ordinary thinking, it never occurs to us to suppose that mental items could occur without a subject, or that their belonging to a subject is not a fundamental aspect of how they should be conceived. And likewise, although we do not spell this out in philosophically precise terms, we ordinarily conceive of mentality as something with its own distinctive nature and as a basic ingredient of how things are. In these respects, then, the Cartesian claims are an endorsement of our commonsense position; and, indeed, to a considerable extent, the considerations to which I have appealed in their support are an elaboration of the intuitions which underlie that position. But, in the case of the third claim, the situation is strikingly different. For, in our ordinary system of thought, what we primarily think of as the subjects of mentality are, as we noted, things with corporeal natures. Thus our standard practice is to ascribe mentality to people and animals, conceived of as entities which have shape, size, and material composition. Nor, at that ordinary level of thinking, does it occur to us that the ultimate subjects might really be certain immaterial and spatially unlocated entities with which these corporeal subjects are in some way associated. So, at this point, unlike the first two, the Cartesian view and our commonsense outlook stand in sharp contrast.

For this reason, we may find ourselves attracted to a position which combines the first two Cartesian claims with a denial of the third—a position which takes mentality to be sui generis and fundamental (Claim 1), and accepts that mental items are to be ultimately represented as elements in the biographies of mental subjects (Claim 2), but thinks of these subjects (the basic subjects involved) as having corporeal natures. This combination has the advantage of being in line with common sense. And, by adopting a corporealist view of the subject, it also avoids some seemingly awkward questions that arise for the Cartesian. In particular, if we take the basic subjects to be wholly nonphysical, what positive specification can we give of their natures? And how do we account for their existence? Defenders of the Cartesian view may find these questions embarrassing.[9]

[9] Though, in the end, I do not think that they need to. On the question of the nature of nonphysical subjects, see *The Immaterial Self*, chap. 7, section 5. The question of what accounts for the existence of these subjects is one which I consider, albeit briefly, in the final section of this paper.

But whatever the initial attractions of the envisaged combination, it seems to me that there are insuperable difficulties in embracing it, and that once we accept the first two claims of the Cartesian view, we are obliged to accept the third claim as well. The reasons for this will emerge as soon as we try to get a clear understanding of the situation which the combination postulates—of a basic but corporeal subject, characterized by dualistically conceived mentality.

We need to begin by drawing a distinction between two ways in which it could be thought that the basic subjects of mentality have corporeal natures. One way would be to suppose that these subjects are just a special category of ordinary material objects. It would be to suppose that when a person or animal is in a mental state, or engaged in some mental activity, the basic subject of the relevant mentality (the entity which is to be ultimately thought of as in that state or engaged in that activity) is simply the biological organism, or perhaps some psychologically crucial part of it. It would be to suppose that, even if the mentality of the subjects cannot be equated with or reduced to anything physical, the entities themselves, which have this mentality, are, in their essential natures, entirely physical—needing nothing other than their physical attributes to exist and preserve their identity through time. I shall speak of this as the *simple* corporealist view. The other possibility would be to suppose that the basic subjects of mentality are radically dual in nature. Like ordinary material objects, they have shape, size, and material composition, and have these essentially. But their essential natures also include a psychological component, which is quite separate from their physical character and is what equips them to be mental subjects. So when a person or animal is in a mental state, or engaged in a mental activity, the basic subject of the mentality is not, on this account, the biological organism, but something qualitatively richer—something which possesses the full physical character of the organism, but has an essential nonphysical character as well. I shall speak of this as the *complex* corporealist view. Someone who wants to adopt the relevant combination of positions—combining the first two claims of the Cartesian account with a rejection of the third—has to decide whether (in rejecting this third claim) he is accepting the corporealist view in its simple or in its complex form. Let us consider each option in turn.

The problem with the first option, which accepts the simple view, is immediately apparent. If something is just an ordinary material object, whose essential nature is purely physical, there seems to be no way of understanding how it could be the basic subject of mentality in the form in which the dualist conceives of it. It is not that the simple view *logically* excludes such a possibility: there is no *logical contradiction* (even implicit) in the claim that an ordinary material object is the fundamental possessor of mentality of a dualistic kind. The difficulty is in understanding how such a thing could be. If something is merely a material object, any understanding of how it is equipped to be a mental subject will presumably have to be achieved by focusing on its physical nature. But focusing on an object's physical nature will only reveal how it is equipped to be in states or engage in activities which are directly to do with its possession of that nature—with its condition as a physical thing. And so it will only help us to understand how the object can be the basic subject of mental states and activities if we accept some form of physicalistic or suitably reductive account of the mentality involved. Focusing on the physical nature of an object simply offers no clue as to how it can be the basic subject of the kinds of mentality which the dualist postulates.

It should be stressed that this point holds irrespective of the kind of material object we are considering. It is no easier to understand how at the fundamental level of description, dualistic mentality could genuinely characterize human beings and animals, construed merely as biological organisms, than to understand how it could characterize such things as trees or stones or pens. It is true, of course, that mentality has an intimate *functional* association with the states and behavior of these organisms which it does not have with other sorts of things. Tread on a human organism's toe and, in normal circumstances, there will be a resulting pain; and when a human organism exhibits goal-directed behavior, this will normally indicate the controlling influence of a mental purpose. These kinds of links are not present in the case of such things as trees, stones, and pens. But the point remains that, without some nondualist account of the mentality involved, such links do not make it any easier to understand how the organism can itself be the *subject*. They do not help us to understand how the material object can be that which *has* the mentality which its states generate or which its behavior expresses—how it can be what genuinely *instantiates* the relevant psychological properties.

It follows that, if there is to be any prospect of making sense of the corporealist view, in the context of a dualist conception of mentality, then this view will need to be taken in its complex form. Here, the basic subjects are thought of as having two sides to their natures. They are corporeal objects, with shape, size, and material composition. But their natures also include a psychological component, which is not an aspect of their physical character, but is equally essential to them. This psychological component is then thought of as what equips the objects to be subjects of dualistic mentality. We cannot understand how such mentality can characterize a *merely* corporeal object, like a biological organism, since it would be entirely extraneous to the object's nature. But, in the new situation, we can take the psychological component of their natures to be precisely what gives the relevant objects the distinctive character of mental subjects, with the capacity to be in dualistic mental states and perform dualistic mental acts.

This complex version of the corporealist view avoids the particular problem of the simple version. But, precisely by avoiding this problem, it becomes vulnerable to an analogous problem at another point. For there is simply no way of understanding how a single object could have this dually endowed nature. Just as there is no way of understanding how a merely corporeal object could be the basic subject of dualistic mentality (because such mentality would have no qualitative connection with the kind of thing the object is), so there is a similar obstacle to understanding how something which is, whatever else, a certain kind of corporeal object could have this additional and quite different side to its nature. After all, suppose I apply the proposal to the case of this pen (the one I am now holding). Suppose I suggest that, in addition to this pen, there is an object which has all the same physical attributes, and has them in the same concretely realized form, but whose essential nature also includes the relevant kind of psychological component, which equips it to be a mental subject. Our reaction to this suggestion would not be, merely, that it is evidentially unwarranted or far-fetched. It would be that we cannot even make sense of it. We just cannot understand how something which has all the physical attributes of the pen, and in the same concretely realized form, could be anything other than the pen itself, which is a purely corporeal object. Focusing on these attributes, we can form no conception of what it would be for them to be hypostatically united with a further qualitative factor to form an object of a richer—psychophysical—kind. But if this is so for the pen, I cannot see how the situation would be different for any other kind of material object. And, in particular, I cannot see how it would be different for a biological organism. As we have said, certain kinds of biological organism have an intimate functional association with the occurrence of mentality; and that certainly makes it easier to explain why we ordinarily think of the basic subjects involved as having corporeal natures. But just as it does not make it easier to understand how an organism as such could be the basic subject of dualistic mentality, so it does not make it easier to understand how something could have the physical character of an organism but possess an essential nonphysical character as well. It does not help to reveal how the relationship between a basic subject and an organism could be closer than the one which the Cartesian envisages, whereby two entities which are ontologically separate and qualitatively contrasting form ingredients of a single functional system.

We cannot make sense of the corporealist view in its complex form, where basic subjects are taken to be dual in nature. And, as we have also seen, we can only make sense of this view in its simple (purely corporealist) form if we combine it with a physicalistic or reductive account of mentality—an account which construes mentality in a way that explicitly reveals how it can characterize something whose nature is purely physical. The upshot is that, in the framework of the dualist conception of mentality, we cannot make sense of the corporealist view at all. And this means that the case I have offered for the first two claims of the Cartesian view becomes a case for accepting the third claim too. If, as I have argued, mentality is something sui generis and fundamental, and if, as I have also argued, it is to be ultimately represented as belonging to subjects, then we have to accept that these subjects are wholly nonphysical. We have to accept that, even though we ordinarily ascribe mentality to corporeal objects (in particular, to human beings construed as members of an animal species), the entities which *fundamentally* qualify as the subjects of the mentality involved (the entities which feature as subjects in the philosophically fundamental account) are wholly nonphysical in their intrinsic nature, and (being thus nonphysical in nature) are without location in physical space.

V. The Role of God

This, then, is my brief defense of the Cartesian view of the mind. As I have already stressed, it is, for the most part, no more than an outline of the defense which I developed in *The Immaterial Self.* And, indeed, in one crucial respect, it even falls short of such an outline. For while it covers the argument by which I tried to establish the truth of the Cartesian view (by covering the arguments which I deployed against the various alternatives to that view), it does nothing to indicate the ways in which I tried to rebut the various objections to which the view might be thought vulnerable. It is true, of course, that if the argument in favor of the view is fully successful, then these objections must be mistaken. But it would be naïve to suppose that the success of the argument could be made manifest without showing how the objections can be met.

There is one point which I did not make in the book, and, in retrospect, I wish that I had. An apparent difficulty for the Cartesian view is that there seems to be no remotely plausible way of accounting, in natural terms, for the existence and functional role of the postulated nonphysical subjects. Biological life begins at conception, when an ovum and a sperm fuse to produce a new unitary organism. But it is hard to see how this process, or the subsequent development of the organism, could create an additional nonphysical substance and functionally attach it to the organism in the relevant way. The answer, it seems to me, is that we should explain these things by appeal to the creative role of God. Whether by a general decree or by specific acts for each occasion, it is God who (in addition to his creation and sustainment of the physical world) creates the nonphysical subjects and arranges for their functional attachment to the appropriate organisms; and, at least in the case of human beings, theology can offer some account of God's purpose in doing this, and of why that purpose is rationally appropriate to his nature. No doubt, at this point, the opponents of the Cartesian view will throw up their hands in horror: if the view requires this theistic underpinning, is not that just one more indication of its intellectual bankruptcy? But I, at any rate, see things the other way. Theism enables the Cartesian to explain the existence and role of the nonphysical subjects; and, because this is the only satisfactory explanation, the argument for the Cartesian view becomes itself a powerful argument for the existence of God. In other words, being confident of the strength of the case for the Cartesian view, I see the need for its theistic underpinning as creating a problem for the atheist rather than for the Cartesian.

JAEGWON KIM

Lonely Souls: Causality and Substance Dualism

I. The Problem

We commonly think that we, as persons, have both a mental and a bodily dimension—or, if you prefer, mental aspects and material aspects. Something like this dualism of personhood, I believe, is common lore shared across most cultures and religious traditions, although such beliefs are not always articulated in the form of an explicit set of dogmas as in some established religions. It is often part of this "folk dualism" that we are able to survive bodily deaths, as "pure spirits," and retain all or most of the spiritual aspects of ourselves after our bodies are gone.

Spirits and souls as conceived in popular lore seem to have physical properties as well, if only vestigially physical ones, and are not what Descartes and other philosophical dualists would call souls or minds—wholly immaterial and nonphysical substances outside physical space with no physical properties whatever. For example, souls are commonly said to *leave* the body when a person dies and *rise upward* toward heaven, indicating that they are thought to have, and are able to change, locations in physical space. And they can be heard and seen, we are told, by people endowed with special virtues and in especially propitious mental states. Souls are sometimes pictured as balls of bright light, causing the air to stir barely perceptibly as they move and even emitting some unearthly sounds. Perhaps, they are

Thanks to David Armstrong, Jerry Katz, Noah Latham, Barry Loewer, Eugene Mills, Timothy O'Connor, Alvin Plantinga, and Ernest Sosa for helpful comments and suggestions. This paper is descended from a paper first presented at a conference on mind-body dualism at the University of Notre Dame in March 1998.

composed of pure immaterial Cartesian souls and some rare and strange matter unknown to science. As is well known, Descartes thought of persons in a similar way—the difference is that for Descartes a person is a combination, or "union" as he called it, of an immaterial soul and a human body composed of ordinary matter, not some weird and ethereal stuff.

But does this conception of a person, as something made up of two radically diverse components, a body and an immaterial soul, make sense, whether the body is made up of ordinary matter or some mysterious ethereal stuff? One contention of this paper is that there is reason to think that such a conception of a person is ultimately unintelligible. My arguments will be principally based on considerations on causation—specifically, I will try to undermine the idea that immaterial souls can causally interact with material bodies, thereby forming a "union" with them. If I am right, it is an idea that we cannot make intelligible. In fact, it will be seen that much of the interest of my discussion, such as it is, concerns issues about mental causation and, more generally, causation itself, and, if the general drift of my arguments is correct, it will cast serious doubts on the usefulness and viability of the very notion of immaterial substance. My claim about the Cartesian "two-component" conception of persons will fall out as a corollary of what I have to say about mind-body causation under substance dualism.

II. Descartes and Mental Causation

Conventional wisdom has it that the downfall of Cartesian mind-body dualism was due to its inability to account for mental causation. In particular, as has often been noted, his radical dualism of mental and material substances was thought to be inconsistent with the possibility of causal transactions between them. Princess Elisabeth of Bohemia famously asked Descartes to explain "how man's soul, being only a thinking substance, can determine animal spirits so as to cause voluntary action."[1] According to one commentator, Richard A. Watson, the perceived inconsistency between the radical duality of minds and bodies and their causal interaction was not only a major theoretical flaw in Cartesianism but also the historical cause of its demise.[2]

The reason standardly offered for the supposed incoherence of Cartesian interactionist dualism is that it is difficult to conceive how two

[1] Margaret Wilson, ed., *The Essential Descartes* (New York: New American Library, 1969), 373.

[2] Richard A. Watson, *The Downfall of Cartesianism 1673–1712* (The Hague: Martinus Nijhoff, 1966).

substances with such radically diverse natures, one in space-time with mass, inertia, and the like and the other lacking wholly in material properties and not even located in physical space, could stand in causal relations to each other. Apparently, various principles about causation, such as that cause and effect must show a certain degree of mutual affinity or "essential likeness," or that there can be no "greater reality" in an effect than there is in its cause, seem to have played a role. Anthony Kenny, for example, writes: "On Descartes' principles it is difficult to see how an unextended thinking substance can cause motion in an extended unthinking substance and how the extended unthinking substance can cause sensations in the unextended thinking substance. The properties of the two kinds of substance seem to place them in such diverse categories that it is impossible for them to interact."[3] That is pretty much all that Kenny has to say about Descartes's troubles with mind-body causation—and, as far as I know, that is pretty much all we get from Descartes's critics and commentators. But as an argument this is incomplete and unsatisfying. As it stands, it is not much of an argument—it hardly gets started; rather, it only expresses a vague dissatisfaction of the sort that ought to prompt us to look for a real argument. Why is it incoherent to think that there can be causal relations between "diverse substances"? Why is it "impossible," as Kenny puts it, for things with diverse natures to enter into causal relations with one another? Just what sorts of diverseness make trouble and why?

It has not been an easy matter to pin down exactly what is wrong with positing causal relations between substances with diverse natures and explain in concrete terms what it is about the natures of mental and material substance that make them unfit to enter into causal relations with each other. And there have been commentators who have defended Descartes against the Kenny-style charge of incoherence. Louis Loeb is one of them.[4] Loeb's defense rests on his claim that Descartes was a proto-Humean about causation—namely that, for Descartes, causality amounted to nothing more than brute regularity, or "constant conjunction," and there can be no a priori metaphysical constraint, such as resemblance or mutual affinity, on what events can be causally joined with what other events. Loeb quotes from Descartes:

> There is no reason to be surprised that certain motions of the heart should be naturally connected in this way with certain thoughts, which they in no

[3] Anthony Kenny, *Descartes* (New York: Random House, 1968), 222–23.

[4] Louis E. Loeb, *From Descartes to Hume* (Ithaca: Cornell University Press, 1981). See 134–49.

> way resemble. The soul's natural capacity for union with a body brings with it the possibility of an association between thoughts and bodily motions or conditions so that when the same conditions recur in the body they impel the soul to the same thought; and conversely when the same thought recurs, it disposes the body to return to the same conditions.[5]

On Loeb's view, then, the fact that soul and body are of such diverse natures was, for Descartes, no barrier at all for their entering into the most intimate of causal relations, to form a "union" that is a person. Taking Loeb's word for it that Descartes was indeed a proto-Humean on the nature of causation, his point seems to me sufficient as a response to the kind of vaguely worded and inchoate objection of the sort that Kenny and many others have advanced. But does the constant conjunction view of causation really help save Descartes? I don't think it does, and the reason, I think, is simple to see and also instructive.

Suppose that two persons, Smith and Jones, are "psychophysically synchronized," as it were, in such a way that each time Smith's mind wills to raise his hand so does Jones's, and vice versa, and every time they will to raise their hands, their hands rise. There is a constant conjunction between Smith's mind's willing to raise a hand and Smith's hand's rising, and, similarly, between Jones's mind's willing to raise a hand and Jones's hand's going up. If you are a pure constant conjunctivist about causation, this would suffice for saying that a given instance of Smith's willing to raise a hand is a cause of the subsequent rising of his hand, and similarly in the case of Jones. But there is a problem here. For we see that instances of Smith's mind's willing to raise a hand are constantly conjoined not only with his hand's rising but *also with Jones's hand's rising*, and, similarly, instances of Jones's mind's willing to raise a hand are constantly conjoined with Smith's hand's rising. So why is it not the case that Smith's volition causes Jones's hand to go up, and that Jones's volition causes Smith's hand to go up?

If, however, you believe in the idea of "causal necessity" and think that constant conjunction, if it is to support a causal relation, must hold with necessity in some form, you have a prima facie answer: the constant and regular conjunction between Smith's mind's willing to raise a hand and Jones's hand's going up is only coincidental, carrying no force of neces-

[5] Anthony Kenny, trans. and ed., *Descartes' Philosophical Letters* (Oxford: Oxford University Press, 1963), 210. I am rather dubious as to whether this passage supports Loeb's Humean interpretation of Descartes, for Descartes is using here causal verbs, "impel" and "dispose," to describe the regularities. But Loeb may well be right, and I am not in a position to challenge him on this point.

sity. And this is perhaps manifest in the fact that there are no counterfactual dependencies between these events: for example, it is not true that if Smith had not willed that a hand should rise, Jones's hand would not have gone up.

But it won't do to say that after all Smith wills *his* hand to rise and that's why his willing causes his hand, not Jones's hand, to rise. It isn't clear what this reply can accomplish, but it begs the question on hand. The reason is that, according to the standard interpretation of Descartes, what makes Smith's hand Smith's, not Jones's—that is, what makes Smith's body the body with which Smith's mind is "united"—is the fact that there is specially intimate and direct causal commerce between the two. To say that this is the body with which this mind is united is to say that this body is the only material thing that this mind can *directly* affect—that is, without other bodies serving as causal intermediaries—and that all changes this mind can cause in other bodies are caused by changes in this body. This is *my* body, and this is *my* arm, because it is something that I can move without moving any other body. I can raise *your* arm only by grabbing it with my hand and pulling it up.[6] And something similar must obtain in the direction of body-to-mind causation as well. The "union" of a mind and a body that Descartes speaks of, therefore, presupposes mental causation. Whether or not this interpretation of Descartes is historically correct, a causal account of "ownership" seems the most natural option for substance dualists, and I do not know of noncausal alternatives that make any real sense.

I have heard some people say that we could simply take the concept of the mind's "union" with a body as a primitive, and that it is simply a primitive fact, perhaps divinely ordained, that this mind and this body are integrated into a proper union that is a person. But I find such an approach unintelligible. For it seems to concede that the notion of "union" of minds and bodies, and hence the notion of a person, are unintelligible. If God chose to unite my body with my mind, just what is it that he did? I am not asking *why* he chose to unite this particular mind with this particular body, or *why* he decided to engage in such activities as uniting minds and bodies at all, or *whether* he, or anyone else, could have powers to do things like that. If God united my mind and my body there must be a relationship R such that a mind stands in relation R to a body if and only if that mind and that body constitute a unitary person. In uniting my mind and my body, God related the two with R. Unless we know what R is, we

[6] Does this exclude telekinesis? Yes. This probably is the main reason why there is something a priori strange about telekinesis. If telekinesis were a widespread everyday phenomenon, that might very well undermine the idea that each of us has a distinct body.

do not know what God did. Again, we are not asking *how* God managed to establish R between a mind and a body—as far as we are concerned, that can remain a mystery forever. We only want to know *what* God did.

III. Causation and the "Pairing" Problem

The difficulty we have seen with Loeb's interpretation of Descartes as a Humean in matters of causation, I believe, points to a more fundamental difficulty in the idea that mental substances, outside physical space, can enter into causal relations with objects in physical space, a difficulty that is not resolved when, as above, some sort of "necessary connection" is invoked as a constituent of causal relations. What is perhaps more surprising, the very same difficulty besets the idea that such nonspatial mental substances can enter into any sort of causal relations, whether with material things or with other mental substances.

Let us begin with a simple example of physical causation: two rifles, A and B, are simultaneously fired, and this results in the simultaneous death of two persons, Andy and Buddy. What makes it the case that the firing of rifle A caused Andy's death and the firing of rifle B caused Buddy's death, and not the other way around? What are the principles that underlie the correct and incorrect *pairings* of cause and effect in a situation like this? We can call this "the causal pairing problem," or "the pairing problem" for short.[7]

Two possible ways for handling this problem come to mind.

1. We can trace a continuous causal chain from the firing of rifle A to Andy's death, and another such chain from the firing of B to Buddy's death. (Indeed, we can, with a high-speed camera, trace the bullet's path from rifle A to Andy, etc.) No causal chain exists from the firing of A to Buddy's death, or from the firing of B to Andy's death.

2. We look for a "pairing relation," R, that holds between A's firing and Andy's death and between B's firing and Buddy's death, but not between A's firing and Buddy's death or B's firing and Andy's death. In this particular case, when the two rifles were fired, rifle A, not rifle B, was located at a certain distance from Andy and pointed in his direction, and similarly with rifle B and Buddy. It is these *spatial relations* (distance, orientation,

[7] I first discussed this problem in "Causation, Nomic Subsumption, and the Concept of Event," *Journal of Philosophy* 70 (1973): 217–36. I was prompted to reflect on the issues involved here by John Foster's "Psychophysical Causal Relations," *American Philosophical Quarterly* 5 (1968): 64–70.

etc.) that help pair the firing of A with Andy's death and the firing of B with Buddy's death. Spatial relations seem to serve as the "pairing relations" in this case, and perhaps for all cases of physical causation involving distinct objects.

The two methods may be related, but let us set aside this question for now.

Let us now turn to a situation involving nonphysical Cartesian souls as causal agents. There are two souls, A and B, and they perform a certain mental action, as a result of which a change occurs in material substance M. We may suppose that mental actions of the kind involved generally cause physical changes of the sort that happened in M, and, moreover, that in the present case it is soul A's action, not soul B's, that caused the change in M. Surely, such a possibility must exist. But ask: What relation might perform the job of pairing soul A's action with the change in M, a relation that is absent in the case of soul B's action and the change in M? Evidently, no spatial relations can be invoked to answer this question, for souls are not in space and are not able to bear spatial relations to material things. Soul A cannot be any "nearer" to material object M, or more appropriately "oriented" with respect to it, than soul B is. Is there anything that can do for souls what space, or the network of spatial relations, does for material things?

Let us now consider the possibility of causality within a purely mental world—a world inhabited only by Cartesian souls. Soul A acts in a certain way at time *t* and so does soul B at the same time. This is followed by certain changes in two other souls, A* and B*. Suppose that actions of A and B are causes of the changes in A* and B*. But which cause caused which effect? If we want a solution that is analogous to case 2 above for rifle firings and dyings, what we need is a pairing relation R such that R holds, say, for A and A*, and for B and B*, but not for A and B*, or for B and A*. Since the entities are immaterial souls outside physical space, R cannot be a spatial, or any other kind of physical, relation. The radical nonspatiality of mental substances rules out the possibility of invoking any spatial relationship for the cause-effect pairing.

Evidently, then, the pairing relation R must be some kind of psychological relation. But what could that be? Could R be some kind of intentional relation, such as thinking of, picking out, and referring? Perhaps, soul A gazes at soul A* and B*, and then pick outs A*, and causes a change in it. But how do we understand these relations like gazing at and picking out? What is it for A to pick out A* rather than B*? To pick out something outside us, we must be in a certain epistemic relationship with it; we must perceive it somehow and be able to distinguish it from other things around it—that is, perceptually identify it. Take perception: What is it for me to perceive this tree, not another tree which is hidden behind it and which is qualitatively indistinguishable from it? The only credible answer is that the tree I perceive is the one that is causing my perceptual experience as of a tree, and that I do not see the hidden tree because it bears no causal relation to my perceptual experience.[8] Ultimately, these intentional relations must be explained on the basis of causal relations (this is not to say that they are entirely reducible to causality), and I do not believe we can explain what it is for soul A to pick out soul A* rather than B* except by positing some kind of causal relation that holds for A and A* but not for A and B*. If this is right, invoking intentional relations to do causal pairings begs the question: we need causal relations to understand intentional relations. Even if intentional relations were free of causal involvements, that would not in itself show that they would suffice as pairing relations. In addition, they must satisfy certain structural requirements; this will become clear below.

We are not necessarily supposing that one single R will suffice for all causal relations between two mental substances. But if the physical case is any guide, we seem to be in need of a certain kind of "space," not physical space of course, but some kind of a nonphysical coordinate system that gives every mental substance and every event involving a mental substance a *unique location* (at a time), and which yields for each pair of mental entities a determinate relationship defined by their locations. Such a system of "mental space" could provide us with a basis for a solution to the pairing problem, and enable us to make sense of causal relations between nonspatial mental entities. But I don't think that we have the foggiest idea what such a framework might look like—what psychological relations might generate such a structure.

What about using the notion of causal chain to connect the souls in the right cause-effect relationships? Can there be a causal chain between soul A's action and the change in soul A*, and between soul B's action and the change in soul B*? But do we have an understanding of such purely mental causal chains? What could such chains be like outside physical space? Hume required that a cause-effect pair of events that are spatiotemporally separated be connected by a causal chain of *spatially contiguous* events. It is difficult to imagine what kind of causal chain might be inserted between events involving two mental substances. Presumably we have to place a third soul, C, between soul A and soul A*, such that A's action causes a

[8] This of course is the causal theory of perception. See H. P. Grice, "The Causal Theory of Perception," *Proceedings of the Aristotelian Society,* supp. vol. 35 (1961).

change in C which in turn causes the change in A*. But what could "between" mean here? What is it for an immaterial and nonspatial thing to be "between" two other immaterial and nonspatial things? In the physical case it is physical space that gives a sense to betweenness. In the mental case, what would serve the role that space serves in the physical case?

One might say: For C to be "between" A and A* in a sense relevant to present purposes is for A's action to cause a change in C and for this change to cause a change in A*. That is, betweenness is to be taken simply as causal betweenness. This of course is the idea of a causal chain, but it is clear that this idea does not give us an independent handle on the pairing problem. The reason is simple: it begs the question. Our original question was: How do we pair soul A's action with a change in soul A*? Now we have two pairing problems instead of one: First, we need to pair soul A's action with a change in a third soul, C, and then pair this change in C with the change in A*. This means that methods 1 and 2 above are not really independent. The very idea of a causal chain makes sense only if an appropriate notion of causation is already on hand, and this requires a prior solution to the pairing problem. This means that method 2 is the only thing we have.

We are, therefore, back with 2—that is, with the question what psychological relations might serve the role that spatial relations serve in the case of physical causation. The problem here is independent of the Humean constant conjunction view of causation, and therefore independent of the difficulty we raised for Loeb's defense of Descartes. For suppose that there is a "necessary," counterfactual sustaining, regularity connecting properties F and G of immaterial mental substances. A mental substance, A has F at *t*, and at *t**, and an instant later, two mental substances, B and C, acquire property G. I think we would like the following to be a possible situation: A's having F at *t* causes B to have G at *t**, but it does not cause C to have G at *t**. If so, there must be an intelligible account of why A acts on B but not on C, and such an account must be grounded in a certain relation, a "pairing relation," holding for A and B but not for A and C. What conceivable psychological or intentional relation, or system of such relations, could serve this purpose? I don't have a clue.

If these reflections are not entirely wrongheaded, our idea of causation requires that the causally connected items be situated in a spacelike framework. It has been widely believed, as we noted, that Cartesian dualism of two substances runs into insurmountable difficulties in explaining the possibility of causal relations across the two domains, mental-to-physical and physical-to-mental—especially the former. But what our considerations show is that there is an even deeper difficulty—substantival dualism is faced with difficulties even in explaining how mental-to-mental causation is possible, how two distinct Cartesian souls could be in causal commerce with each other. Perhaps Leibniz was wise to renounce all causal relations between individual substances, or monads—although I have no idea as to his actual reasons for this view. A purely Cartesian world seems like a pretty lonely place, inhabited by immaterial souls each of which is an island unto itself, totally isolated from all other souls. Even the actual world, if we are immaterial souls, would be a lonely place for us; each of us, as an immaterial entity, would be entirely cut off from anything else, whether physical or nonphysical, in our surroundings. Can you imagine any existence that is lonelier than an immaterial self?

IV. Causation and Space

The fact, assuming this to be a fact, that the causal pairing problem for physical causation is solved only by invoking spatial relations tells us, I believe, something important about physical causation and the physical domain. By locating each and every physical item—object and event—in an all-encompassing coordinate system, this framework imposes a determinate relation on every pair of items in the physical domain. Causal structure of the physical domain, or our ability to impose a causal structure on it, presupposes this space-time framework. Causal relations must be selective and discriminating, in the sense that there can be two objects with identical intrinsic properties such that a third object causally acts on one of them but not the other (this can be stated for events as well), and, similarly, that there can be two intrinsically indiscernible objects such that one of them, but not the other, causally acts on a third object. If so, there must be a principled way of distinguishing the two intrinsically indiscernible objects in such causal situations, and it seems that spatial relations provide us with the principal means for doing this. Although this isn't the place to enter into detailed discussion, spatial relations have the right sorts of properties; for example, causal influences generally diminish as distance in space increases, and various sorts of barriers can be set up in the right places in space to prevent or impede propagation of causal influences (though perhaps not gravity!). In general, causal relations between physical objects or events depend crucially on their spatiotemporal relations to each other; just think of the point of establishing alibis—"I wasn't there," if true, is sufficient for "I didn't do it." And the temporal order alone will not be sufficient to provide us with such a basis. We need a full space-time framework for this purpose. It wasn't for nothing, after all, that Hume included "contiguity" in space and time, as well as constant conjunction, among his conditions for causal relations. From our present perspective, Hume's contiguity condition can be seen as a response to the pairing problem.

If this is right, it gives us one plausible way of vindicating the critics of Descartes who, as we saw, argued that the radically diverse natures of mental and material substances preclude causal relations between them. It is of the essence of material substances that they have determinate positions in the space-time framework and that there is a determinate spatiotemporal relationship between each pair of them. Descartes of course talked of extendedness in space as the essence of matter, but we can broadly construe this to include other spatial properties and relations for material substances. Now consider the mental side: as I take it, the Cartesian doctrine has it that it is part of the souls' essential nature that they are outside the spatial order and lack all spatial properties, though they do belong to the temporal order. And it is this essential nonspatiality that makes trouble for their participation in causal structures. What is interesting is that it isn't just mind-to-body causation but also mind-to-mind causation that is put in jeopardy.

We have already seen how difficulties arise for mind-to-body and mind-to-mind causation. Unsurprisingly, body-to-mind causation fares no better. Let's quickly run through this: Consider a physical object causally acting on a mental substance, causing it to have property F at time *t*. Suppose that there is another mental substance that begins to have F at *t*, but not as a causal result of the physical object's action. How might the pairing problem be solved in this case? To solve it, we need to identify a relation R that holds between the physical object and the mental substance it causally affects but which does not hold between the physical object and the second mental substance. The only relation that can do this for physical objects is the spatial relation, but the very essence of a mental substance excludes it from any and all spatial relations. Moreover, given the fact that we could not devise a system of pairing relations for the domain of mental substances, it seems out of the question that we could generate a system that would work across the divide between the mental and material realms. If this is true, not even epiphenomenalism is an option for the substance dualist.

I am not claiming that these considerations are what motivated the anti-Cartesian argument that mind-body causal interaction is incoherent given the radically diverse natures of minds and bodies, or the absence of similarity or affinity between them. I am only suggesting that this may be one way to flesh out the critics' worries and show that there is a real and concrete basis for these worries. Causal interaction is precluded between mental and material substances because of their diverse essential natures—more specifically, because of the essential spatiality of bodies and the essential nonspatiality of minds. Causality requires a pairing relation, and this diversity between minds and bodies does not permit such relations connecting minds and bodies. What the critics perhaps didn't see was the possibility that essentially the same difficulty bedevils causal relations *within* the realm of the minds as well.

V. Can We Locate Souls in Space?

These reflections might lead one to wonder whether it would help the cause of substance dualism if mental substances were at least given spatial locations, not as extended substances like material bodies but as extensionless geometric points. After all, Descartes spoke of the pineal gland as "the seat" of the soul, and it is easy to find passages in his writings that seem to give souls positions in space, although this probably was not part of his official doctrine. And most people who believe in souls, philosophers included, appear to think that our souls are in our bodies at least—my soul in my body, your soul in your body, and so on. But I would hazard that this conviction is closely associated with the idea that my soul is in direct causal contact with my body and your soul with your body. The pineal gland is the seat of the soul for Descartes, as I take it, only because it is where unmediated mind-body causal interaction takes place. If all this is right, this confirms my speculation that mind-body causation generates pressure to somehow bring minds into space, which, for Descartes, is exclusively the realm of the matter.

In any case, putting souls into physical space may create more problems than it solves. For one thing, we need a principled way of locating each soul at a particular point in space. It is difficult to imagine how this can be done (why can't we locate all the souls in the world in one place, say in this empty coffee mug on my desk, like the many angels on the head of a pin?). It would obviously beg the question to locate my soul where my body, or brain, is on the ground that my soul and my body are in direct causal interaction with each other. Second, if locating souls in space is to help with the pairing problem, it must be the case that no more than one soul can occupy an identical spatial point; for otherwise spatial relations would not suffice to uniquely identify each soul in relation to other souls in space. This is analogous to the so-called principle of "impenetrability of matter," a principle whose point can be taken as the claim that space provides us with a criterion of individuation for material things. According to it, material objects occupying exactly the same spatial region are one and the same. What we need is a similar principle for souls, that is, a principle of "impenetrability of souls": Two distinct souls cannot occupy exactly the same point in space. But if souls are subject to spatial exclusion, in addition to the fact that the exercise of their causal powers are constrained by spatial relations, why aren't souls just material objects, albeit of a very special, and strange, kind? Moreover, there is a prior question: Why should we think that a principle of spatial exclusion applies to immaterial souls? To solve the pairing problem for souls by placing them in space requires such a principle, but that's not a reason for thinking that the principle holds; we cannot wish it into being—we need independent reasons and evidence.

Moreover, if a soul, all of it, is at a geometric point, it is puzzling how it could have enough structure to account for all the marvelous causal work it is supposed to perform and explain the differences between souls in regard to their causal powers. You may say: A soul's causal powers arise from its mental structure, and mental structure doesn't take up space. But what is mental structure? What are its parts and how are the parts configured in a structure? If a soul's mental structure is to account for its distinctive causal powers, then, given the pairing problem and the essentiality of spatial relations for causation, it is unclear how wholly nonspatial mental structure could give an explanation of a soul's causal powers. To go on: If souls exclude each other for spatial occupancy, do souls exclude material bodies as well? If not, why not? It may be that one's dualist commitments dictate certain answers to these questions. But that would hardly show they are the "true" answers. We shouldn't do philosophy by first deciding what conclusions we want to prove, or what aims we want to realize, and then posit convenient entities and premises to get us where we want to go. When we think of the myriad problems and puzzles that arise from locating souls in physical space, it is difficult to escape the impression that whatever answers that might be offered would likely look ad hoc and fail to convince.

I have tried to explore considerations that seem to show that the causal relation indeed exerts a strong, perhaps irresistible, pressure toward a degree of homogeneity over its domain, and, moreover, that the kind of homogeneity it requires probably includes, at a minimum, spatiotemporality, which arguably entails physicality. The more we think about causation, the clearer becomes our realization, I think, that the possibility of causation between distinct objects depends on a shared spacelike coordinate system in which these objects are located, a scheme that individuates objects by their "locations" in the scheme. Are there such schemes other than the scheme of physical space? I don't believe we know of any. This alone makes trouble for serious substance dualisms and dualist conceptions of personhood—unless, like Leibniz, you are prepared to give up causal relations for substances altogether. Malebranche denied causal relations between all finite substances, reserving causal powers exclusively for God, the only genuine causal agent that there is. It is perhaps not surprising that among the dualists of his time, Descartes was the only major philosopher who chose to include minds as an integral part of the causal structure of the world. In defense of Descartes, we can ask: What would be the point of having souls as immaterial substances if they turn out to have no causal powers, not even powers to be affected by things around them? Before we castigate Descartes for his possibly unworkable metaphysics, therefore, we should applaud him for showing a healthy respect for common sense in his defense of mental causation and his insistence on making sense of our intuitive dualistic conception of what it is to be a person.

TIMOTHY O'CONNOR

Causality, Mind, and Free Will

Whatever the totality of our nature might be, we human beings have bodies that situate us in a physical space. Many of our actions are at least partially constituted by causally connected sequences of events within such bodies. Do these evident facts constrain, on purely conceptual grounds, the account we advance concerning the metaphysical nature of our minds, from which our actions spring?

One familiar affirmative answer to this question holds that these facts suffice to entail that Descartes's picture of the human mind must be mistaken. On Descartes's view, our mind or soul (the only essential part of ourselves) has no spatial location. Yet it directly interacts with but one physical object, the brain of that body with which it is, "as it were, intermingled," so as to "form one unit" (Meditation VI). The radical disparity posited between a nonspatial mind, whose intentional and conscious properties are had by no physical object, and a spatial body, all of whose properties are had by no mind, has prompted some to conclude that, pace Descartes, causal interaction between the two is impossible. In the preceding chapter Jaegwon Kim has given a new twist to this old line of thought. In the present essay, I will use Kim's argument as a springboard for motivating my own favored picture of the metaphysics of mind and body and then discussing how an often vilified account of freedom of the will may be realized within it.

A version of this paper was read at the University of North Carolina at Chapel Hill and Davidson College. For helpful comments, I thank Louise Antony, John Carroll, John Heil, William Lycan, Al Mele, David Robb, Dan Ryder, and Peter Unger.

I. Kim's Argument

Kim contends that the existence of a spatial framework, or something strongly analogous to such a framework, is a necessary condition on causal interaction among objects. He supports this thesis by an analysis of the "pairing problem," which invites us to give a principled way of identifying individual causal relationships in a scenario in which parallel sequences occur. Suppose rifles A and B are fired simultaneously and result in the simultaneous deaths of Andy and Buddy. Kim asks two questions (which he does not clearly distinguish): (1) What makes it true that A's firing killed Andy and not the other way around? (2) What principles or criteria would lead us to correctly pair individual causes with their effects? Kim answers both these questions in terms of the spatial relations among the rifles and the two individuals. Rifle A's distance from, and orientation in relation to, Andy, is an important general feature of the situation that both made it possible for A to result in Andy's death and gives us a principled reason for supposing these two items to be causally paired, rather than A with Buddy and B with Andy.

I think Kim's treating these two questions as inextricably linked is unwise. He gives no reason to suppose that there could not be a situation in which objects are so distributed that their patterns of causal interactions exhibit a deep symmetry, making it impossible to decide the true causal pairings on empirical grounds. It is instead the first of Kim's questions, concerning the truthmaker for individual causal pairings, that interests me. Kim is implicitly supposing that causality necessarily exhibits a kind of *generality*. If an object or system A acts on B at time *t*, this will be due to general characteristics of B: its being the right sort of thing for A to act upon and its being in the right relationship to A at the time. Had it been a different object C that had those characteristics at *t* (both intrinsic and in relation to A), then A would have acted on it instead. Causality, we might say, is *non-haecceitistic:* objects do not have a primitive disposition to act on certain other individual objects; they are instead disposed to act on any objects having the right characteristics. At different times, the same object will achieve much the same effect on different tokens of some general type.

I accept this thesis about causal generality.[1] Kim wields it against Cartesian dualism as follows: we can imagine two nonphysical minds with identical intrinsic states at time *t0*. Yet one acts on body B1 and the other acts on body B2. Why? Given that the minds bear no spatial relationships with

[1] It is denied by "singularists" who hold that causation is first and foremost a relation between particular events, and the holding of that relation in a given instance has no implications (strict or probabilistic) for what happens elsewhereor elsewhen. C might cause E even

these bodies, we must find some other kind of external relationship that explains the causal selectivity. Kim can think of none and concludes that there probably couldn't be one. So if causation cannot be haecceitistic, selective dualistic interaction (one mind with one body, and vice versa) appears to be impossible. Note that an appeal to God as the one who ordains certain permanent mind-body pairings will not help. For just as God cannot make a round square, likewise God cannot create a haecceitistic model of an essentially non-haecceitistic make.

Kim goes further. He suggests that the same consideration should lead us to suppose that causal interaction even solely *among* nonphysical minds is probably incoherent. For what kind of relationship could play the role of a structuring environment that is played by space for physical objects? If none is proffered, and we embrace the Eleatic linkage of existence with causal powers, we should suspect the coherence of the very idea of a nonphysical mind altogether.

II. A Souler System?

It will be profitable to begin our assessment of the options for dualistic causality with a quick look at this last, fanciful scenario of a monistic

---

though no other C-type event causes or has a tendency to cause an E-type event. It may *happen* to be true of our world that all causal transactions fall into patterns of certain types, but this, for the singularist, is at best owing to some contingent feature of the way causation is manifested in our world. There might have been ubiquitous causation in a chaotic, anomic world—including causal patterns between pairs of objects that are not amenable to general analysis of the sort Kim requires.

The implausibility of this view is apparent when one considers the ultimate positions on the nature of causation in the actual world held by the two contemporary philosophers who have most emphatically argued that causation is a singular relation—positions which look decidedly *anti*-singularist to the causal observer. David Armstrong has responded to a serious problem for earlier versions of his position by holding that causation is manifested in our world as a relation among *types* of states of affairs. (See *A World of States of Affairs* [Cambridge: Cambridge University Press, 1997].) And Michael Tooley's "speculative proposal" in response to that same problem is to posit unusual features in the mereology of transcendent universals. If it is a law of nature that all things having property *P* have property *Q*, then, he says, we might suppose that *P* "exists only as the conjunctive universal, *P and Q*" (*Causation: A Realist Approach* [Oxford: Clarendon, 1987], 124). It would then follow that *any* time *P* is instantiated, *Q* is as well. Although these moves are critical to salvaging their respective theories of the general nature of causal processes in our world, they insist that these are merely contingent facts about causation, so as to preserve the singularist "intuition" that there might have been instances of causation in an anomic world—in a world where events having the effects they do has nothing to do with the kind of events they are. This contingency is mysterious and unmotivated.

system of interacting souls. Kim rather quickly places it outside the bounds of intelligibility, due to the lack of spatial relations that could structure the conditions of selective interaction. But there are other forms of order. One can readily imagine a scenario in which such an alternative to spatial relationships serves to structure the interactions of nonphysical minds, provided they have a suitably rich psychology. Suppose that God, in generating a series of souls, ordains that in their initial state they conform to a mathematically describable array, with each soul carrying the information of its present location in the array as a primitive intentional state. Souls 'move' through the array over time by forming intentions to occupy a specified location. Among the basic laws of this souler system is a dynamical one that governs the actual rearrangements as a function of all such intentions. (Perhaps, analogous to a time-sharing condominium arrangement, souls continually form ordered preferences as to their subsequent location. The dynamical law might factor in previous success in obtaining highly ranked preferences, give a certain weight to preferences to remain in one's present "neighborhood," and so forth. The reader is invited to fill in the details as he wishes.) Causal capacities come in two basic types: the ability to form specific intentions concerning oneself or another and the ability to modify the intentional state of another via one's own intentions. I shall say more about the basic ability to generate intentions later. Let us concentrate now on the effect of such intentions on one's fellows. An example might be this: by intending to communicate to Jaegwon the thought that it would be nice to have a body as humans do, I cause him to register this thought, along with a belief that it is *my* thought that he is now entertaining. Again, there will be some sort of dynamical law that governs the degree of success in bringing about such states in others: perhaps it will be directly proportional to the recipient's attentiveness and inversely proportional to his present informational load and "distance" in the array. Perhaps instead of a function dictating continuously diminishing clarity and accuracy in the reception of the thought, these features of the effect will be measurable in discrete quanta of only a few magnitudes.

It will be noticed that I have used spatial metaphors to characterize the ordering that structures the interaction of souls in a nonspatial world. This should not in itself be objectionable, however. It is analogous to the nonliteral talk of phase space in quantum mechanics. We find it natural and easy to encode information in spatial terms. Propositional logic can be given a spatially encoded formalization, but we can do so without supposing that the logical relationships so represented are actually spatial. One might, though, shape the worry about reliance on spatial metaphor into the following objection: You have not actually described a framework of objective external relations. Instead, you have merely gestured at an abstract formalism and asserted without argument that there could be a kind of external relation so characterizable that is distinct from spatial relations and holds among nonphysical minds. Your reference to divine decree in instituting the array seems ineliminable, and in consequence the changing sequence over time that you described smacks of occasionalism, rather than real interaction.

In reply, I grant that a mathematical characterization of an objective ordering does not disclose the qualitative character of the ordering it is meant to describe, in the way that we ordinarily suppose ourselves to directly apprehend suitable instances of spatial relations. The only such external relations among concrete objects that we do seem to apprehend in this way—setting aside the contentious relation of causation itself—are spatial and temporal. Nonetheless, sketching the picture as I did above encourages the thought that there might be other possible instances of such mathematical structures. (Indeed, if one accepts relativity theory as a straightforward guide to the metaphysics of space-time, one is committed to denying, contrary to appearances, that space and time are objective relations and accepting instead an underlying reality—the space-time interval—that is *not* directly apprehended in experience.)

If necessary, we might mount a further defense of the possibility of soul-soul interactions that exploits the fact that it is easier for us to accept the existence of intrinsic properties that are alien to our world. (Why? Probably because we are committed to the existence of a wider range of such properties together with the fact that we can functionally specify properties in terms of their causal role within a system, whereas external relations merely provide a background, or structured framework, within which properties manifest their dispositional character.) So suppose one remains skeptical of the very possibility of external relations within a system of nonphysical souls. One could recast my description of such a system by eschewing external relations within an array in favor of a primitive sort of intrinsic informational state had by each soul, such that it knows "where" it is "in relation to" all the others. (Here, of course, the relational talk is merely metaphorical for a primitive, quantifiable, and intrinsic feature.) Whether a given soul may act upon another will depend in part on these informational states, along with their other intrinsic properties. In such a scenario, all causal interactions would be a function entirely of intrinsic properties, without reference to any structuring external relations. But I do not see that it can be dismissed on that account; for the necessary *role* that external relations play in our world's physical transactions—providing an objective structuring of objects that allows for completely general dispositional tendencies to work selectively from context to context—*is* carried out in the envisioned scenario.

III. The Trouble with Cartesian Interactionism

Can the strategy just employed on behalf of the coherence of a parliament of souls be adapted to the picture of the Cartesian dualist? It seems not. We should require not just the system of ordered relations among the nonphysical souls, along with the system of spatial relations among the physical objects, but also a cross-grid mapping of the two, identifying in general terms which body will impact which mind, and vice versa, in terms of their locations within their respective systems. And the trouble here is that on the Cartesian picture, we continually have the same pairings of individual souls and bodies, despite constant relational changes on at least the physical space side of the duality. The Cartesian picture of causal interaction seems unrepentantly haecceitistic.

(Is there the barest of possibilities in the following scenario? Suppose a two-dimensional mind-body array, involving external relations on both sides—*not* including spatiality—in which individual minds and bodies never in fact *change* locations. In consequence, they always act on the same object cross-gridwise. Meanwhile, the bodies are acting and acted upon by constantly changing physical objects as their spatial relations change. We may suppose the souls lack potentiality for soul-soul interaction. In principle—at least by the power of God—souls and bodies could be reconfigured within the two-dimensional array, coming to act on different objects of the other category. If this scenario were coherent, it would involve the most exquisitely small distance from the objectionable idea of haecceitistic causality. Whether truly possible or not, for it to be true of our world, we must assume a system of physical relations entirely hidden from ordinary observation and indeed irrelevant to body-body interaction. I judge this sufficiently high a price to motivate the alternative presented in the sequel.)

What the dualist needs, as even Descartes saw but failed to provide, is a metaphysics on which the mind and body constitute a unified natural *system*. We want a plausible picture on which a particular mind and body are not independent objects that somehow continually find one another in the crowd of similar such objects, but instead constitute a unified single system whose union is grounded independently of particular mental-physical interactions. For note that Kim's argument does not anywhere address *self*-causality—a single object or natural system's acting upon itself. The problem of generality does not sensibly arise in this context, apart from the easily satisfied requirement that if a given system has the propensity to act upon itself in a certain manner, a similar propensity should be had by a qualitatively identical system.[2]

IV. Mind and Emergence

Here is a way individual souls and bodies might constitute a single natural system. At some specific juncture in the development of the human organism, the body generates the soul, a nonphysical substance. Provided the requisite degree of structural complexity and life-conserving functions of the body are preserved, the soul will likewise persist. Thus, it is completely dependent on the body not just for its coming to be but also for its continuing to be. Given such a baseline, asymmetrical dependency-of-existence relation, it is not arbitrary that these two entities should also interact continuously in more specific ways over time. On this picture, the soul is not entirely an entity in its own right, but is more properly seen as an aspect of the overall, fundamentally biological system that is the human person.

While I do think this emergentist variety of substance dualism is able to overcome Kim's objection to the traditional variety, the kind of causal capacity it attributes to the requisite biological systems is extraordinary. Differentiating details aside, causal agents of every sort in the universe are taken to act by introducing a qualitative change (or sustaining a persisting qualitative state) within themselves or other entities. The present sort of emergence, by contrast, would involve the generation of fundamentally new substance in the world—amounting to creation ex nihilo. That's a lot to swallow. Note that it's not sufficient, for addressing Kim's problem, that one retreat to supposing a preestablished harmony. For then the apparent dependence of the soul on the body is not real, the two do not constitute a single natural system, and the pairing problem is not solved.

[2] I note in passing that one might suppose that the problem presently under consideration applies equally to the classical conception of God as a nonphysical mind who causally acts upon the physical universe. But this would be a mistake. The physical universe is not a pregiven object which, as it happens, God encounters, as on the Cartesian picture the soul is an originally independent substance in its own right and is then "fitted" to a specific body. Instead, God's acting on the universe in particular ways at particular times is of a piece with His giving being to the universe at that time: the universe is entirely dependent on Him at all times for its very existence and character, and there is no neutral environment akin to space in which He and it and possibly other entities coexist, which might prompt the question of the general conditions that govern selective interaction among them.

I suggest instead that those of us with dualist predilections try to live with a weaker form of dualism, on which token mental events are ontologically sui generis, distinct from any complex token physical state, without there being any substance distinct from the body which is the direct bearer of those events. This is a substance monism on which human persons are fundamental biological entities that also have emergent mental states. In the present section, I will sketch in formal terms the notion of emergence I have in mind.[3] In the remainder of the chapter, I will address one reason some traditional dualists are dissatisfied with the weaker form of emergence: its implications for freedom of the will.

The informed reader is admonished that what we want in an account of emergence in the present context is quite different from other, epistemologically rooted conceptions of emergence employed in some contemporary theories of mind in philosophy and cognitive science. Our notion is ontological. We shall say that a state of an object is emergent if it instantiates one or more simple, or nonstructural, properties and is a causal consequence of the object's exhibiting some general type of complex configuration (whose complexity will probably be a feature of both its intrinsic and functional structure). By calling a property "nonstructural," I mean that its instantiation does not even partly consist in the instantiation of a plurality of more basic properties. By calling the emergent state a "causal consequence" of the object's complex configuration, I mean this: in addition to having a locally determinative influence in the manner characterized by physical science, fundamental particles or systems also naturally tend (in any context) toward the generation of such an emergent state. But their doing so is not discernible in contexts not exhibiting the requisite macrocomplexity, because each such tending on its own is "incomplete." It takes the right threshold degree of complexity for those tendings, present in each microparticle, to jointly achieve their characteristic effect, which is the generation of a specific type of holistic state.

So far I have given only a sufficient condition for a state's being emergent. The reason is that the picture becomes more complicated once we consider not just the generation of an emergent state, but the kinematics of an object's having one or more emergent features for a period of time. Think of the above as a baseline case, involving just such an initial generation of an emergent state. Then consider that, as a fundamentally new kind of feature, it will confer certain causal capacities on the object

[3] I explain this less formally and address objections not considered here in chapter 6 of my *Persons and Causes: The Metaphysics of Free Will* (New York: Oxford University Press, 2000).

that go beyond even the summation of capacities directly conferred by the object's microstructure. Its effects might include directly determining aspects of the microphysical structure of the object as well as generating other emergent states. In setting forth a general account of how this might go, I am guided not by abstract intuition about how it must go in any possible emergent scenario, but by a natural conjecture about how it goes with respect to our own mental life, on the supposition that qualitative and intentional features of our mental states are emergent.

On that supposition, it is plausible that there are enduring baseline mental states that partially underwrite more specific and often momentary mental states. Suppose, then, that when a neurophysiological system H comes to have a certain kind of complex configuration P^* at time $t0$, the baseline emergent state E is the direct result at $t1$. (P^*, of course, will have to be of a sufficiently general type as to persist through constant and dramatic change.) P^* will also partly determine the underlying physical state of H at time $t1$. Let $P0$ be the remaining aspect of H's intrinsic state at $t0$, and $P@$ be the summation of those factors in H's immediate environment that will bear upon the physical state of H at $t1$. Letting "$\rightarrow$" represent the causal relation, we have

$$P^* \text{ at } t0 \rightarrow E \text{ at } t1$$

and

$$P^* + P0 + P@ \text{ at } t0 \rightarrow P^* + P1 \text{ at } t1$$

(the latter conjunction being the total intrinsic physical state of H at time $t1$, with $P1$ being the remainder beyond P^*). Now E at $t1$ will help to determine in part the physical state of H at the subsequent moment, $t2$, but not its continuing to exhibit P^*, of course, as that would involve causal circularity. E, we may suppose, will also help to determine the occurrence at $t2$ of another emergent state, $E2$. Diagrammatically, the overall picture is this:

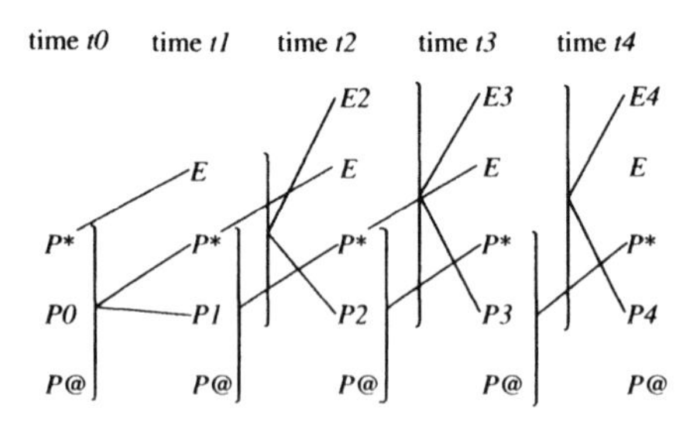

(For simplicity of representation, I'm treating *P@* schematically; at each moment it represents the sum total of those immediate environmental factors bearing on the intrinsic state of H at the subsequent moment.)

We are now in position to answer two standardly asked questions about any doctrine of mental causation. First, do the emergent properties of H supervene on its physical properties? By "supervenience" I here mean a synchronic relation between families of properties. The family of emergent properties would supervene on the family of physical properties just in case having an emergent property implies, of causal necessity, that (1) an object has some physical properties and that (2) its having any specific set of physical properties suffices to determine which, if any, emergent properties it has.

The first condition on supervenience is evidently satisfied. The slogan used to capture the second condition is: No mental difference without a physical difference. Consider first the status of our baseline emergent feature *E*, with reference to times *t0* and *t1* in the diagram. *E* is absent at *t0* and present immediately thereafter. The underlying physical properties are different, too, but that is not the reason for the difference in emergent properties. For the differentiating factors (*P0*, *P1*, and the variable *P@*) are, by hypothesis, not directly relevant to the occurrence of *E*. *P** alone is so relevant. Yet *E* is absent at the first time, since *P**'s obtaining at *t0* causally determines what will occur not at that very time but immediately thereafter. So at the first instant of its instantiation in H, H will not bear *E*. This indicates that there might be two objects having identical intrinsic physical properties (including *P**) and existing in the same external circumstance, yet one has *E* and the other lacks it.

But this is only a slight departure, restricted to the first instant at which the "base" property *P** occurs. More interesting divergence between emergent properties in the face of physical similarity can be seen when we turn from the baseline emergent property *E* to the more specific features *E2*, *E3*, and *E4*. Consider *E2* at time *t2*. You might have the underlying physical properties *P** and *P2* without having had *E2*. For *E2* is a causal product of the immediately prior state of H at *t1* (comprised of *P**, *P1*, and *E*). This prior state presumably could have been different (such that *E2* would not then occur at *t2*), consistent with the same physical state at *t2*, given a suitably fortuitous change in the environmental circumstance *P@*. The possibility of a difference with respect to *E2* without an underlying physical difference is clearer when we instead suppose a case in which the causal connections are probabilistic only. For then we can hold fixed the immediately prior state of H, and suppose a scenario in which it causes the same underlying physical state at *t2* but, owing to a different chancy outcome, causes the occurrence not of *E2* but of some distinct property, *E**2, at the emergent level.

So emergent states do not in general supervene on physical states. A second question we might have is whether they are epiphenomenal, at least with respect to the purely physical states of H and its immediate environment. Is the system in its purely physical aspect—is physics more generally—causally closed? Here, too, the answer is no. *P3*'s obtaining at *t3* is in part a product of *E* and *E2*'s obtaining at *t2*. Had one or both of these failed to obtain at that previous time, something other than *P3* would have occurred subsequently. Consistent with this, it is true in an emergentist scenario that everything that occurs rests on the *total* potentialities of the physical properties. For the occurrence of any emergent properties are among those potentialities, and so the effects of the emergent features are indirectly a consequence of the physical properties too. The difference that emergence makes is that what happens transcends the immediate, or local, interactions of the microphysics.

In summation, we have seen that property emergentism allows for a form of dualism that escapes Kim's problem, since the mental-physical interactions it posits occur within the context of a natural unitary system, and hence is a form of self-causality, rather than multiple-object transaction. I now turn to one test of its being sufficiently robust: whether it is consistent with the kind of freedom of will to which many dualists subscribe.

V. Causal Generality and Free Will

Freedom of the will, in my judgment, involves the exercise of a distinctively personal form of causality, one which differs in certain respects from the mechanistic form of causation operative in impersonal causal forces.[4] In the mechanistic case, objects have specific causal powers, or dispositional tendencies, associated with their fundamental intrinsic properties. The powers might concern a unique outcome or a range of possible effects that is structured by a specific probability measure. Either

[4] I have argued this in several places, most recently in the book cited in the previous note. When I say that agent causation is "purposive," and thereby contrasts with "mechanistic" causation, I don't mean to imply that it is not law-governed in any way. (See the following note.) Nor do I mean to imply that were reasons directly to cause choices, the activity would be nonpurposive in the ordinary sense. Rather, I intend to highlight the fact that agent causation is essentially purposive, whereas mechanistic causality is not. Agent causality is triadic—it involves an agent's causing an intention for a reason. The dyadic form of mechanistic causality is indifferent to whether the causes be reasons or impersonal states.

way, they exercise certain of these causal powers as a matter of course when they are placed in the appropriate circumstances. Such circumstances either stimulate a latent mechanism or remove inhibitors to the activity of a mechanism already in a state of readiness. Strictly speaking, the cause here is the *event* of the object's having these power-conferring properties in those circumstances.

According to some of us, there is another species of the causal genus, involving the characteristic activity of purposive free agents. Such agents can represent possible courses of action to themselves and have desires and beliefs concerning those alternatives. Against that background motivational framework, they themselves directly bring about immediately *executive* states of intention to act in various ways. This direct causing by agents of states of intention goes like this: As with mechanistic causes, the distinctive capacities of agent causes ("active powers") are grounded in some set of properties. So any agent having the relevant internal properties will *have it directly within his power to* cause any of a range of states of intention delimited by internal and external circumstances. However, these properties function differently in the associated causal process. Instead of being associated with direct causal functions from circumstances to effects, they (in conjunction with appropriate circumstances) *make possible* the agent's producing an effect. These choice-enabling properties ground a different type of causal power or capacity—one that in suitable circumstances is freely exercised by the agent himself. (One might say that agent causation is essentially purposive, whereas mechanistic causality is not. Agent causality is triadic—it involves an agent's causing an intention for a reason. The dyadic form of mechanistic causality is indifferent to whether the causes be reasons or impersonal states.)

Now given his concern with causal generality, Kim might wonder whether I am trying to have things both ways by embracing the causal powers account of mechanistic causation while also defending agent causation. The causal powers account is resolutely "anti-singularist" in the sense discussed above. Yet I have purported to identify as one of its species something (involving agent causation) that seems to imply singularism. But there is not really a problem here, except perhaps with the way some draw the singularist / anti-singularist distinction. Mechanistic and agent causation both require generality with respect to the grounding of causal powers. A given particular has a given type of causal power because of its intrinsic properties, and properties are universals. Where agent and mechanistic causal capacities diverge is in their *exercise*. The exercise of mechanistic capacities conforms to tendencies of some measure (the limiting case being deterministic). In the agent causal case this is not necessarily so, at least as a conceptual matter. Agents may choose any of the options within the range of their power at a given time without having some fixed probabilistic tendency to do so. (There are some contingent features of human agents that indicate that the exercise of active power has further causal structure in the way reasons govern it. Reasons move us to act, and some do so much more strongly than others. My current proposal, elaborated elsewhere, is that we think of the agent's states of having reasons to act in various ways as structuring the agent causal capacity, such that the agent's freely choosing an action type will have some objective tendency to occur, one which fluctuates over time. Even if this is accepted, it is true that, in contrast to mechanistic causation, it remains up to the agent to decide how to act. The tendency-conferring state of having a reason does not itself generate the action; it disposes the agent himself to initiate an action sequence.) Whether or not we add this wrinkle, the important point here is that the basic view does not fall afoul of Kim's stricture on non-haecceitistic causal tendencies, since agent causation is grounded in generalized capacities and is a form of self-causality within a unitary system.

Can we make sense of agent causation as an *emergent* capacity of a fundamentally biological system? Note that such a theorist is committed to the emergence of a very different sort of property altogether. Instead of producing certain effects in the appropriate circumstances itself, of necessity, this property enables the individual that has it in a certain range of circumstances to freely and directly bring about (or not bring about) any of a range of effects. It might be thought that because of this distinctive character, it isn't possible that it could naturally emerge from other properties. Such a property could be instantiated only in a very different kind of *substance* from material substances, as on the problematic Cartesian view.

This thought does not bear up well under scrutiny, however. Given that there is nothing inconsistent about the emergence of an "ordinary" causal property, able to causally influence the environments in which it is instantiated, it is hard to see just why there could not be a variety of emergent property whose novelty consists in enabling its possessor directly to effect changes at will (within a narrowly limited range, and in appropriate circumstances). If properties are able, as a matter of nomological necessity, to produce an entirely novel type of property, what reason do we have to assert that, when it comes to the property / kind distinction just noted, properties can spawn others of their own kind alone? At least, this would seem to be an empirical, not philosophical or conceptual, matter.

Still, taking the agency theory seriously within an emergentist framework raises several theoretical problems. The most fundamental of these is determining the precise underlying properties on which an agent-causal capacity depends. Put differently, what types of features—either functionally or intrinsically characterized—constitute a physical system's being a free agent in the technical sense? Conversely, what structural transformations in the human nervous system would result in long-standing (or permanent) loss of the agent-causal capacity generally? This is an empirical matter (one answerable only by neurobiological science) and does not lie within the province of philosophical action theory. Yet even a casual acquaintance with how neurobiologists approach their craft is enough to give an appreciation of the enormous difficulty this most basic issue poses. A plausible general conjecture is that such a capacity is bound up with the capacities for action representation and for conscious awareness, in their specifically human (and probably certain other mammalian) manifestations. It is highly plausible that this self-determining capacity strictly requires each of these other abilities, since they appear to follow from the very characterization of active power as structured by motivating reasons and as allowing the free formation of executive states of intention in accordance with an action representation.

If there are agent-causal events, there is no neat and simple way of dividing those events from mechanistic-causal ones. It surely must be allowed that some human behavior, even conscious behavior, is directly brought about by mechanistic-causal factors. (Not all action is *free* action, and I intend agent causation to account only for the latter.) This is likely to be true of behavior governed by unconscious factors and highly routinized actions. Precisely to what extent, then, is an ordinary human's behavior directly regulated by the agent himself, and to what extent is it controlled by subpersonal processes? Even when I act freely, I am usually not trying to control directly the precise degree of muscle contraction, limb trajectory, and so forth. This makes it plausible to hold that our memory system stores action sequences that we simply activate through conscious choice. (It also explains the facility of an experienced performer in carrying out complex movements, such as a sequence of dance steps.)[5] It is likely that these choices are at times brought about event-causally, while we simply monitor the result and retain the capacity to agent-causally redirect things as need be.

[5] An early philosophical discussion of the implications of this for theories of action is A. Farrer's *The Freedom of the Will* (London: Adam & Charles Black, 1958). Concrete proposals for how to account for such phenomena within recent cognitive science models may be found in S. Kosslyn and O. Koenig, *Wet Mind* (New York: Free Press, 1992), and in Donald Norman and Tim Shallice, "Attention to Action: Willed and Automatic Control of Behavior," in *Cognitive Neuroscience: A Reader*, ed. Michael Gazzaniga (Oxford: Blackwell, 2000), 376–90.

Finally, one might also worry that free will requires the emergence of a degree of indeterminism far beyond what we have any reason to believe is operative (as a function of quantum indeterminacy) at the complex level of neural structures. My reply is that since an emergent property has, relative to its underlying properties, a unique, nonstructural nature, we have no a priori reason to think it must result in processes exhibiting precisely the same degree of indeterminism as is present in its sustaining lower-level processes. Still, we are not supposing "something's coming from nothing," as many have thought: the presence of any emergent feature, on the view I have sketched, will be determined by more fundamental features of its possessor. What it does allow is a stable set of processes giving rise, at certain critical junctures, to a somewhat different order of affairs via "top-down" controlling features. It is just this possibility that allows the right sort of emergentist view to overcome the opposite complaint from Cartesian sympathizers that agents with such emergent capacities are "ontologically superficial"—not among the truly basic entities whose activities determine the way the world is.[6] While it is true, on my picture, that the presence of agent-causal capacities in select complex entities has always been among the potentialities of the world's primordial building blocks, the way those potentialities are exercised is not so prefigured. The agents themselves determine these outcomes. In consequence, any way of completely characterizing what happens in the world must make reference to these agents and their distinctive capacities. This is as ontologically "deep" as any entity that is not necessary being could aspire to.

[6] This complaint occurs in some recent unpublished work by Peter Unger.

CHARLES TALIAFERRO

Emergentism and Consciousness: Going beyond Property Dualism

In the second half of the twentieth century, the philosophy of mind was carried out largely in the service of a materialist project. As Jaegwon Kim observes, "The shared project of the majority of those who have worked on the mind-body problem over the past few decades has been to find a way of accommodating the mental within a principled physical scheme, while at the same time preserving it as something distinctive—that is, without losing what we value, or find special, in our nature as creatures with minds."[1] A recurrent move in the field was to test the most ambitious forms of materialism: physicalism without any hint of dualism. But whether this materialist project was in the hands of radical behaviorists like John Watson or the more recent eliminativists from Quine to the Churchlands, the majority of English-speaking philosophers occupied more modest positions for the sake of values or "common sense." These modest positions have themselves been difficult to define and stabilize philosophically. Identity theorists face the threat of epiphenomenalism. Functionalists face problems of qualia that do not show any sign of abating. A growing number of materialists have yielded ground to allow for a modest form of dualism: a dualism of properties.

According to property dualism, there are some mental properties (activities, states, events—depending on the preferred categories) that are not identical with physical properties. On this view, being in pain is

I thank the Department of Philosophy, New York University, and the Department of Religion, Princeton University, for comments on an earlier version of this paper.

[1] Jaegwon Kim, *Mind in a Physical World: An Essay on the Mind-Body Problem and Mental Causation* (Cambridge: MIT Press, 1998), 2.

inextricably bound up with and caused by certain brain processes, but it is not the very same thing as the brain process. This view has been defended by Thomas Nagel, Colin McGinn, Roderick Chisholm, and others. Many advocates of supervenience theories of mind accept a distinction between mental and physical properties. And despite their insistence on a firmly grounded physicalist identification of the person as a biological animal, neo-Aristotelians like David Wiggins still allow for a conceptual distinction between the mental and the physical.

In this chapter I canvass some of the appeal of property dualism, highlight some of its difficulties, and then propose, instead, a more radical, dualist philosophy of mind.

I. The Virtues of Property Dualism

Many materialist philosophers acknowledge that substance dualism is the most widely held position among the untutored. It is the philosophy of the person on the street. A sampling of materialists who variously acknowledge the dominance and, to some extent, the initial plausibility of dualism includes Michael Levin, Daniel Dennett, David Lewis, Thomas Nagel, J. J. C. Smart, Richard Rorty, and Donald Davidson.[2] The latest to join these ranks is Colin McGinn who, in *The Mysterious Flame: Conscious Minds in a Material World*, agrees that dualism is the commonsense view. He grants that it has some prima facie plausibility and that, to some extent, dualists are right.[3] "The dualists are right to doubt that the brain as currently conceived can explain the mind."[4]

Property dualism has the advantage of taking on at least a big section of this "commonsense" outlook. Property dualism is thus pitted against the more extreme eliminativist attack on "folk psychology." There is no need for property dualists to launch a thoroughgoing error theory against our customary descriptions and explanations of ourselves in terms of beliefs, desires, and sensation. Property dualists can capitalize on observations such as this: "Consciousness certainly *seems* quite different from a mere brain process. My hearing of a loud bang, say, presents itself as a different *kind* of thing from electrical activity in a certain part of my brain. And thinking about a trip to the beach does not *feel* like the spiking of

[2] Charles Taliaferro, *Consciousness and the Mind of God* (Cambridge: Oxford University Press, 1994), 26.

[3] Colin McGinn, *The Mysterious Flame: Conscious Minds in a Material World* (New York: Basic Books, 1999), 23, 29.

[4] Ibid., 29.

innumerable neurons in my cortex."[5] And property dualism has the added advantage of avoiding the problems that beset substance dualism.

According to a fairly standard form of substance dualism, persons are not metaphysically identical with their bodies nor any physical object or process. A person is a nonphysical, concrete thing, enduring over time, and causally interactive with his body. In the case of a well-functioning embodiment (for example, someone who has sensations, the ability to act, and so on), the person is so sensorially bound up with his body that he senses the world through and with his body, he has a sensory awareness of his body from within (proprioception), he acts in the world as his body (his moving across the street is an event that essentially involves bodily movements), and the functioning of his thinking, feeling, sensing, and agency all depend causally upon the functioning of his body. Dualists sometimes argue for their position on the grounds that while the person and body are intimately causally bound together, it is metaphysically possible for the person to exist without his body and it is possible for his body to exist without him. This Cartesian, modal argument has contemporary defenders.[6]

Substance dualism has been attacked on many fronts. Its weaknesses provide grounds for property dualism. With eliminativism and substance dualism both ruled out, property dualism appears to be a good compromise. In this chapter I will concentrate largely on McGinn's four objections to substance dualism and then on the strengths and weaknesses of his property dualism.

First, there is the charge that substance dualism leaves us with an exaggerated picture of the mind-body relation. McGinn argues that while property dualism may not be able to account in precise scientific terms for how it is that the brain produces and sustains consciousness, nonetheless it locates consciousness more firmly in the natural, material world. Substance dualism instead saddles us with a mind that functions with too much independence from the brain. According to McGinn, substance dualists are akin to pretechnological primitives who fail to grasp the radical dependency of the mental on the physical. He refers to this outlook as "theistic dualism" rather than just "dualism" for reasons that will become apparent shortly.

> The trouble with theistic dualism is that it vastly exaggerates the gap between mind and brain. The mind is far more dependent on the brain than

[5] Ibid., 24.

[6] See Richard Swinburne, *Evolution of the Soul* (Oxford: Oxford University Press, 1986); W. D. Hart, *The Engine of the Soul* (Cambridge: Cambridge University Press, 1988); Taliaferro, *Consciousness*.

> the theory acknowledges. Imagine being a primitive human confronted with a modern stereo system. Being unable to understand how the sound comes out of the speakers, you might be tempted to think that the gleaming machinery in front of you plays no role in producing the sound. But that would be a mistake on your part. And you would quickly learn your error if you took a hammer to the system and noticed the changes in emitted sound. The fact is that we know that the brain produces consciousness, we just don't know how it does this.[7]

Whatever the problems facing property dualism in accounting for consciousness, the problems are far more extreme in the case of substance dualism.

Second, McGinn argues that dualism leads to epiphenomenalism, the view that the physical affects the mental but not vice versa. He calls this the zombie problem. "The zombie problem is that dualism allows us to subtract the mind from the brain while leaving the brain completely intact. Consider your brain now, whirring and chugging away, and consider your present state of consciousness. Dualism says that we can coherently imagine that your brain stays the same while we 'suppose' your consciousness away."[8] McGinn maintains that a philosophy of mind which leads to epiphenomenalism is disastrous.

> Epiphenomenalism is the claim that mind doesn't matter, that it makes no difference what happens in the world, that it does not cause behavior. My zombie twin behaves just like me but has no mind at all. How then can it be that *my* mind affects my behavior? My mind must be like a lazy halo floating over my brain, unable to influence the course of events. This problem is particularly acute when we consider what I say about my own mind. Suppose I say the words "I am having an experience of red" just when I am in fact experiencing red. It is overwhelmingly natural to suppose that it is my experience of red that explains my saying those words: I am simply reporting my current experience. I say what I do because of what I experience. But my zombie twin says the same words, since he is a physical duplicate of me, and yet he has no experience of red, no experience at all. So in his case the explanation of his saying those words is not that he is having an experience of red. Rather, the explanation relies on the physical events in his brain and the way they trigger his speech mechanisms. But then surely my words must have the same explanation, because the same effects must have the same explanation, and certainly just those physical events were going on in me.[9]

[7] McGinn, *Mysterious Flame,* 88.
[8] Ibid., 25.
[9] Ibid., 25, 26.

Actually, the case McGinn describes is even worse than standard epiphenomenalism. Most epiphenomenalists would allow that the physiology of seeing colors might prompt the mental activity of speaking; they would simply deny that mental activity can in turn play the causal role of initiating physical processes. If McGinn is right, dualists seem straddled with a disjointed parallelism. Whatever the cause of McGinn's saying "I see red," it is not the physical network of his body. This argument charges that we cannot accept substance dualism without, in Kim's terms, "losing what we value or find special, in our nature as creatures with minds."

Third, McGinn maintains that substance dualism leads to incoherence. This may be called the "ghost problem." If dualists believe that a person (or mind or soul) is nonphysical, they must believe it is coherent to suppose that there could be a disembodied person or mind.

> How could such a mind be located anywhere without a body to anchor it? How can it have effects in the physical world? How could we manage to pick out and describe one disembodied mind rather than another? We can hardly point to a disembodied mind. When we picture a ghost to ourselves we indulge in a contradictory mishmash of the immaterial and the corporeal, an entity that can be seen but not touched, that can walk through walls yet can pick things up, that produced sounds from no vocal apparatus, that has a surface but no interior organs.[10]

Ghosts are incoherent. Therefore substance dualism is false.

Fourth, substance dualism is at odds with our background beliefs. At the back of much philosophy of mind lies a metaphysical picture of the nature of the cosmos that is materialist to the core. As Paul Churchland writes, "Most scientists and philosophers would cite the presumed fact that humans have their origin in 4.5 billion years of purely chemical and biological evolution as a weighty consideration of expecting mental phenomena to be nothing but a particularly exquisite articulation of the basic properties of matter and energy."[11] And McGinn similarly underscores a materialist metaphysic. "Consider the universe before conscious beings came along: the odds did not look good that such beings could come to exist. The world was all just physical objects and physical forces, devoid of life."[12] But while Churchland's project is eliminative, McGinn does allow for consciousness, and thus must face a puzzle or mystery. By his

[10] Ibid., 27.

[11] Paul Churchland, *The Engine of Reason, the Seat of the Soul* (Cambridge: MIT Press, 1995), 211.

[12] McGinn, *Mysterious Flame,* 14.

lights, we can allow this emergence, this rupture in an otherwise thoroughly material cosmos, and live with the mystery. But substance dualists face a more formidable problem, and the chief resource that is used by these dualists to address the problem of emergence is problematic: theism.

Theism, of course, may be advanced to assist not just substance dualists but property dualists as well. McGinn puts the problem this way: "How did evolution convert the water of biological tissue into the wine of consciousness?"[13] Like a number of naturalists—Galen Strawson, Jerry Fodor, Ned Block—McGinn is not at all impressed by naturalist explanations of the emergence of consciousness from matter. "We have a good idea how the Big Bang led to the creation of stars and galaxies, principally by the force of gravity. But we know of no comparable force that might explain how ever-expanding lumps of matter might have developed an inner conscious life."[14] This would seem to lend weight to theism. If, as McGinn notes, the odds are not in favor of the emergence of consciousness given a materialist background, perhaps we should switch our background beliefs. R. M. Adams, Richard Swinburne, and others have advanced theistic arguments based on the existence of consciousness. The emergence of consciousness in nature appears to be natural given that nature itself exists in virtue of an all good, conscious Creator.[15]

But, so McGinn argues, to bring theism into the picture would simply enlarge the mystery. McGinn writes: "A brain is a celestial object with more bizarre properties than any black hole or red dwarf or infinitely dense singularity."[16] We get nowhere if we explain the bizarre brain in light of an even more bizarre, larger brain or spirit. The appeal to theism at this juncture would be a classic case of explaining the obscure in light of the more obscure.

> It is indeed a deep mystery how sentience arises from the brain, but it does not follow that we have to postulate objective miracles in the world. If the mystery arises from our cognitive limitations, then it is mistaken to try to plug the explanatory gap by introducing God into the picture. Imagine a clever monkey trying to understand plant growth. She might well be tempted to suppose that God is the force behind this phenomenon, since

[13] Ibid., 13.

[14] Ibid., 15.

[15] See Richard Swinburne, *The Existence of God* (Oxford: Oxford University Press, 1979); R. M. Adams, *The Virtues of Faith* (Oxford: Oxford University Press, 1987); J. P. Moreland, "Searle's Biological Naturalism and the Argument From Consciousness," *Faith and Philosophy* 15 (1998): 1.

[16] McGinn, *Mysterious Flame,* 16.

> she cannot grasp the theory of photosynthesis. But it would be more rational for her to infer that her explanatory troubles spring from a cognitive lack on her part, and not from magic in the plant itself. In the same way, we can appeal to our cognitive limitations as an alternative to the supernatural story.[17]

And "magic" seems to be what theists advance. They believe, McGinn assumes, that God performs separate acts, creating each individual mind or soul and then linking it to a body. "God created your soul and adjoined it to your body for the duration of your mortal life. Each soul is itself a local miracle, a sign of God's supernatural power in the empirical world." The result is a metaphysic that involves too much divine interference. McGinn puts the point tersely: "Nature abhors a miracle." "Theistic dualism takes minds to be created whole by God, with the brain playing no constructive role in this process."[18]

Theism is also shown to be inadequate from the standpoint of the distribution of consciousness throughout nature. "How strange, then, that we need God to explain its presence [consciousness] in animals and yet we don't need God to explain more complex traits of animals." Invoking theism for humans but not for nonhuman animals appears ad hoc. "The God hypothesis begins to seem arbitrary and unexplanatory." Theism offers no more of an explanation of consciousness than McGinn's naturalism "because it is equally mysterious how God's actions produce conscious minds."[19]

Substance dualism may be attacked on other grounds. For example, there is the famous private language argument. I think McGinn has identified the four most substantial objections, however, and so I will address these here and then propose a more radical dualist schema.[20]

II. A Case for Substance Rather Than Property Dualism

Property dualism may not have the burden of arguing for the coherence, let alone the plausibility, of theism, but it does face the problem of accounting for the emergence of conscious states from physical states and processes. "Consciousness is rooted in the brain via *some* natural property

[17] Ibid., 84, 85.

[18] Ibid., 83, 84, 91, 230.

[19] Ibid., 87, 88.

[20] I discuss the private language argument and other antidualism arguments in *Consciousness and the Mind of God.*

of the brain tissue, but it is not explicable in terms of electrochemical processes of the familiar kind."[21] Insofar as property dualists hold that the mental and physical are not identical, there is a gap between the two that is very difficult to bridge. A further difficulty facing property dualism is the apparent contingency of the mind-body relation. It is hard to understand how it is that the mind and body are necessarily so related in the face of their apparent contingency. In an earlier book, *The Problem of Consciousness*, McGinn highlights the problem.

> How is it possible for conscious states to depend upon brain states? How can technicolour phenomenology arise from soggy grey matter? . . . How could the aggregation of millions of individually insentient neurones generate subjective awareness? We know that brains are the *de facto* causal basis of consciousness, but we have, it seems, no understanding of how this can be so. It strikes us as miraculous, eerie, even faintly comic.[22]

I will return to this difficulty after replying to McGinn's four objections.

Do substance dualists exaggerate the distinction between person and body? Certainly forms of dualism have been advanced that do in fact offer a splintered picture of the mind-body relationship. But is there any necessity to follow this? I suggest there is not. McGinn does not object in principle to interaction between the physical and nonphysical, and so long as there can be *some* interaction, why not construe the interaction as altogether thorough? For a person with a well-functioning embodiment, to act, think, and feel one's way in the world is, certainly, to do so as an embodied being. There is no reason for dualists to cast the person or mind as a "lazy halo" (or a very active halo!) floating over the brain.[23]

McGinn's analogy of the stereo system is curious. Yes, the speakers et cetera produce sound, but this admits of analysis. By McGinn's own lights, isn't the sound (what someone hears) different from the physical stuff that causes it? Yes, we can understand why the smashing of the machine would lead to the loss of the music, but we can also easily imagine the music continuing as the sound is heard due to the echoes. The sound is not the very same thing as the music box or the state and activity of the listener's brain.[24] Substance dualists need not deny that the destruction of the

[21] McGinn, *Mysterious Flame*, 29.

[22] Colin McGinn, *The Problem of Consciousness* (Oxford: Blackwell, 1990), 1.

[23] Taliaferro, *Consciousness*.

[24] Recall Peter Strawson's treatment of the hypothesis that there might be a world of just sound; *Individuals* (Garden City, N.Y.: Doubleday, 1963), chap. 2. Plato, famously, discusses

body leads to the destruction or annihilation of consciousness and the person. Some dualists have denied the continuance of consciousness after death, while others have been agnostic (C. D. Broad, C. J. Ducasse). Substance dualists have argued for a different point: the annihilation of the body does not *entail* the annihilation of the body. One may accept this thesis and yet hold that there is no conscious, personal life without certain configurations of physical states.

What about the charge of epiphenomenalism? McGinn assumes that the same event must have the same cause; if McGinn's physiological states cause him to consciously utter a sentence, then the matching physiological states of another being must cause him to consciously utter a matching sentence. McGinn advances this as a *necessary* state of affairs. If the zombie twin is a bona fide possibility, then the relationship between McGinn's physiology and his conscious states is not necessary, and therefore not causal. But why assume that all causal relations are necessary? Why rule out the bare possibility that while event A causes B, it is metaphysically possible that the laws of nature could change and A not cause B? Many philosophers before and after Hume have cast causal relations in contingent terms. David Lewis, who is very far from being a dualist writes:

> Things might have been different, in ever so many ways. . . . I might not have existed at all—neither I myself, nor any counterpart of me. Or there might never have been any people. Or the physical constants might have had somewhat different values, incompatible with the emergence of life. Or there might have been altogether different laws of nature; and instead of electrons and quarks, there might have been alien particles, without charge or mass or spin but with alien physical properties that nothing in this world shares. There are ever so many ways that a world might be; and one of these many ways is the way this world is.[25]

When the dualist claims it is metaphysically possible for bodies and minds to be configured differently then we find them (as in a zombie twin, for

---

the relation of music and instruments in the *Phaedo*. Substance dualists will not cast the mind-body relation as a relation of music to a stereo system or to instruments, since music is a process or activity rather than a concrete substance. But McGinn's example nonetheless invites the observation that the music qua something heard by concertgoers is not the same thing as any physical activity. At least, that is the reasonable conclusion given McGinn's recognition of the distinctive character of consciousness vis-à-vis our best picture of the physical world.

[25] David K. Lewis, *On the Plurality of Worlds* (New York: Blackwell, 1986), 1, 2.

instance), the dualist need not assert that this is a possibility *given the present laws of nature*. The dualist may rather be calling into question whether the laws of nature are themselves metaphysically necessary—could it be, for example, that carbon could have had different causal properties than it does in our cosmos?

As I cited him earlier, McGinn thinks that "Nature abhors a miracle." Perhaps this is a colorful way of underscoring the uniformity of the laws of nature. Let it be conceded that miracles do not happen; why go further and claim they are metaphysically impossible? Until McGinn establishes the metaphysical necessity of causal relations, he has yet to establish that substance dualism entails epiphenomenalism.

What about the coherence of a disembodied being? Several replies are in order. The first is to question how sensible and clear our grasp is of the physical world. In an instructive review of McGinn's book, Galen Strawson proposes that it is not *consciousness* that is mysterious but the physical world. We grasp the character of consciousness clearly in our own states; the physical cosmos is the more mysterious. Strawson takes issue with a key assumption in McGinn's work:

> This is the assumption that we have a pretty good understanding of the nature of matter—of matter in space—of the physical in general. It is only relative to this assumption that the existence of consciousness in a material world seems mystifying. For what exactly is puzzling about consciousness, once we put the assumption aside? Suppose you have an experience of redness, or pain, and consider it just as such. There doesn't seem to be any room for anything that could be called failure to understand what it is.[26]

Strawson then charges that physics has displaced McGinn's more Newtonian picture of matter. "It's been a long time since the 18th century since . . . Priestley pointed out that there are no scientific grounds for supposing that the fundamental constituents of matter have any truly solid central part, and the picture of grainy, inert particles has effectively disappeared in the strangeness of modern quantum theory and superstring theory."[27]

Contemporary physics is not now positing ghosts, but it does allow theoretical items that lack mass, determinate location, and weight, and it admits things (fields and waves) that can go through walls, cannot be seen

[26] Galen Strawson, "Little Gray Cells," *New York Times Book Review*, 11 July 1999, 13.
[27] Ibid.

through ordinary means, and exercise physical effects. As Bas van Frassen writes: "Do concepts of the soul . . . baffle you? They pale beside the unimaginable otherness of closed space-times, event-horizons, EPR correlations, and bootstrap models."[28] Notions of disembodiment may seem less odd than the posits of contemporary physics.

Finally, what is so bad about theism? The charge that it is circular to invoke theism seems based on an odd assumption. If theism is true, then there is an omniscient, omnipotent, good being, without origin or end, who creates and sustains the cosmos in existence. Most philosophical theists hold that God exists necessarily, and most of them who endorse the cosmological argument contend that any evidence that this contingent cosmos owes its existence to a noncontingent, intentional reality is evidence for the existence of God. McGinn is right: "There is nothing about the intrinsic structure of lumps of mere matter that suggests a divine origin. When we look at rocks through a microscope, no trace of the divine greets the eye. Asteroids and black holes show no tell-tale signs of a divine creator."[29] But what theists endeavor to do is to argue from the *contingency* of rocks, matter and energy, et cetera, to the existence of God. They do not argue for theism from some kind of mark or sign on a rock, like the signature of a supreme perfect artist.

McGinn puts the charge of circularity as follows: "The theory takes for granted the existence of the conscious agent who is held to explain the existence of all other conscious agents. But if there is a problem about how the conscious beings we see around us come to exist, therein there is equally a problem about how the conscious being who creates each of those conscious beings came to be."[30]

But this is not a matter of theistic philosophers unfairly taking something for granted. They are hypothesizing that if there is a God, then we may understand the emergence of consciousness as the outcome of a conscious, intentional being. Nontheists are welcome to choose their own starting points and explain consciousness and the cosmos *tout court* from their vantage point.

If theism is accepted as part of the account of the existence of consciousness, does the emergence of each person amount to a miracle? No. Theologically a miracle has been understood along two lines: miracles are religiously significant events brought about by God in vio-

[28] See Paul Churchland, ed. *Images of Science* (Chicago: University of Chicago Press, 1985), 285.

[29] McGinn, *Mysterious Flame*, 79.

[30] Ibid., 86.

lation of a law of nature, or miracles are religiously significant events that are different from God's regular, sustained acts. Either way, theistic dualists need not characterize the emergence of consciousness in nature or in individuals as miracles. Presumably the most elegant way for a theist to construe the genesis of consciousness is by appeal to divinely willed natural laws. Just as God wills carbon to exist with all its properties, God also wills certain causal relations such that when there are certain physical configurations and structures these bring about consciousness. The emergence of consciousness can be likened to any law of nature, and certainly it can be held to reflect sustained, ongoing Divine intentions.

A comprehensive, theistic reading of nature will link all natural laws in terms of God's intentions. Alvin Plantinga's comment is representative: "The very causal laws on which we rely in any activity are no more than the record of God's regular, constant and habitual dealings with the stuff of the universe he has created."[31] What about the charge that theistic dualism is left with a chauvinist picture of nature, viz., only humans are to be understood dualistically? Most contemporary dualists take a dualist reading of nonhuman animals, so this charge is bypassed.

Is there parity, then, between property dualism and substance dualism? McGinn thinks "consciousness depends upon an unknowable natural property of the brain."[32] He underscores how we are limited in our grasp of causal, natural relations and the properties of the brain. He contends we are not "forced" to accept theism. "Instead of concluding that God has to be brought in to explain sentience, we can always remind ourselves that it might be that there is something about the mind-brain nexus that we fundamentally do not grasp. . . . There is thus nothing that forces us to accept supernatural explanations about consciousness, even if the human mind cannot in principle remove its mystery."[33] But when is a philosophical argument so powerful that it *forces us* to accept it? Veterans in philosophy know that philosophical positions are often advanced incrementally–not by knockout arguments but by a cluster of favorable reasons, matched by a cluster of problems facing the alternatives. If theism is incoherent or found to be antiscientific or profoundly inferior to naturalism on philosophical grounds, a

[31] Alvin Plantinga, *Does God Have a Nature?* (Milwaukee: Marquette University Press, 1980), 3.

[32] McGinn, *Mysterious Flame*, 28.

[33] Ibid., 85.

combined theistic dualism is unacceptable. But if, as many of us have argued, theism is in far better shape as a contender, then it can come into play as forming a powerful, comprehensive account of the mind in the material world, balancing what "we value, or find special, in our nature as creatures with minds" (Kim) with what we know about the world and ourselves scientifically.[34]

I have not sought to *establish* theistic dualism in this essay. I have instead sought to underscore the appeal of property dualism, reply to some forceful objections to substance dualism, and then suggest that substance dualism can be supported by a comprehensive metaphysic, theism, which has greater credibility than McGinn charges. McGinn acknowledges the apparent contingency of the mental and physical, the initial plausibility of substance dualism, and the problem of accounting for the emergence of consciousness. Dualistic theism preserves the contingency of the mental and physical, and by placing consciousness at the very center of reality it is unhampered by the problem of explaining the origin of consciousness.

In closing, I underscore a key element in theism. Classical theists in Judaism, Christianity, and Islam understand God's action in terms of goodness. God creates and conserves the cosmos, consciousness and all, because it is good to do so. Theistic dualists like Descartes further understood the mind-body relation in terms of goodness: being materially embodied is good. Theistic dualists like Descartes also acknowledged the ways in which one's embodiment can go wrong, the ways in which we may make perceptual errors, lose our powers of agency and sensation. Many of the observations that McGinn has made about the exaggerated remoteness of mind and body can be viewed as a break down of the good functional unity of person and body in theistic dualism.

I have proposed that dualists are not committed to believing that the mind somehow floats above the body. Even so, one needs to grant that there are cases in which people may be so damaged emotionally, so repelled by their bodies, that they act *as if* they are not truly present, not truly embodied. Isn't it possible also to be so disconnected from one's life that one verges on becoming the zombie twin, not losing consciousness altogether yet being sufficiently conscious only to perform the most routine, mechanical acts? As for McGinn's ghosts, can't one have feelings that are akin to ghosts in their elusiveness? Or have emotions that are a mishmash of incompatible impulses that can't be touched or

[34] Charles Taliaferro, *Contemporary Philosophy of Religion* (Oxford: Blackwell, 1998). I am quoting Kim in *Mind in a Physical World*, 2.

pointed to? I suggest the answer to these questions is yes! Substance dualism easily accommodates these cases, and theistic dualism provides a further metaphysic and theory of values by which one may see these cases to be impairments or breakdowns in the functional unity of an embodied person.[35]

[35] See *Consciousness and the Mind of God* for further observations on McGinn. In "The Virtues of Embodiment," forthcoming in the journal *Philosophy*, I offer an arctic, or virtue-based, understanding of embodiment.

ERIC T. OLSON

A Compound of Two Substances

Cartesian or substance dualism is the view that concrete substances come in two basic kinds. There are material things, such as biological organisms. These may be either simple or composed of parts. And there are immaterial things—minds or souls—which are always simple. No material thing depends for its existence on any soul, or vice versa. And only souls can think.

Cartesian dualism is usually discussed as a theory of mind: as an account of the ultimate nature of the mental, and its relation to the physical. But it is also an account of our own ultimate nature: an account of what we are, fundamentally and metaphysically. There is disagreement, however, about what Cartesian dualism says that we are. According to some, it says that we are souls: wholly immaterial things. According to others, it says that we are things made up of a soul and a body. We have a dual nature: partly immaterial, but also partly material. Each of us is a compound of two substances.

I will call the first view *pure dualism*. It says that the material object by which you perceive and act in the physical world—the thing we call your body—may be as intimately connected with you as you like; but it is not a part of you. The second I will call *compound dualism*. It says that both soul and body are parts of you, though only the soul is essential to you: you could outlive your body if your soul continued to exist, but no one

For help with this paper I am grateful to audiences at Cambridge, Keele, Notre Dame, and Oxford, and to Arif Ahmed, Keith Allen, Jim Baillie, André Gallois, Simon Harrison, Katherine Hawley, David Mackie, Trenton Merricks, Derek Parfit, Richard Swinburne, Dean Zimmerman, and two anonymous referees.

could survive the destruction of one's soul. Plainly, if you are a soul, you can't also be a thing made up of that soul and something else; so the two views are incompatible. These seem to be the only options: there is nothing else that you could be, given Cartesian dualism.

There is little agreement about which is the right way to understand Cartesian dualism. Undergraduates almost invariably state it as compound dualism. Professionals often do so as well, whatever their sympathies toward dualism per se. Here is a typical statement: "I understand by substance dualism the view that those persons which are human beings living on Earth, have two parts linked together, body and soul. . . . On the dualist account the whole man has the properties he does because his constituent parts have the properties they do. I weigh ten stone because my body does; I imagine a cat because my soul does."[1] A smaller number of philosophers take Cartesian dualism to be pure dualism. Many appear unaware of the difference between the two views. This may explain why so many respected figures say inconsistent or incoherent things about the matter. Ryle, for instance, says that on Cartesian dualism a person is both "a ghost mysteriously ensconced in a machine"—pure dualism—and "an association between a body and a non-body," which sounds like compound dualism.[2] Descartes himself, in the Sixth Meditation, says, "it is certain that I am really distinct from my body," and that "I and the body form a unit" (I and the body, not the soul and the body); yet he describes himself a few lines later as "a combination of body and mind."[3] Others describe Cartesianism as the view that a person is two things, a mind and a body—which taken literally would violate the logic of identity.[4]

The difference may seem trivial. I think it is extremely important. Pure dualism is often thought to be less attractive than compound dualism because it implies that we are wholly immaterial. We aren't really visible or tangible. We don't grow larger in our youth or more wrinkled in old age. Strictly speaking, we aren't even human beings—men or women. (I take it

[1] Richard Swinburne, *The Evolution of the Soul* (Oxford: Clarendon, 1997), 145.

[2] Gilbert Ryle, *The Concept of Mind* (London: Hutchinson, 1949), 18, 189.

[3] René Descartes, *The Philosophical Writings of Descartes,* vol. 2, trans. J. Cottingham et al. (Cambridge: Cambridge University Press, 1984), 54, 56.

[4] Ryle, *Concept of Mind,* 11; Roger Scruton, *Modern Philosophy: An Introduction and Survey* (London: Sinclair-Stevenson, 1994), 36; Richard Taylor, *Metaphysics,* 4th ed. (Englewood Cliffs, N.J.: Prentice Hall, 1992), 14. Gordon Baker and Katherine Morris say that "Descartes characterized an individual person as a composite thing, a combination of a body . . . and a rational soul"; yet, for Descartes, "The logical form of any judgement that exhibits my *conscientia* must be that I (the soul) have a mode of thinking" (Baker and Morris, *Descartes's Dualism* [London: Routledge, 1996], 60, 110–11). Unless I am not a person, these views are inconsistent.

that a human being must be at least partly material.) The truth of the matter is that certain human animals relate to us in such a way that we call them our bodies, and it is those things that we see and touch and which bear those physical properties we naïvely attribute to ourselves. It may still be in some sense correct to say that Olson is a 150-pound human being; at any rate that is not the sort of mistake you would make if you were to say that I was an 800-pound walrus. But this is at best a loose and potentially misleading description of me. In sober truth I weigh nothing at all. Compound dualism, on the other hand, seems to imply that we are visible and tangible, and have the physical properties we ordinarily take ourselves to have.

For all that, I believe that there is no good reason for Cartesians to be compound dualists, and every reason for them to be pure dualists. I will argue that compound dualism faces two serious problems that have nothing to do with the usual criticisms of Cartesian dualism, and that do not arise for pure dualism. The difficulties may appear simple and obvious, and can be stated briefly (sections 1 and 5). But many more complex and less obvious things can be said in response to them, and these take up the bulk of the chapter. Finally, I will argue briefly that the apparent attractions of compound dualism are unreal. (I won't discuss the merits of Cartesian dualism per se.)

I. The Problem of the Thinking Soul

The most evident problem with compound dualism is its claim that, although it is souls that think, we are not souls. How can the thing that "thinks in me" be something other than myself?[5] I will call this the *problem of the thinking soul.* In fact it is a cluster of problems, or perhaps one problem with many faces.

First, compound dualism entails that there are at least twice as many thinking things as we thought there were. You are a compound of a body and a soul. But that soul is itself rational and conscious. So there are two thinking beings sitting in your chair, a soul and a compound, reading an essay that was co-written by a simple and a compound philosopher.

Second, compound dualism rules out any plausible account of what it is to be a person. My soul has all the mental properties I take myself to have.

[5] The phrase is Locke's. Much the same problem has been raised against his view that, although there are thinking substances, *people* are something else (see Harold Noonan, *Personal Identity* [London: Routledge, 1989], 71–72).

So why isn't it a person? It satisfies all the best-known definitions of the term. Surely there couldn't be non-people with the same mental properties as genuine people? Rational, self-conscious, morally responsible non-people that run for office, write novels, and fall in love, just as we do? That would make the difference between being a person and not being a person far less interesting and important than anyone thought. Yet if my soul *were* a person, we couldn't say that each embodied human person was a compound of a soul and a body, as compound dualism says. At most every second person would be such a compound.

Further: If souls aren't people, I ought to wonder whether *I* am a person. I could easily be mistaken. At least half of those who take themselves to be people are mistaken. More generally, on compound dualism I ought to wonder whether I am the compound of my soul and my body or just my soul. How could I ever know? My soul has the same reasons for believing itself to be a compound as I have for believing myself to be one. Yet if it has that belief it is mistaken. But then for all I know I am the one who is mistaken. If I *were* a soul and not a compound, I should believe that I was a compound all the same. So even if compound dualism were true, it looks as if no one could ever know that it was.

But the heart of the problem of the thinking soul is the idea that something numerically different from me does my thinking. That is what compound dualism says: the compound of my body and my soul, which is what I am, thinks only insofar as it has a part, the soul, that thinks. The soul thinks in a completely straightforward sense. You and I think only in a derivative sense. But surely I don't need anything else to think for me. *I* am the thing that thinks my thoughts in the strictest sense. That's what makes them mine. Roderick Chisholm famously made the same point in a different context:

> There is no reason whatever for supposing that I hope for rain only in virtue of the fact that some other thing hopes for rain—some stand-in that, strictly and philosophically, is not identical with me. . . . If there are thus two things that now hope for rain, the one doing it on its own and the other such that its hoping is done for it by the thing that now happens to constitute it, then I am the former thing and not the latter thing.[6]

Naturally there are some properties that we have in a derivative sense. We are tattooed insofar as our skin is tattooed. But thinking is not like this. When we think 'I', don't we *mean* the being, if there is one, who

[6] Roderick Chisholm, *Person and Object* (La Salle, Ill.: Open Court, 1976), 104.

thinks that thought? Consider the *Cogito*. One might challenge the inference from 'I think' to 'I exist' on the grounds that there could be thought but nothing thinking it. Or one might challenge the premise on the grounds that there is no such thing as thought because the "folk" theory underlying that notion is false. But no one ever suggested that, although *something* is thinking, strictly speaking it may not be I but something else.

I'm not sure whether this counts as an argument for the claim that you and I think if anything does, or only a forceful assertion of it. But can you really believe that something else does your thinking for you?

We can see now why no analog of the problem of the thinking soul arises for pure dualism. You may wonder how any substance dualist could avoid the conclusion that there are twice as many thinkers as we thought there were, both souls and soul-body compounds. Or how the pure dualist can avoid saying that the compound, though not a person, is mentally indistinguishable from a person. Or how we could know that we are souls, if that is what we are. The answer is simple: it is only the soul that really thinks. At best the compound of the soul and its body can be said to think insofar as it has a thinking part. But then we might as well say that it doesn't think at all—any more than something made up of you and me, or of you and your chair, would think. So there aren't two thinking things for every human being. No nonperson is psychologically indistinguishable from you. The compound of your soul and your body doesn't mistakenly believe itself to be a person, or a soul. The pure dualist has worries enough, but not that worry.

That is the problem of the thinking soul. I will consider three possible replies on behalf of the compound dualist.

II. Unthinking Souls

We might deny that the soul can think. The compound thinks, but the soul doesn't. I don't imagine a cat because my soul does; at most I imagine a cat because my soul does something else, something nonpsychological. Perhaps I think with my soul in something like the way that I see with my eyes: my eyes don't themselves see, but only do something necessary for my seeing.

But why can't the soul think? Apparently because you need more than just a soul to produce thought, just as you need more than just eyes to see. Descartes thought that some mental activities required a body as well as a soul, so that a disembodied person would lack many of the mental capacities that embodied people enjoy. Perhaps all mental activity is like this.

The soul and the body each produce something sub-psychological, and thought arises only when the two ingredients come together.

Well, maybe. But if the soul must cooperate with a body to produce thought, then all thought must be partly physical. Disembodied thought would be impossible. (At least for us, though gods or angels might manage it.) This would undermine the most common arguments for Cartesian dualism, which appeal to our ability to imagine becoming disembodied. If you couldn't possibly be conscious when disembodied, then you can no more imagine being disembodied than you can imagine being in a coma.

More seriously, if it took both a soul and a body to produce thought, the soul would not be in any sense a thinking substance or a mind. At any rate it would be no more a thinking substance than the body is a thinking substance. The soul would have no more to do with a person's ability to think than the body has. Although this view is a metaphysical dualism of some sort, it is not mind-body dualism. (And if the soul has neither mental nor physical properties, we can only wonder what sort of properties it does have.)

Or perhaps we don't need a body to think. The properties or activities of the soul, unlike those of the body, are sufficient to produce thought. But the soul doesn't itself think. Rather, its activities confer thought and other mental properties on the person whose soul it is. The soul is not so much a thinking thing as a "thought-enabling" thing. It is a producer but not a subject of thought. I find this idea baffling. If a thing's activities are sufficient for anything to think, they ought to be sufficient for it to do so. What could prevent the soul from being the subject of the thoughts and experiences it produces? For that matter, what is the difference between producing thought and thinking? Until these questions are answered, there is little we can say about this proposal.

III. The Problem of the Thinking Person-Stage

Technically minded philosophers will point out that the problem of the thinking soul is not unique. Consider, for instance, the ontology of temporal parts, endorsed by such highly respected philosophers as Quine and Lewis.

On that view, persisting things are made up of different temporal parts that are just like those persisting things save for being temporally shorter. A persisting thing has a property at a time by virtue of having a temporal part or "stage," located at just that time, that has that property *simpliciter*. So if you imagine a cat at noon (assuming that you persist through time and are not yourself a momentary stage), you do so because the "noon" part of you imagines a cat. This means that, strictly speaking, there are far more thinking beings around than the census takers report. We will have to ask why they aren't people, and how we could know that we aren't stages. Most important, you and I don't think in the strictest sense: something else, namely your current temporal part, does your thinking for you.[7] But if the "problem of the thinking person-stage" doesn't embarrass the temporal-parts theorist, why should the problem of the thinking soul worry the compound dualist?

Well, the ontology of temporal parts has all sorts of implausible consequences. No one ever accepted that view because it is intuitively obvious. Those who accept it do so because they think powerful arguments support it, and that the alternatives are worse. That suggests that dualists should be compound dualists only if they can argue that pure dualism is even worse. And they haven't.

IV. The Problem of the Thinking Brain

Here is a third reply: "The problem of the thinking soul is no more serious than the analogous 'problem of the thinking brain' facing materialism. If you are a human animal (or something 'constituted by' a human animal), you think by virtue of the activities of your brain. Thus, by your argument, your brain does your thinking for you, ought to be a person, and so on. Since that is absurd, you must be a mere brain if you are a material object at all. But no materialist worries about the problem of the thinking brain. So presumably it has a solution. Why not apply that solution to the problem of the thinking soul? In any case, compound dualism is no worse off than materialism, and most philosophers are happy to be materialists."

This objection leads into deep waters. The problem of the thinking brain is hard, and it is not obvious what materialists ought to say about it. Three suggestions come to mind.

One is to deny the existence of such things as undetached human brains (those attached in the usual way to the rest of a human being). The particles "arranged cerebrally" within your skull don't make up any larger

[7] On "overpopulation" see David Lewis, "Survival and Identity," in *The Identities of Persons,* ed. A. Rorty (Berkeley: University of California Press, 1976), 26–29; David Lewis, "Many, but Almost One," in *Ontology, Causality and Mind,* ed. J. Bacon et al. (Cambridge: Cambridge University Press, 1993). On other aspects of the problem see Noonan, *Personal Identity,* 75–76; Harold Noonan, "Animalism versus Lockeanism: A Current Controversy," *Philosophical Quarterly* 48 (1998): 316.

material object (or a thing of any other sort). I know of no compelling reason to suppose that there are such arbitrary undetached parts of human beings as brains, and the problem of the thinking brain seems to me a good reason to suppose otherwise.[8] Obviously the compound dualist cannot solve the problem of the thinking soul in an analogous way by denying the existence of embodied souls.

Another idea is to accept that there are undetached human brains but deny that they can think. We use our brains to think. The goings-on in our brains are causally necessary for us to think, just as what goes on in our eyes is necessary for us to see. But our brains don't themselves think, any more than our eyes see. The thing that thinks and sees is the whole human being. Why, then, if the brain is in some sense causally sufficient to produce thought, doesn't it itself think? Well, what is the most salient candidate for being the subject of what we naïvely call a human being's thoughts and experiences? The brain? But what brain? There are many things that could with equal justice be called your brain. (Consider the fact that anatomists must divide the brain arbitrarily from the upper spinal cord.) Surely the best candidate is the whole human being. Whatever the merits of this reasoning, the analogous solution to the problem of the thinking soul would be to deny that the soul can think, which as we have seen is not an option for the compound dualist.

Failing that, one might accept that the brain thinks, but deny that the whole human being thinks only in the derivative sense of having a brain that thinks. The brain and the human being both think in the strictest sense—as, presumably, do any other undetached parts of the human being that include the brain. One way to argue for this would be to ask why anyone should suppose that the brain alone thinks, and not the whole human being. Presumably it is because the human being has parts—hands, for instance—that are in some sense not directly involved in producing thought. I could think without hands, but not without a brain. But it will not be easy to say in what sense my brain alone is "directly involved in producing thought." I can no more think without a heart or lungs than I can without a brain. Of course, I could think if my heart and lungs were replaced with inorganic substitutes. But then I may be able to think if my brain were replaced with an inorganic substitute. Moreover, the thing the anatomists call the brain has many structures that are no more directly involved in producing thought than the heart is. And anyway, why suppose that a

[8] Eric Olson, "Why I Have No Hands," *Theoria* 61 (1995): 182–97; I mention another reason in section 7 below.

genuine thinker may only have parts that are directly involved in producing thought?

Naturally this view would not solve the overpopulation problem, the personhood problem, or the epistemic problem; but it would at least avoid the absurdity of saying that you and I think only insofar as some other thing thinks in itself. In any case, there is no help here for compound dualism, which states explicitly that the compound thinks by having a part, the soul, that thinks.

So the compound dualist can take little comfort in the fact that materialists face something analogous to the problem of the thinking soul.

V. The Problem of Disembodied Survival

Now for the second problem. Suppose that my body is destroyed at the end of Monday and that my soul continues to exist without a body on Tuesday. If Cartesian dualism is true, this must be possible, for the soul needn't be attached to a body to exist. And if my thinking soul could survive this, surely I could survive it. But in what form could I survive? As a soul, of course. What else could I be, after the destruction of my body, if not my soul? It is the only serious candidate for being me that still exists on Tuesday. But I couldn't be my soul, for according to compound dualism I wasn't my soul on Monday, but a compound of my soul and my body. Compound dualism has the absurd consequence that one could come to be identical with something that was previously only a part of one.

We might put it like this. According to Cartesian dualism, I could survive the destruction of my body at the end of Monday; that is,

1. The thing that is I on Monday is the thing that is I on Tuesday.

In that case, I should be my soul on Tuesday:

2. The thing that is I on Tuesday is the thing that is my soul on Tuesday.

But obviously

3. The thing that is my soul on Tuesday is the thing that is my soul on Monday.

From this it follows that

4. The thing that is I on Monday is the thing that is my soul on Monday,

which contradicts compound dualism. I will call this the problem of disembodied survival. Obviously it doesn't arise for the pure dualist, who says that I was identical with my soul all along.

VI. Implausible Solutions

Can the problem be solved? Someone could subvert the logic of the argument by relativizing identity to times: I am not identical with my soul now, but I shall be identical with it after my death.

Or one might reject the possibility of disembodied survival, denying (1). My soul could exist without my body, but *I* couldn't. It won't do to say only that I couldn't survive this in the course of nature, or that I couldn't survive it *as a person*. It must be absolutely impossible for any human person to carry on existing after the destruction of her body. But then my body would be essential to me, contrary to compound dualism.

Perhaps I could survive without *this* body, but not without any body at all: I could survive the destruction of my body only by acquiring a new body. Though this may be consistent with the letter of compound dualism, it certainly goes against the spirit of Cartesianism. It would mean that every human person was essentially made up of parts, and essentially partly material.[9]

But these are drastic measures. A more conservative solution would say that I could survive the destruction of my body as a wholly immaterial thing numerically different from my soul, contrary to (2) (but without resorting to the ontology of temporal parts discussed earlier). Let us consider this.

I should have to survive it as a substance: I take it that nothing can be a substance at one time and a nonsubstance later on. So there must be at least *two* immaterial substances on Tuesday: my soul and I. The soul, of course, was always immaterial. The other substance was formerly made up of my soul and my body. (Something will have to make one of those immaterial thinking things a person and the other a nonperson. But we've been through that already.)

[9] Hart *defines* substance dualism as the view that we can become disembodied (W. D. Hart, *The Engines of the Soul* [Cambridge: Cambridge University Press, 1988], 5).

The challenge will be to explain how the disembodied person relates to her soul, if they are not one and the same. It seems clear that the person must at least continue to have her soul as a part. Surely nothing can survive the loss of all its parts in one go. I may be able to survive gradual replacement of parts, but if you take away all of my parts at once, you take away all of me. So if I am made up of a body and a soul throughout Monday, and if I exist at the beginning of Tuesday when neither that body nor any of its parts are parts of me, then my soul, at least, must remain a part of me then. Moreover, it is hard to see how the existence of my soul could be essential to me, as Cartesian dualism says it is, if I could survive without having it as a part. If the survival of the soul is essential to my survival, then destroying it would necessarily destroy *me*. But how could the destruction of one substance logically entail the destruction of another, unless they at least share a part? And since my soul has no parts other than itself, the only part we could share is the soul itself.

Suppose, then, that I can survive the destruction of my body as a wholly immaterial substance that continues to have my soul as a part. In that case a disembodied person would have to have some other immaterial part besides her soul. Nothing can have just one part—one "proper" part, that is, one part other than itself. The whole must be greater than the part. It belongs to the very idea of parthood that if x is a proper part of y, then y must also have some other part or parts that don't share a part with x.[10] So a disembodied person must be made up of her soul and at least one other immaterial thing. To survive death, I must exchange my material body for some new immaterial part: a "spiritual body," we might say.

Where could this new, immaterial part come from? The only players on the stage before my death are my soul, my body and its parts, and myself. Afterward my soul is still a soul, my body has perished, and I, supposedly, am made up of the soul and something else. The destruction of my material body can't logically entail the existence of some new immaterial thing. It seems that disembodied survival would require some sort of deus ex machina. That might fit naturally with the Christian doctrine that survival of death requires a miracle, and is no part of the course of nature. We could then say, in part at least, what that miracle would have to involve: for me to survive the destruction of my body, the Higher Powers would have to provide me with a spiritual body to take its place.

This proposal is implausible at best. First, what would make the spiritual body a part of the disembodied person? What makes your material

[10] See Peter Simons, *Parts: A Study in Ontology* (Oxford: Clarendon, 1984), 26.

body a part of you, according to compound dualism, is presumably the special causal relations you bear to it: you can move it just by intending to do so, and alterations to it affect you in an especially direct way, so that you can perceive and act through it. Other material objects—your shoes, say, or my body—are not parts of you because they don't relate to you in that way. This suggests that your spiritual body is a part of you when you are disembodied because you bear some analogous causal relation to it and to no other immaterial thing. But what relation could that be?

The proposal also implies that some immaterial substances (souls) are essentially wholly immaterial, while others (disembodied people) are only contingently and temporarily so. I should have thought that any immaterial thing was essentially immaterial.

Another implication is that, although souls may be simple and indivisible, each of us—each human person—is necessarily composite and divisible. But the Cartesian thought that the soul must be indivisible is just the thought that you and I are indivisible. Such arguments as there are for the simplicity of the soul are also arguments for *our* simplicity.

Our having an immortal and substantial soul is usually taken to imply that *we* are immortal. The current proposal denies this: although the survival of your soul may be necessary for you to survive, it is not sufficient. Your soul could survive without a spiritual body, in which case you would perish. Your soul could outlive you. In fact your soul could survive without any intrinsic alteration whatever, continuing to think and be conscious, retaining its apparent memories of your life, and so on, without your surviving. But why should your survival require anything more than the survival of the thing that thinks in you? The natural view for the Cartesian to take, surely, is that the survival of the soul is both necessary and sufficient for the person to survive.

Finally, if your soul can survive without your surviving, why suppose that the person made up of your soul and a new body, spiritual or otherwise, would be you? For all you know, your soul might once have been the soul of someone else. Locke apparently held this view. But he was able to hold it only because he denied that people were substances. In any case he didn't make many converts.

None of these worries arise for pure dualism.

VII. Constitution and the Amputation Paradox

As far as I can see, there is no other solution to the problem of disembodied survival open to the compound dualist. But someone may object: "The problem has nothing to do with compound dualism per se. It is an instance of what we might call the 'amputation paradox.' Suppose you lose your left hand. How would you (or, if you like, your body) then relate to your 'left-hand complement'—the thing previously made up of all your parts save those that share a part with your left hand? Your argument about disembodied survival implies that you would have to be identical with it. But you couldn't be: you are not your left-hand complement before the amputation, so you can't be it afterward. A thing can't come to be identical with something that was previously only a part of it. Because this has nothing to do with any special features of you or your left hand, your argument implies that nothing could survive the loss of any part. A similar argument would show that nothing could ever gain parts. Since this is absurd, your argument must be wrong. Presumably it goes wrong at the same place as the 'hand' argument goes wrong. So any solution to the amputation paradox—and there must be one, since almost no one accepts its conclusion—will equally solve the problem of disembodied survival."

Well, let us see how the amputation paradox might be solved, and whether this suggests a solution to the problem of disembodied existence.

We could relativize identity to times or adopt an ontology of temporal parts.[11] These are open to the compound dualist as well. A third option is to grit our teeth and deny that anything can ever have different parts at different times.[12] Even more drastically, we could deny that there are any composite objects. These are both inconsistent with compound dualism.

Another solution is to deny that there was ever any such object as your "hand complement."[13] The idea is not that your hand complement is something other than an "object," or that it is not a part of you. It would be an object, and a part of you, if it were there at all. But there simply are no hand complements, or other arbitrary, undetached parts of human beings. Why suppose that there are? More generally, you have no proper part that you could "survive as": no amputation that you could survive would result in your coming to coincide exactly with an object that was formerly a proper part of you. This doesn't mean that you have no parts at all. You may have nonarbitrary parts, such as cells or elementary particles. (Because of this solution I prefer to call the amputation paradox the "problem of

[11] On the latter see Mark Heller, *The Ontology of Material Objects* (Cambridge: Cambridge University Press, 1990), 19.

[12] Chisholm, *Person and Object*, 145–58.

[13] Peter van Inwagen, "The Doctrine of Arbitrary Undetached Parts," *Pacific Philosophical Quarterly* 62 (1981): 123–37; Olson, "Why I Have No Hands."

undetached parts.") The analogous solution for the compound dualist would be to deny the existence of the soul, which is of course not an option.

At least one philosopher solves the problem by denying that your hand complement could survive the amputation of your hand.[14] For if it could, something that is first a mere hand complement could come to be something of a radically different kind—a person—which is impossible. To adopt this suggestion, the compound dualist would have to deny that one's soul could survive the destruction of one's body. That is incompatible with Cartesian dualism.

So far we have found no help for the compound dualist. But there may be another solution. Some philosophers believe that when you lose your hand, you come to occupy the same space and to share all of your matter with your hand complement, but without being identical with it. The amputee relates to her hand complement as a person relates to her body (if people are material), or as an organism relates to the mass of matter that coincides with it any moment, or as a clay statue relates to the lump of clay it is made out of. The hand complement *constitutes* the handless person.

This metaphysic is just as contentious as the other proposed solutions to the problem of undetached parts.[15] But let us suppose for the sake of argument that there is such a thing as "material constitution," and that the solution works. Could we then solve the problem of disembodied survival by saying that after my body's destruction my soul constitutes me without being identical with me? This is a hard question. Constitution is poorly understood. If we go by what the philosophers of constitution typically say, though, the answer is clearly no.

It is supposed to belong to the nature of constitution that a constituting thing can outlive the thing it constitutes. The lump of clay would outlive the statue it constitutes if it were crushed, for instance. If the soul constitutes the disembodied person, then your soul could survive without your surviving. Likewise, the same soul could constitute different people at different times, much as the same lump of clay could constitute first one statue and later another. As we have seen, this is implausible at best. Worse, constitution theorists generally agree that a constituted thing can

[14] Michael Burke, "Dion and Theon: An Essentialist Solution to an Ancient Puzzle," *Journal of Philosophy* 91 (1994): 129–39. For what it's worth, my response is "Dion's Foot," *Journal of Philosophy* 94 (1997): 260–65.

[15] See, e.g., Michael Burke, "Copper Statues and Pieces of Copper," *Analysis* 52 (1992): 12–17; Eric Olson, "Composition and Coincidence," *Pacific Philosophical Quarterly* 77 (1996): 374–403.

be constituted by different things at different times: different masses of matter successively constitute the same organism, for instance. If this belongs to the nature of constitution, then a person could be constituted by different souls at different times. Hence your soul would not be essential to you.

It seems to belong to the idea of constitution that nothing can constitute itself, and that a constituted thing must always be constituted by something. And constitution in the relevant sense is a one-to-one relation: two things cannot jointly constitute a third. So if your soul constitutes you after your death, some one thing must constitute you before your death: presumably another compound of soul and body, though one of a different kind from you. That is absurd.

Finally, a constituted object must be made of the same matter, or have the same proper parts, as the thing constituting it. At any rate they must have the same parts at some level of decomposition: they must be made of the same elementary particles, for instance. But a soul and a disembodied person cannot share their matter or their parts. An immaterial soul isn't made of matter, or of some spiritual stuff analogous to matter. It isn't made of anything. And the soul, being simple, has no parts to share.

So much for constitution. Let us consider one final suggestion. Someone might say that the person simply has two parts before her death, a body and a soul, and one part afterward, a soul. A disembodied person has a soul as her *only* proper part. The soul, all by itself, makes up two things, itself and the person.[16] As we saw earlier, this would mean giving up the natural idea that the whole must be greater than the part. There would then be two ways for something to be simple and uncompounded: it may fail to have any parts at all, other than itself; or it may merely fail to have any nonoverlapping parts. A simple, uncompounded thing in the second sense could have as many parts as you like, as long as they all overlap: you could be made up of a soul, and the soul could be made up of some third thing, and so on.

This view seems to suffer from a sort of ontological double vision. When I try to contemplate it, I lose my grip on what it is for one thing to be a part of another. Whatever the relation of simple soul to simple person might be, it couldn't be that of part to whole. Or if it could be, then the notion of parthood is so poorly understood as to make the proposal almost uninformative. In any case, it seems to offer no real advantage over the proposal reached at the end of the previous section.

[16] This idea was put to me by Richard Swinburne.

Thus, despite their formal similarities, the problem of disembodied survival is considerably more difficult than the amputation paradox. And the latter is quite troublesome enough.

I have shown that compound dualism faces two serious worries, neither of which arise for pure dualism.

Of course, pure dualism may have troubles of its own that compound dualism avoids. The most obvious place to look for them is our readiness to attribute physical properties to ourselves. Pure dualism implies that we have physical properties only in a derivative sense: we borrow them, so to speak, from things numerically different from ourselves. We don't have mass in the same straightforward sense as we are people, or as rocks have mass. But then compound dualism has the same consequence, for it says that we have physical properties only in the sense of having a body that has those properties straightforwardly. The tangible, visible thing that bears my physical properties in the strictest sense is not I, but something numerically different from me, just as it is on pure dualism. The only difference is that that thing is a part of me on compound dualism and not on pure dualism. But why should that matter?

Despite initial appearances, then, there seems to be little reason to prefer compound dualism over pure dualism, and the widespread tendency to do so is founded on confusion. The source of the confusion may lie in the unfortunate word "mind," which suggests both "thinking thing" and "thing that one has." It is a word that philosophers would be better off without.

STEWART GOETZ

Modal Dualism: A Critique

The following is an argument (call it the Simple Argument) for substance dualism (dualism, for short):

1. I am essentially a simple entity (I have no separable parts).
2. Any physical body is essentially a complex entity (any physical body has separable parts).
3. Principle of Indiscernibility of Identicals: If two entities, A and B, are identical, then whatever is a property of A is a property of B.
4. Therefore, I am not identical with my (or any) physical body.

The Simple Argument is valid but its soundness is vigorously disputed. Though few quarrel with premises 2 and 3, many dispute 1.

Now, consider another argument for dualism. Commonly termed the Modal Argument for dualism, this argument can be formulated as follows:

3. Principle of Indiscernibility of Identicals: If two entities, A and B, are identical, then whatever is a property of A is a property of B.
5. I have the essential property of being such that I possibly survive (exist) disembodied (without my or any other physical body).
6. No physical body has the essential property of being such that it possibly survives disembodied.
4. Therefore, I am not identical with my (or any other) physical body.

I am indebted to William Hasker, Philip Quinn, Charles Taliaferro, Dean Zimmerman, and an anonymous reader for commenting upon earlier drafts of this paper and making several important contributions.

Like the Simple Argument, the Modal Argument is valid, though its soundness is greatly contested. While few quarrel with premises 3 and 6, many contest 5.

According to the modal dualist (a proponent of the Modal Argument), support for my believing premise 5 is provided by my being able to conceive of myself existing without my physical body. In section 1 of this chapter, I argue that my being able to conceive of my possible disembodiment provides support for premise 5 only if I am already aware of or believe in my distinctness from my (or any other) physical body.[1] In other words, rather than premise 5 providing support for statement 4, statement 4 is a necessary support for 5. This renders the Modal Argument epistemically circular (where an argument is epistemically circular if one or more of its premises can be defended only by tacitly assuming the truth of the conclusion).

An awareness of myself and my physical body as distinct entities requires that they exhibit and I be aware of properties which enable me to apprehend their distinctness. In section 2, I suggest as examples of such properties the properties of being simple and being complex, as exemplified by myself and my physical body respectively. An awareness of these properties would render the Modal Argument epistemically circular by means of the Simple Argument. An additional concern, however, is whether there are properties other than being simple and being complex which might ground an awareness of myself and my physical body as distinct entities. Though no formal proof is provided, through consideration of the properties of being spatial and being nonspatial I suggest that an awareness of any other properties relevant to the issue of apprehending one's distinctness from one's physical body would ultimately presuppose an awareness of one's simplicity and the complexity of one's physical body. If this is correct, the Simple Argument is the central argument for dualism.

Since the simplicity of the self is seemingly a central consideration in arguing for the truth of dualism, sections 3 and 4 are devoted to a brief treatment of it. Though most opponents of the Simple Argument contest premise 1, some (also) question premise 2. For example, atomists argue that not every physical body is essentially complex, but only those bodies that are ultimately composed of atoms which are themselves simple. Although the atomist's view is itself greatly disputed, for the sake of discussion its truth is assumed in section 3, and the suggestion that I am a simple entity which is identical with such an atom is considered. Section

[1] For stylistic simplicity, I will normally speak of (being aware of) the distinction between me and my physical body and omit the words "or any other physical body."

4 concludes the paper with some general thoughts about the possible simplicity of the self and an awareness of it.

I. The Modal Argument's Circularity

The Modal Argument involves some fairly uncontroversial assumptions. For example, it captures the intuitively plausible principle that no physical thing can become nonphysical (every physical thing is essentially physical). Otherwise, my physical body could survive as a nonphysical entity. Also, the argument assumes that I am a particular entity, thing, or substance, as opposed to a property (an abstract entity). Moreover, 'I' and 'my physical body' are used as referring expressions which pick out their referents directly or in a *de re* manner.

It is important to clarify what the essential property of being such that I possibly survive disembodied does and does not entail. It does entail that I am not identical with any physical object. Were I to have a different physical body from the one I presently have, I would still have the property of being such that I survive possibly disembodied because it is an essential property. Indeed, given my exemplification of this property, I can survive and no physical objects exist. What is not entailed by the essential property of being such that I possibly survive disembodied is that I have existed in the past or will exist in the future without a physical body. All the proponent of premise 5 claims is that it is possible that I exist disembodied.

As was stated earlier, the Modal Argument is valid. But it is doubtful that one can justifiably believe or know that premise 5 is true without already justifiably believing or knowing that the conclusion (statement 4) is true. So the argument is epistemically circular. To understand why it is plausible to believe that knowledge of statement 5 assumes a knowledge of statement 4, consider premise 5, which entails that there is a contingent relation between my physical body and me. According to the modal dualist, my reason for believing that 5 is true is that, though embodied, I can conceive that I exist without my physical body (where what I can conceive is my most reliable test for what is possible). There is much debate about just what it is to conceive of something, and some suggestions are pretty obviously nonstarters.[2] For present purposes, I will understand 'conceivability' as 'what can be coherently supposed'.

[2] For example, 'conceivability' cannot mean 'understandability' (what can be understood) because I can understand necessary falsehoods such as 2 + 2 = 5. If I did not understand such a falsehood, I could not know that it is necessarily false. Hence, conceivability as understandability cannot support possibility because what is necessarily false is not possible. Similarly, 'conceivability' cannot mean 'believability' (what can be believed) because it seems

Colin McGinn has pointed out that while it is true that each person can conceive of himself existing without his physical body, being able to conceive this supports the truth of premise 5 only if it is reasonable to think that one could be either introspectively or sensorially aware of a necessary relation between oneself and one's physical body (such a relation would entail that one could not survive disembodied), provided that such a relation exists. McGinn claims that if a necessary relation between my body and me obtains, it is not something of which either introspective or sensory investigation could make me aware. Stated differently, I am not aware of being contingently related to my physical body but at best fail to be aware of being necessarily related to it. But the failure to be aware of this relation does not count as evidence against its presence. In general, the failure to be aware of a relation or property counts against its obtaining only if it is reasonable to think that one could be aware of it, if it is present. Thus, in the case of being aware of an elephant, it is reasonable to conclude that nothing in the room exemplifies the property of being an elephant if I am unable to see, feel, smell, or hear an elephant. However, a necessary relation between oneself and one's physical body is not like the property of being an elephant in the sense that the former is not accessible to any kind of awareness (introspective or empirical) by its possessor. Hence, the failure to apprehend it does not support the dualist position.

> The reason we feel the tug of contingency, pulling consciousness loose from its physical moorings, may be that we do not and cannot grasp the nature of the property that intelligibly links them. The brain has physical properties we can grasp, and variations in these correlate with changes in consciousness, but we cannot draw the veil that conceals the manner of their connection. Not grasping the nature of the connection, it strikes us as deeply contingent; we cannot make the assertion of a necessary connection intelligible to ourselves. There *may* then be a real necessary connection; it is just that it will always strike us as curiously brutish and unperspicuous. We may thus, as upholders of intrinsic contingency, be the dupes of our own cognitive blindness.[3]

---

that I can believe what is necessarily false. For example, some people might believe that Goldbach's conjecture (that every even number greater than two is the sum of two primes) is true while others might believe that it is false. It would seem that members of one group believe what is necessarily false. If one were to respond that we can believe only what is possible, then one would have to have some other way besides believability to ascertain what is possible so that one could determine what it is that a person really believes. For an excellent discussion of these matters, see Paul Tidman's "Conceivability as a Test for Possibility," *American Philosophical Quarterly* 31 (1994): 297–309.

[3] Colin McGinn, *The Problem of Consciousness* (Oxford: Basil Blackwell, 1991), 20; McGinn's emphasis.

On McGinn's view, there is a property which links consciousness to the physical world, and he thinks the link is necessary. Since we are not aware of this property and the link it provides, we can conceive our disembodiment. But this conceivability of disembodiment provides no support for possible disembodiment and for premise 5 of the Modal Argument because the relevant property and link are not the kinds of things of which we can be aware. In short, one's ability to conceive of surviving disembodied is not explained by one's awareness or grasp of the property of being contingently related to one's physical body. It is explained by the fact that the necessary relation between oneself and one's body is in principle beyond one's ken.

Charles Taliaferro, who is a proponent of the Modal Argument, believes that an adequate response to McGinn must begin with a distinction between weakly conceiving something and strongly conceiving it. Something is weakly conceivable for a person when he reflects on it and believes it to be possible on the grounds that he does not see (fails to see) that it is impossible. Something is strongly conceivable for a person when he judges that it is possible "on the basis of a more positive grasp of the properties involved [in the present case, the properties of a person and his physical body] and the compatibility of [these] with what [he] knows about the world and so on."[4] This more positive grasp of the properties involved consists of a person's not being intellectually negligent, where a person is not intellectually negligent if he attends to certain important features that would be apparent to him after some further expected attention that is within his power.[5] Given this distinction between weak and strong conceivability, Taliaferro makes the following response to McGinn:

> Isn't the simplest explanation of why we feel the "tug of contingency," and even feel that there is a "deep contingency" between person and body, that the relation truly is contingent? The ground for thinking a relation is contingent is typically the conceivability . . . of the relation failing to hold. We can, so I believe, strongly conceive of the person-body relation being radically altered, and, on this basis, I propose that the reason why we do not grasp the necessary tie between person and body is that it is not there.[6]

On Taliaferro's notion of strong conceivability, to conceive strongly that we can survive disembodied requires that we have a positive grasp of the

[4] Charles Taliaferro, *Consciousness and the Mind of God* (Cambridge: Cambridge University Press, 1994), 137.

[5] Ibid., 137–38.

[6] Ibid., 195.

properties which are involved in the contingency relation between ourselves and our physical bodies. A question of central importance for his position is this: What properties that I exhibit are involved in the contingency relation which I conceive between me and my physical body such that my having a positive grasp of them explains my being able to conceive strongly my possible disembodiment? How Taliaferro would answer this question is not obvious. It might seem initially plausible to maintain that the relevant properties are psychological ones such as thinking and experiencing pain which I exemplify. Taliaferro, however, rejects this proposal. According to him, though it is the case that psychological properties (events) are irreducibly distinct from or not identical with physical properties, this does not entail that they cannot all be exemplified by one entity.[7] On the basis of my awareness of psychological properties that I exemplify, I cannot be confident of anything stronger than property dualism. While I fail to apprehend a necessary link between psychological and physical properties, which would require that they be exemplified by a single entity, I also fail to apprehend a contingency relation between them, which would entail that they could be exemplified by distinct entities. Thus, my ability to conceive of them as properties of different substances is a case of weak, not strong, conceivability, and this weak conceivability will not support the truth of premise 5.

Taliaferro fails to specify what is positively grasped in strongly conceiving possible disembodiment. It is plausible to suggest that if I can strongly conceive my possible disembodiment, what I grasp is the distinctness between myself and my physical body, where this grasped distinction is based in an actual awareness of the distinctness of the two entities. To support this suggestion, consider two examples of contingency relations which I can strongly conceive but which presuppose an awareness of the ontological distinctness of the terms of the contingency relations. First, consider an example of a contingent spatial relation. Though I presently live east of Chicago, I can strongly conceive of living west of Chicago. I am able to conceive this strongly because I am aware of both myself and Chicago as distinct entities in a common spatial framework and of my standing in the contingent spatial relation of living east of it. My being able to conceive strongly that I can live west of Chicago also requires that I exemplify and be aware of the modal property which is the power to move in space.

Second, consider the relational property of being president of the college at which I teach. Though I presently am a term in the contingent

[7] Ibid., 54, 57, 84, 161.

relation of being a philosophy professor at this college, I can strongly conceive of myself being the president of it because I am aware of both it and myself as ontologically distinct entities. At a minimum, this awareness involves my being aware of it as an organizational structure whose administrative hierarchy contains the position of president and that I have various modal properties such as the power to think, the power to choose, and so forth, which provide me with the requisite qualifications or credentials for occupying that position.

What these examples suggest with respect to my possible disembodiment is that if I can strongly conceive of myself existing disembodied, this is because I am aware of myself and my body as distinct entities. Awareness of what is actual, not conceivability, is the source of modal belief.

At this point, the burden for the modal dualist is to specify the properties he exhibits and positively grasps, properties that ground his ability to conceive his possible disembodiment strongly but do not presuppose an awareness of being distinct from his physical body. While failure on the modal dualist's part to say anything informative on this issue is not a decisive argument against his view, it leaves one without a reason to think that his account of the conceivability of possible disembodiment is closer to the truth than McGinn's. Failure on the part of the modal dualist to specify any properties he exemplifies that can ground his claim of strong conceivability raises the question about how he can be confident that he is strongly, and not weakly, conceiving his possible disembodiment. At best, his claim and that of McGinn are equally justified, and neither position is more persuasive than the other.

It is relevant to note that it will not help the modal dualist avoid this standoff to say that instead of my grasping the properties involved in the contingency relation between myself and my physical body, I grasp the absence of the property of being necessarily related to my physical body. The problem with this answer is that a grasping of this absence entails a grasping of the contingency relation between my physical body and me, and this generates the problem of epistemic circularity all over again. The reason a grasping of the absence of the property of being necessarily related to my physical body entails a grasping of the contingency relation between it and me is as follows: I am aware of having a physical body. So, I am aware of being possibly embodied. To grasp the absence of the property of being necessarily related to my physical body is to grasp being possibly not embodied. But to grasp both being possibly embodied and being possibly not embodied is to grasp being contingently embodied.

In an attempt to defend the Modal Argument against the charge of epistemic circularity, Taliaferro has noted that in addition to dualists many nondualists are able to conceive of their being disembodied, but none of them believes that statement 4 is true.[8] Hence, believing or knowing that one is not identical with one's physical body (statement 4) cannot be a necessary condition of justifiably believing in the possibility of disembodiment.

If my argument against Taliaferro is correct, then nondualists who maintain that they can conceive of their possible disembodiment do not assent to premise 5 because such an assent requires the support of a strong conception of disembodiment which is based in an awareness of the distinctness between oneself and one's physical body. Rather than strongly conceiving their possible disembodiment, these nondualists must only be weakly conceiving it. To evaluate the position that nondualists who claim they can conceive of being disembodied do not accept statement 5, consider the materialist D. M. Armstrong's account of the conceivability of disembodiment. According to Armstrong,

> disembodied existence seems to be a perfectly intelligible supposition. . . . Consider the case where I am lying in bed at night thinking. Surely it is logically possible that I might be having just the same experiences, and yet not have a body at all? No doubt I am having certain somatic, that is to say, bodily, sensations. But if I am lying still these will not be very detailed in nature, and I can see nothing self-contradictory in supposing that they do not correspond to anything in physical reality. Yet I need be in no doubt about my identity.[9]

Elsewhere, Armstrong notes (without dissent) Descartes's view that one is not aware that one's mind is extended or material.[10] In light of one's failure to be aware that one's mind is extended or material, one can conceive that one exists and no bodies exist. Moreover, given the Cartesian thesis that the mind is self-intimating in the sense that if something is a property of one's mind at time *t*, then one is aware at *t* that this something is a property of one's mind,[11] one's failure to be aware of one's mind being extended or material at *t* implies that it is not extended or material at *t*. Armstrong, however, claims that there is no reason to believe that the mind is self-intimating. Thus, it does not follow from one's failure to be aware that the mind is

[8] Ibid., 197.

[9] D. M. Armstrong, *A Materialist Theory of Mind* (London: Routledge and Kegan Paul, 1968), 19.

[10] D. M. Armstrong, *The Mind-Body Problem: An Opinionated Introduction* (Boulder, Colo.: Westview, 1999), 22.

[11] Ibid., 15.

extended or material that it is so. Failure to be aware that one's mind is extended or material is the basis for only a weak form of conceivability.

Armstrong himself defends a functionalist conception of the mind where a mind is whatever satisfies a certain functional specification of causal inputs and outputs. For example, a mind is, in part, whatever feels pain from the input of skin tissue damage and produces the output of bodily withdrawal from the source of the damage. This functionalist understanding of the mind is complemented by a lack of awareness of the intrinsic nature of what it is that realizes the mental functions. Armstrong claims that, given that mental properties are functionally (relationally) specified and that he has no awareness of his intrinsic nature, he could, for all he knows, be a soul. For all he knows, however, he might be his central nervous system.[12] In light of the empirical discoveries of science (which inform us about the intrinsic features of our mental functions), he claims that it is most reasonable to think that his central nervous system is what realizes or instantiates the functionally defined mental properties and that he is this piece of matter.[13]

In virtue of his denial of the Cartesian thesis that the mind is self-intimating and his own functionalist understanding of the mind, it is clear that Armstrong will maintain that his conception of his disembodiment is weak in nature. Because he does not have an awareness of himself as an entity which is distinct from his physical body, he is unable to conceive his possible disembodiment strongly.

Taliaferro maintains that functionalists such as Armstrong possess the same modal intuition as dualists. He believes that they develop their functionalist view of the mind as a way of avoiding drawing a dualist conclusion from the modal intuition which they want to harmonize with materialism. He also believes that this way of avoiding drawing the dualist conclusion is implausible. Thus, in response to Armstrong, he says that

> I see no good reason to claim that in having the reflections [about disembodiment] Armstrong recounts, I am simply holding that whatever it is that occupies such-and-such a causal role among physical objects could become . . . disembodied. Rather, it seems to me that *I* may exist spatially unextended. I believe with respect to myself that I could be disembodied and thereby attribute a modal property to myself in a *de re,* direct fashion. I do not simply subscribe to a *de dicto* proposition like "Whatever satisfies such-and-such functional analysis could be disembodied."[14]

[12] Armstrong, *Materialist Theory of Mind,* 120 ff.

[13] Ibid., 79.

[14] Taliaferro, *Consciousness and the Mind of God,* 198.

Taliaferro insists that it seems to him that *he,* as opposed to *whatever* occupies a particular causal role, may exist disembodied. Stated differently, he believes that his dualist interpretation of a common modal intuition is more plausible than Armstrong's functionalist one. The problem for Taliaferro is that if there is a common modal intuition shared by nondualists and dualists, Armstrong will assert that it consists of weakly conceiving possible disembodiment and that Taliaferro needs to explain why it is that he, Armstrong, is wrong about this matter. Without being able to say something positive or informative about the properties he exhibits and grasps which make it plausible to believe that he is strongly conceiving his possible disembodiment, it is difficult, if not impossible, for Taliaferro to make a convincing case for the additional claim that there is a common modal intuition which is that of strongly conceiving possible disembodiment. This does not imply that Armstrong has made a more convincing case for his position. But it does mean that neither position is more compelling than the other.

Like Taliaferro, Stephen Yablo is a proponent of the Modal Argument. For Yablo, a proposition *p* is conceivable for me if I can *imagine* a situation which I take to verify *p* (of which I truly believe that *p*).[15] When I imagine a situation which I take to verify *p,* it appears to me that *p* is possible. With respect to the Modal Argument, I have support for the position that it is possible for me to exist disembodied because I am able to conceive of my possible disembodiment, where conceiving of my possible disembodiment is imagining myself existing disembodied such that my belief that I exist disembodied is true.

To understand 'conceivability' as 'imaginability' raises the problem of the indeterminacy of what can be imagined. To understand what this problem is, consider in more detail Yablo's explanation of what is involved in conceiving a proposition *p*. In imagining a situation which will verify *p* (a situation of which I truly believe that *p*), I implicitly acknowledge that this situation is embedded in a larger reality which, if thoroughly complete in every detail, is a possible world. Obviously, it is not possible for me to imagine every feature of a possible world because of the limitations of my power of imagination. But it is possible for me "to imagine a *p*-verifying world while leaving matters visibly irrelevant to *p*'s truth value unspecified."[16] This imagining is hopelessly unforthcoming about matters beyond the immediate situation relevant to verifying *p,* but this is nonproblematic because these irrelevant matters are indifferent to *p*'s truth value.

[15] Stephen Yablo, "Is Conceivability a Guide to Possibility?," *Philosophy and Phenomenological Research* 53 (1993): 1–42.

[16] Ibid., 29.

The problem with this account of conceivability and, thus, for the Modal Argument is knowing what is relevant and what is irrelevant to *p*'s truth value, and making sure that I have included all of the former in what I imagine. How can I be sure, when imagining a situation of which I believe that I exist disembodied, that I have not left out something relevant to my identity with my physical body which is such that, were I aware of it, it would make imagining my disembodiment impossible? In other words, in recognizing the indeterminate nature of what I can imagine, Yablo is faced with the problem of weak conceivability posed by McGinn. As with Taliaferro's claim to be able to conceive strongly his possible disembodiment, there is a conspicuous absence in Yablo's defense of the Modal Argument of any statement specifying the properties I exemplify whose grasp by me explains my being able to imagine (strongly) my possible disembodiment.

Yablo denies that what I can imagine (conceive) presupposes an awareness of the distinctness of my physical body and myself. He maintains that the denial that I am identical with my physical body is not the basis for but a result of what I can conceive.[17] However, his own comments on another example of what is conceivable belie his position on conceiving possible disembodiment. Thus, in describing the fact that the ancients were able to conceive that Hesperus could have existed without Phosphorus, Yablo states that they could do so "only because they falsely believed that Hesperus and Phosphorus were distinct. . . . [T]he ancients could conceive it as possible that Hesperus should exist without Phosphorus . . . only because they denied the truth . . . that they were identical."[18] In other words, though the ancients' belief about the distinctness of Hesperus and Phosphorus was erroneous, without it they could never have conceived what they did. Contrary to what Yablo maintains, the example of Hesperus and Phosphorus suggests that the same kind of necessary condition for conceivability holds with respect to the Modal Argument. If I am able to conceive of my possible disembodiment strongly, this is only because I am aware of and / or already believe that I and my physical body are distinct.[19] It is not the strong conceivability of my possible disembodiment which produces the belief that I am not identical with my physical body. It

[17] Stephen Yablo, "The Real Distinction between Mind and Body," *Canadian Journal of Philosophy,* supp. vol. 16 (1990): 184, 185.

[18] Ibid., 182.

[19] Compare the following statement by Yablo: "Absent specific grounds for doubt, *p*'s conceivability as possible prima facie justifies me in the belief that *p* is possible. Outside of philosophy, this would hardly require argument. Imagine that you claim to be able to conceive of a situation in which you exist, but the Washington Monument does not. Assuming that we

is the awareness of or belief that I am not identical with my physical body which explains the strong conceivability of my possible disembodiment.

A proponent of the Modal Argument might try to defend his position by distinguishing between genuinely strongly conceiving something (as in the case of my conceiving living west of Chicago) and illusorily strongly conceiving it (as in the case of Hesperus and Phosphorus). Thus, in the case of the ancients, they thought that they were genuinely strongly conceiving of the possible existence of Hesperus without Phosphorus, while in reality they were not. Nevertheless, though their conception was illusory, it was still good, but defeasible, evidence for their believing that it was possible that one exist without the other. Similarly, in the case of my possible disembodiment, though my strongly conceiving of it is defeasible and might be illusory, this conceivability is still good evidence for my believing that it is possible.

In the case of Hesperus and Phosphorus the distinction between genuinely and illusorily conceiving something presupposes that the ancients already believed in the distinctness of Hesperus and Phosphorus. What was defeasible in this case was the belief in their distinctness. The ancients thought that this belief was true, when it was false. With genuine strong conceivability, one truly believes in the distinctness of the relevant entities.[20] With illusory strong conceivability, one falsely believes that two entities are distinct. But in neither case does strong conceivability serve as evidence for the possible existence of one of the entities without the other. Belief in their distinctness is presupposed by strong conceivability.

II. Simplicity and Complexity

To be able to conceive my possible disembodiment strongly, it appears that I will need to be aware of myself as an entity which is distinct from my

ourselves find no difficulty in the conception, are we still in a position seriously to question the possibility of yourself without the Monument?" (ibid., 181). As Yablo contends, the obvious answer to this question is no. But what he does not appreciate is that I can conceive of a situation in which I exist, but the Washington Monument does not, only because I am already aware and believe that I am distinct from (not identical with) it.

[20] Compare the following example given by W. D. Hart: "Each of us not now at Victoria Station is convinced that he could have been there, and what convinces him seems patently that he can imagine having gone there. It is easy to generate endlessly many uncontroversial examples like this" (W. D. Hart, *The Engines of the Soul* [Cambridge: Cambridge University Press, 1988], 30). What Hart seems not to realize is that such examples undercut the Modal Argument. To imagine oneself being at Victoria Station presupposes that one already believes in the distinctness of oneself and Victoria Station and that one has the power to move in space with respect to it.

physical body. Of interest, now, is the following question: If I am able to conceive my possible disembodiment strongly, what properties do my physical body and I exhibit such that by being aware of them I am able to apprehend my distinctness from my physical body? I can be aware of myself as an entity distinct from my physical body, it is clear, if I am aware of myself as a simple entity and of my body as a complex entity. This is the Simple Argument for dualism. If it is the case that in order to conceive my possible disembodiment strongly I must be aware of the properties of being simple and being complex as exemplified by myself and my physical body respectively, then the Modal Argument presupposes the Simple Argument. However, one might wonder whether there are other properties whose apprehension would enable one to distinguish between oneself and one's physical body.

As examples of such properties, consider being nonspatial and being spatial, which are frequently ascribed to the self and its physical body respectively by dualists. If one believes that one's physical body is essentially spatial, then the fact that one exemplifies essentially the property of being nonspatial is sufficient for being able to distinguish between oneself and one's physical body. But it is doubtful that one could be aware of exemplifying the property of being nonspatial without already being aware of one's simplicity. This is because there is good reason to believe that an awareness of the latter property is the inferential basis for an awareness of the former. To illustrate this point, consider Descartes's reasoning about the self's nonspatiality. In reflecting initially on what the mind is, he says that it seems to be in space:

> I imagined that it was something extremely rare and subtle like a wind, a flame, or an ether, which was spread throughout my grosser parts. . . . Nature . . . teaches me by these sensations of pain, hunger, thirst, etc., that I am not only lodged in my body as a pilot in a vessel, but that I am very closely united to it, and so to speak so intermingled with it that I seem to compose with it one whole. . . . [T]he whole mind seems to be united to the whole body.[21]

Though the mind seems to be in space, upon reflection Descartes believed that it is not. This is because he thought that any entity (a substance as opposed to, say, a property) which is in space is a body, and a body is essentially extended. That which is extended is divisible. Thus, if the self were

[21] Descartes, *Meditations*, in *The Philosophical Works of Descartes*, vol. 1, trans. Elizabeth S. Haldane and G. R. T. Ross (Cambridge: Cambridge University Press, 1911), 151, 192, 196.

in space, it would be divisible. But since it is simple, it is indivisible. Hence it must be nonspatial.

In other words, not even Descartes claimed to be directly aware of exemplifying the property of being nonspatial. Rather, he inferred that he exemplified it on the basis of his belief about his simplicity and the essential natures of spatial entities and bodies. Thus, not only would an awareness of one's being essentially nonspatial render the Modal Argument epistemically circular, but also it would do so by means of the Simple Argument.

For the sake of discussion, let us continue to assume that there is no support for premise 5 of the Modal Argument that does not depend on an awareness of one's distinctness from one's physical body. Is it plausible to think that such an awareness could only be had in virtue of an awareness of the properties of being simple and being complex? In support of the position that this is not plausible, consider a case where you are lying on an operating table and have an experience of seeing your body falling away from you as you ascend above the operating table. In such a situation, can you not be aware of yourself as distinct from your physical body without being aware of your simplicity?[22]

There is good reason to think that even in a case of actual disembodiment one would have to be aware of one's simplicity in order to be aware that one is not identical with any physical entity. The dualist thesis is not merely that the self is not identical with its actual physical body, but that it is not identical with any physical body. Thus, while an out-of-body experience of the kind just described does establish that I am not identical with the entirety of my physical body, it does not establish that I am not identical with any part of my physical body. Perhaps I am identical with a portion of my brain which is now out of my body. To know or believe that I am not identical with that or any other part of my physical body, it seems that I must be aware of exemplifying the property of being simple. Here, the McGinn-like distinction between not being aware of being a physical body and being aware of not being a physical body is important. The latter is the stronger epistemic position and requires an awareness of one's simplicity. Without such an awareness, one is left in the former and weaker epistemic position.

In the end, while an out-of-body experience might convince one that one is not identical with but distinct from the entirety of one's present physical body, it would not convince one that one is not identical with any part of that physical body. An awareness of some other properties is required for this. Clearly the properties of being simple and being complex,

[22] I owe this example to Dean Zimmerman.

possessed respectively by oneself and one's physical body, will fulfill the requirement. But if one is aware of being a simple entity, then one does not need an out-of-body experience to be convinced that one is not identical with one's physical body.

III. Atomism

In maintaining that an awareness by a person of his simplicity will support the strong conceivability of his possible disembodiment, it is being assumed that a person's physical body is a complex entity. But what if a person's complex physical body is made up of simple atoms? In this case, while a person is not identical with his physical body as a whole or a combination of two or more of its parts, might he not be identical with one, but no more than one, of its simple proper parts? If he is identical with such an atom, is it not the case that he cannot strongly conceive of his possible disembodiment with respect to it?[23]

If we assume that an 'atomic person' has an objective physical nature which is knowable from a third-person perspective, in addition to having a subjective nonphysical nature which is knowable without observation, and if we also assume that such a person either is unaware of this objective nature or is aware of it but cannot discern a necessary connection between it and his subjective nature, then it is not possible for him to conceive strongly of his possible disembodiment with respect to it. At most, his possible disembodiment with respect to it is weakly conceivable.

That a person is a spatially located entity is something that classical dualism as expressed by Descartes and his followers has found problematic. Whether or not a simple self could be or is spatially located is an issue which is beyond the scope of this paper. Hence, it will have to suffice for now to say that if a person is a simple self that is located in space and if his physical body is ultimately composed of simple atoms, then the possibility that he is identical with one of these atoms cannot be ruled out a priori.

IV. Of What Is One Aware?

In closing, it is appropriate to address briefly the issue I have avoided so far: Is it reasonable for a person to believe that he is aware of being a simple

[23] Philip Quinn and Dean Zimmerman have raised this possibility with me.

entity? Many will find an affirmative answer to this question thoroughly implausible. While they might concede that it has been convincingly argued that all of us think of ourselves as simple entities,[24] they will maintain that it is nevertheless wrong to maintain that this belief is rooted in an awareness of our simplicity. The position of a large number of contemporary philosophers is that rather than being aware of one's simplicity, one fails to be aware of one's complexity.

In contemporary literature on the philosophy of mind, the empirical consideration most frequently raised against the simplicity of the self is the evidence from commissurotomy cases. Those who suggest or take seriously the idea that it is possible to be aware of one's simplicity are chided by critics for not taking more seriously these empirical data against such a supposed awareness. Those who take such empirical data seriously are equally chided by dualists for dismissing too quickly one's apparent awareness of one's simplicity on the basis of data which are open to other interpretations. As of now, there does not seem to be any way to arbitrate this disagreement or the question of whether or not it is possible to be aware of one's simplicity, provided one is a simple entity. What does seem to be the case, however, is that if there is a successful argument for dualism, it is the Simple, and not the Modal, Argument.

[24] See Thomas Nagel's *The View from Nowhere* (Oxford: Oxford University Press, 1986), 32–34; and Derek Parfit's *Reasons and Persons* (Oxford: Clarendon, 1987), 472.

PART II

Alternatives to Cartesian Dualism

WILLIAM HASKER

Persons as Emergent Substances

In this chapter I propose to do three things. First, I will argue that the prevalent materialisms concerning persons and consciousness are in a state of incipient crisis—a crisis, to be sure, which as yet is inadequately recognized and acknowledged, yet its lineaments are gradually becoming clear. Second, I will argue that the traditional dualisms—Cartesian or Thomistic—offer no adequate alternative, because of internal difficulties that render them all too vulnerable to the materialist critique. And finally, I offer a few suggestions about how we might begin to transcend the impasse and progress toward a better understanding. I will speak, then, about the Crisis of Materialism, the Dilemma of Dualism, and the Middle Way.[1]

I. The Crisis of Materialism

To illustrate the crisis of materialism I call upon the views of two philosophers from opposite ends of the materialist spectrum: the eliminative materialist Paul Churchland and the "new mysterian" Colin McGinn. It may seem odd to some of you to cite eliminativism as evidence for a crisis of materialism. Is this not rather the most bold and assertive of materialisms, the one which most effectively drowns out protest and deprives its critics of the resources needed to raise objections? In one sense, this is certainly true. The eliminativist idea, roughly, is this: our ordinary discourse about

[1] For a complete account of persons as emergent, see William Hasker, *The Emergent Self* (Ithaca: Cornell University Press, 1999).

the mind and its contents is said to constitute a theory, namely "folk psychology." Folk psychology was developed long ago as an attempt of primitive humans to explain human thought and behavior, and it has remained largely unchanged ever since. But, like other "folk theories"—folk physics, folk biology, folk astronomy, and the like—it is largely false and is destined to be supplanted by a properly scientific theory of the mind framed in terms of neurophysiology. Objections against this thesis stated in terms of our ordinary understanding of the mental beg the question by appealing to the very folk psychology that eliminativism proposes to replace. To be sure, the replacement is not actually available as yet. But this situation, while regrettable, is no real embarrassment to the eliminativist: it's just a fact that science is hard work and takes time.

I am reminded here of another philosophical school which was likewise bold and assertive and which, like eliminative materialism, seemed able to deprive its critics of the resources needed to mount an effective challenge against it. I am referring, of course, to logical positivism, which almost literally "took the words right out of the mouth" of its critics by demonstrating that their contrary theses were devoid of cognitive meaning. Fortunately, those days are now past, and my present purpose is not a refutation of positivism but rather a diagnosis. What happened, I submit, was this: committed to a rather extreme and dogmatic variety of empiricism, the positivists saw clearly that their empiricism simply could not account for large ranges of human thought and discourse—morality, religion, metaphysics, and even (as it turned out) a great deal of scientific discourse. Rather than revise their empiricism to accommodate these data of human experience, they simply ruled them out of court, while leaving the door open for their recovery, as "emotive language," in a form which voided most of their original significance. Eventually, of course, reality reasserted itself. Nowadays ethics, religion, metaphysics, and science all go about their business largely untroubled by the positivist assault, which is well on its way to becoming a distant memory.

My proposal is that something similar to this has been happening in the philosophy of mind. Over the past several decades we have seen a profusion of efforts by materialists to account for the phenomena of the mind. Many of these efforts have been impressive in conception and technically dazzling in execution. Yet signs are not lacking that we may have here a research program which is degenerative rather than progressive. The movement from logical behaviorism to type-identity to token-identity to functionalism to supervenience can't readily be characterized as a progression from "less adequate" to "more adequate" accounts; rather, it is a series of replacements of theories which seem clearly wrong by others which, by dint of novelty, seem for a while to have a better chance of success. Particularly resistant to a properly materialist account is the sheer fact of consciousness itself. Either consciousness is conspicuous by its absence (as in behaviorism and, arguably, in functionalism), or it is present but the account is not sufficiently "materialist" (as in some varieties of supervenience). Under these circumstances, the move made by eliminativism seems like a stroke of genius: rather than endure the unresolved tension between theory and data, proclaim that the data in question are themselves contaminated with bad theory and thus ineligible for incorporation in a proper science of the mind. In fact, eliminativism is even more successful than positivism in protecting itself from a hostile critique. The positivist recasting of (for example) moral language was at least available for inspection, and for many its deficiencies were readily apparent. But the eliminativist account of the life of the mind—that is to say, the eliminativist replacement for the account given by folk psychology, which is marked for elimination—remains hidden from us, and so it retains the mystery, allure, and invulnerability to criticism of all such "promised lands."

At the other end of the materialist spectrum from eliminativism—indeed, perhaps a little beyond that spectrum—lie the recent views of Colin McGinn. The contrast between the two approaches is evident in McGinn's dictum that "a test of whether a proposed solution to the mind-body problem is adequate is whether it relieves the pressure towards eliminativism."[2] McGinn observes that, in contrast with progress in some other areas of the philosophy of mind (for example, in the account of intentional content), the problem of giving a materialist account of consciousness remains intractable: "How is it possible for conscious states to depend on brain states? How can technicolour phenomenology arise from soggy grey matter?"[3] McGinn's contribution is not to provide a "constructive solution" for the problem, but rather to explain why no such solution is possible. His proposal is that the property—whatever it is—in virtue of which the brain is the basis of consciousness, is "cognitively closed" to human beings. That is to say, our concept-forming powers are simply inadequate to enable us to grasp or comprehend this property. McGinn appeals here to Thomas Nagel's version of realism, which asserts that there is no guarantee that it lies within the conceptual powers of human minds to comprehend all of reality; he also notes that

[2] Colin McGinn, "Can We Solve the Mind-Body Problem?" in *The Problem of Consciousness* (Cambridge: Blackwell, 1991), 18.

[3] Ibid., 1.

traditional theists have acknowledged "conceptual closure" in relation to God, in that humans are incapable of grasping certain of the divine attributes. McGinn argues at length that the same conclusion should be drawn with regard to our ability to comprehend the brain-mind connection. Yet in spite of this McGinn remains naturalistic: "Resolutely shunning the supernatural, I think it is undeniable that it must be in virtue of some natural property of the brain that organisms are conscious. There just has to be some explanation for how brains subserve minds."[4] But given that our minds are constituted as they are, the needed explanation will remain forever beyond our grasp.

My purpose here is not to discuss McGinn's case for this proposal, but rather to remark on the fact that he considers it to be a "solution"—albeit a "non-constructive" solution—for the mind body problem. His position is that "the nature of the psychophysical connection has a full and non-mysterious explanation in a certain science, but . . . this science is inaccessible to us as a matter of principle. . . . This removes the philosophical problem because it assures us that the entities *themselves* pose no inherent philosophical difficulty."[5] I wonder how many other philosophers will perceive this as a "solution." The assurance that the entities themselves pose no inherent difficulties has to be accepted by an act of faith; presumably this resolves the problem because we have been shown that, in the nature of the case, faith-assurance is the only kind we could expect to have.

Am I justified in asserting that McGinn's position reveals materialism "in crisis"? I think a good many materialists would indeed find themselves in crisis if forced to give up (as McGinn thinks they must) the claim that "every property of mind can be explained in broadly physical terms."[6] McGinn's effort, of course, is to reassure these philosophers by explaining to them that the mind-brain connection, while unavoidably mysterious to us, is in no way supernatural. What is striking here is that he seems unaware of—or perhaps indifferent to—the possibility that his position may be open to criticisms from opponents of naturalism. The truth of naturalism is simply taken for granted; what is needed is for McGinn to assure his fellow naturalists that his apparently heretical position does not endanger their common faith.

I would argue that a naturalistic position such as McGinn's—one, that is, that recognizes the reality and importance of consciousness while admitting

[4] Ibid., 6.

[5] Ibid., 17.

[6] McGinn cites this as the "standard contemporary view of naturalism" in the philosophy of mind, though it is not a definition to which he himself subscribes (see McGinn, "Consciousness and Content," in *Problem of Consciousness*, 23).

that we are unable to give an explanation of consciousness in physical terms—is indeed vulnerable to an anti-naturalistic critique. I do not want to lay too much stress on the irreducible mystery which McGinn acknowledges in his position, since I don't think any view in the philosophy of mind can avoid mystery without denying part of the data. Instead, among the several lines of argument which might be pursued here, I choose to develop the unity-of-consciousness argument.

On any materialist view, there is no "substance," no concrete individual being, involved in our mental operations other than the human body, in particular the brain and nervous system. Whatever mental properties and experiences we recognize to exist, then, must somehow be properties of the brain and nervous system. Now of course the brain is an extremely complex organ, made up of many identifiable sub-organs, and further of some billions of neurons and other cells, each of which is itself extremely complex. But here is the point: the brain *consists of* these parts; there *is no* brain "over and above" the parts of which it consists; and so whatever is *done by* the brain must also "consist of" the properties of, and relations between the parts of the brain. But when we apply this to conscious experience, an anomaly results. It is a fact of experience that when I am, for instance, viewing a complex scene, my viewing of that scene is experienced *as a unity*; it is simply unintelligible how this experience can consist of the activities of and relations between parts of the brain each of which does *not* have the experience in question. What needs to be accounted for is the *unity of conscious experience,* and I submit that this *cannot* be accounted for by materialism unless it is willing to countenance the existence of some "unified consciousness" which is *not* simply the resultant of the combined functioning of the various parts of the brain and nervous system. Such an argument, to be sure, needs additional elaboration to make it fully convincing, but I believe it raises considerations which must not be overlooked as we are seeking an adequate account of the mind.

II. The Dilemma of Dualism

I have no doubt that many of you are reading this critique of materialism with the comfortable—or perhaps not so comfortable—thought that it is paving the way for the triumphant return of dualism. Maybe so—but not, I think, dualism in the familiar Cartesian version. I do not, to be sure, wish to press here the familiar, and greatly overrated, objections based on the "problem of mind-body interaction." Let me say it plainly: there are no compelling philosophical principles from which it follows that the interaction of minds and bodies, construed in broadly Cartesian terms, is impossible.[7] And while Cartesian dualism does leave this interaction quite mysterious, that is no very strong objection against the theory. As we saw in our discussion of McGinn, our topic is one which provides us with a surfeit of mystery whichever way we turn; the only theories which can avoid it are those that deny or ignore part of the data.

My complaints against Cartesian dualism are basically two. The first is that it cannot plausibly account for the extensive and intimate dependence of mind on brain that we find to exist. Some forms of dependence, of course, are readily understandable on Cartesian assumptions. The immaterial mind will be dependent on the brain as the channel for sensory information, and as the control center for bodily movement. It is therefore to be expected that sensory and motor capacities will be brain-dependent, and that impairment of brain function will interfere with those capacities. But why should *consciousness itself* be interrupted by a blow to the head, or a dose of medication? And why should a personality be drastically altered—sometimes temporarily, sometimes permanently—by injury to the brain or a chemical imbalance in the brain?

Scientific discoveries reveal additional, previously unknown aspects of mind-brain dependency. There are, for example, the "split-brain" phenomena exhibited by commissurotomy patients, which strongly suggest that *consciousness itself* can be divided as a result of an operation on the brain. Another striking piece of evidence is found in the phenomenon of "visual agnosia." As a result of specific types of brain damage, there are persons of whom it is true that (1) their visual capacity as such is largely undamaged (they are able to discriminate visual detail); (2) their general intelligence is unimpaired; but (3) they are in important ways unable to "make sense" of what they are seeing—unable to read words, even though they can discern the letters, unable to recognize familiar faces or to "read" the expressions on people's faces. What this shows is that the functioning of the brain, and indeed of quite specific regions within the brain, is required for and intimately involved in some highly sophisticated mental processes; we do not have a situation, as Cartesian dualism might lead us to suppose, in which the body and brain merely serve up raw perceptual data which is then understood and interpreted by the immaterial mind. I believe, therefore, that an adequate theory of the mind must allow for the dependence of mental activity upon brain function in a way that is stronger than Cartesian dualism can readily accommodate.

[7] This is shown convincingly by Keith Yandell in "A Defense of Dualism," *Faith and Philosophy* 12 (1995): 548–66. See also the contributions to this volume by Kim and O'Connor.

Another area of difficulty for dualism is the relationship between human beings and other animals. Cartesian souls, of course, cannot be replicated through biological reproduction; they must be directly created by God. And, given the universal divine activity of conservation, they are "naturally immortal." This fact seemed to Descartes good reason to deny souls to the beasts; thus his infamous doctrine that animals are mere automata. Surely we cannot follow Descartes in this; a contemporary Cartesian must assign souls to the animals as well as to human beings. Presumably, then, God creates souls individually for the myriads of mosquitoes that spawn every summer—and then (assuming we draw the line at immortal mosquitoes) he annihilates the mosquitoes' souls every time one of them falls victim to a bugzapper. Yet another problem arises in the case of those creatures (such as starfish) that can be divided into parts, with each part then developing into a complete organism. At first, we have one starfish and one soul; then, two starfish and two souls—but where does the second soul come from? And there does not seem to be any plausible way to incorporate Cartesian souls into the story of biological evolution.[8] I believe that any form of dualism which gives a coherent and plausible account of these phenomena will have to differ considerably from Cartesianism.

It may occur to some of you that if Cartesian dualism is in trouble in the ways mentioned, the solution lies ready to hand in the more Aristotelian dualism of Thomas Aquinas. I agree in part; Aquinas's doctrine does facilitate a closer tie between soul and body, and also between human beings and the rest of nature, than is possible on Cartesian assumptions. But while there is something right in the spirit of Aquinas's view, that view as it stands just is not a viable option for contemporary philosophers. The great difficulty here lies in the transition from Aristotelian physics, which is teleological and hylomorphic, to modern physics, which is determinedly nonteleological and refuses to allow a place for Aristotelian "substantial forms." If the "form" is interpreted merely as an arrangement of physical particles and forces—as a "configurational state" of matter, in Eleonore Stump's phrase,[9] then we have simply another variety of materialism, one which may or may not have advantages over other varieties but is

[8] Richard Swinburne's defense of dualism is titled *The Evolution of the Soul.* But he has admitted that this is a misnomer; on his view, souls do not and cannot evolve (discussion at the Wheaton Philosophy Conference, September 1990).

[9] See Eleanor Stump, "Materialism without Reductionism and Non-Cartesian Substance Dualism," in *Faith and Philosophy* 12 (1995): 505–31. This essay is the best attempt I know of to present Aquinas's doctrine as a viable option in the contemporary debate.

certainly remote from the intention of Aquinas. If on the other hand the form is itself a concrete individual—in Stump's phrasing, a "configured configurer"—then we have in effect a substance dualism which does not differ radically from that of Descartes.[10] One difference that does exist lies in the fact that while the souls of humans are specially and individually created by God, animals have souls which are produced by natural processes. Another difference lies in the fact that Aristotelian souls are responsible for energizing bodily functions such as digestion, growth, and reproduction as well as for consciousness, sensation, and reasoning; this runs head-on into the commitment of contemporary biology to mechanistic explanations of such biological processes. It is not out of the question that further tinkering with this view might produce something that would be worthy of consideration in the contemporary debate. Such tinkering, in fact, might result in a view not greatly dissimilar to the one to be sketched in the latter part of this essay. But the result of all this would certainly not *be* Aquinas's view, however much it might be indebted to his view.

And so ends our "lightning review" of options in the philosophy of mind. Materialism, I have argued, is in crisis because it reduces mentality to a function of the physical organism in ways that do not, in the end, account for the mind as we know it to be. And dualism faces a dilemma in that it needs to provide an account of the human mind and spirit without so divorcing mind from matter that the connection between them—and indeed, the connection between human beings and the entire world of nature—becomes almost entirely mysterious. There is need, in short for a middle way in the philosophy of mind, a perspective which reduces the gulf between mind and matter without doing violence to the nature of either.

III. The Middle Way

In the remainder of this chapter I will sketch out a theory of the mind which meets these desiderata. I shall not claim either that this theory provides the only possible solution to the problem of the nature of persons, or that it is without difficulties of its own. I will count myself successful if I can leave you with the perception that this is a view that merits further consideration—that it may offer a way forward through the thicket of difficulties which perplex us.

[10] Oddly, Stump does not seem to recognize that these are two incompatible doctrines; both halves of her title are meant to apply to one, supposedly consistent, theory of Aquinas.

We begin by stipulating that we take the well-confirmed results of natural science, including research on neurophysiology, just as we find them. Attempts to resolve the problem through a nonrealistic interpretation of the sciences, as in idealism and some forms of phenomenology, are deeply implausible and provide no lasting solution to our problems.[11] We need not assume that the sciences give us a *complete account* of the nature of the world, even an "in-principle" complete account. But what they do give us, in the form of their well-confirmed results, must be acknowledged as true and as informative about the real nature of things.

But if our theory should be "realistic" about the results of the sciences, it should also be "realistic" about the phenomena of the mind itself. John Searle has noted that a great deal of recent philosophy of mind is extremely implausible because of its denial of apparently "obvious facts about the mental, such as that we all really do have subjective conscious mental states and that these are not eliminable in favor of anything else."[12] It's true that we do not, in the case of the mind, have well-confirmed scientific theories comparable to the powerful theories that have been developed in the physical sciences. But we do have a vast amount of *data* concerning mental processes, events, and properties, and we should begin with the presumption that we are going to take that data as it stands, rather than truncate it in order to tailor it to the requirements of this or that philosophical scheme.

So far, perhaps, so good. But stating that we are realists both about the physical and about the mental brings to the fore once again the vast differences between the two: the chasm opens beneath our feet. Cartesian dualism simply accepts the chasm, postulating the soul as an entity of a completely different nature than the physical, an entity with no essential or internal relationship to the body, which must be added to the body *ab extra* by a special divine act of creation. This scheme is not without initial plausibility from a theistic point of view, but I believe it carries with it insuperable difficulties.

In rejecting such dualisms, we implicitly affirm that *the human mind is produced by the human brain and is not a separate element "added to" the brain from outside.* This leads to the further conclusion that mental properties are "emergent" in the following sense: they are properties that

[11] The mind-body problem arises, in large part, because of the apparent incongruity between the well-confirmed results of the natural sciences and what seems to be experientially the case with regard to the mind. Giving a nonrealistic interpretation of the sciences simply moves the incongruity to another place, between the manifest content of the scientific disciplines and the philosophical interpretation which is given of that content.

[12] John Searle, *The Rediscovery of the Mind* (Cambridge: MIT Press, 1992), 3.

manifest themselves when the appropriate material constituents are placed in special highly complex relationships but which are neither observable in simpler configurations nor derivable from properties which are thus observable.

But while property emergence is necessary for the kind of view being developed here, it is not sufficient. For the unity of consciousness argument, cited above, claims to show not only that the properties of the mind cannot be explained in terms of the properties exhibited by matter in simpler, nonbiological configurations; it also claims that these properties cannot be explained in terms of any properties of, and relations between, the material constituents of the brain. A conscious experience simply is a unity, and to decompose it into a collection of separate parts is to falsify it. So it is not enough to say that there are emergent properties here; what is needed is an *emergent individual,* a new individual entity which comes into existence as a result of a certain functional configuration of the material constituents of the brain and nervous system. As an analogy which may assist us in grasping this notion, I suggest the various "fields" with which we are familiar in physical science—the magnetic field, the gravitational field, and so on. A magnetic field, for example, is a real existing concrete entity, distinct from the magnet which produces it. (This is shown by the fact that the field normally occupies a region of space considerably larger than that occupied by the magnet.) The field is "generated" by the magnet in virtue of the fact that the magnet's material constituents are arranged in a certain way—namely, when a sufficient number of the iron molecules are aligned so that their "micro-fields" reinforce each other and produce a detectable overall field. But once generated, the field exerts a causality of its own, on the magnet itself as well as on other objects in the vicinity. (In an electric motor, the armature moves partly because of the magnetic fields produced by itself.) Keeping all this in mind, we can say that *as a magnet generates its magnetic field, so the brain generates its field of consciousness.* The mind, like the magnetic field, comes into existence when the constituents of its "material base" are arranged in a suitable way—in this case, in the extremely complex arrangement found in the nervous systems of animals. And like the magnetic field, it exerts a causality of its own; certainly on the brain itself, and conceivably also on other minds (telepathy?) or aspects of the material world (telekinesis?).

To be sure, this analogy has its limitations. The properties of the magnetic field and the other fields identified by physics do not seem to be emergent in the strong sense required for the properties of the mind. Nor does it seem that these fields possess the kind of unity that is required for the mind, as shown by the unity-of-consciousness argument. The analogy with the magnetic field is useful in enabling us to conceive of the ontological status of the mind according to the present theory. But the analogy can't bear the full weight of the theory, which must rather commend itself in virtue of its inherent advantages over both materialism and Cartesian dualism.

The theory's advantages over dualism result from the close natural connection it postulates between mind and brain, as contrasted with the disparity between mind and matter postulated by dualism. In view of this close connection, it is natural to conclude that the emergent consciousness is itself a spatial entity. And there is evidence both from subhuman animals and from human beings (for example, commissurotomy) that the field of consciousness is capable of being divided as a result of damage to the brain and nervous system. Both of these points, of course, mark important breaks with Cartesianism. Beyond this, the theory makes intelligible, as Cartesian dualism does not, the intimate dependence of consciousness and mental processes on brain function. And, finally, it is completely free of embarrassment over the souls of animals. Animals have souls, just as we do: their souls are less complex and sophisticated than ours, because generated by less complex nervous systems.

The theory's advantages over materialism will depend on which variety of materialism is in view. As compared with eliminativist and strongly reductive varieties of materialism, our theory has the advantage that it takes the phenomena of mental life at face value instead of denying them or mutilating them to fit into a Procrustean bed. The view proposed here has more affinity with "property dualism" and views which postulate a strong form of property emergence—but these are views to which many will hesitate to accord the label "materialist." Be that as it may, the present view differs from property dualism and property-emergence views in its postulation of the mind as an *emergent individual,* thus providing it with an answer, which those views lack, to the problem posed by the unity of consciousness argument.

The resemblance to property-emergence views does, however, suggest a name for our theory. Formerly I have referred to it simply as "emergentism," but that label could lead to misunderstanding because it is most commonly used for theories of property emergence. I suggest, then, "emergent dualism" as a name which brings to the fore both the theme of emergence and the undeniable affinities between the "soul-field" postulated here and the mind as conceived by traditional dualism.

Finally, what of eternal life? In principle, emergent dualism leaves open the question of life after death for human beings. Certainly the theory provides no metaphysical guarantee of survival. If anything, the field analogy cuts the other way: stop the generator, destroy the magnet, and the magnetic field disappears. It seems however, that there is at least the *logical possibility* for the field to continue without its supporting magnet; it is, after all, a distinct individual. No doubt an omnipotent God could annihilate all of the electromagnets in a particle accelerator, and instantaneously replace them with others, while causing the identical field to persist in being. Or, he could directly sustain the field by his own power, without the need for a material "generator" of any kind. Perhaps there is no reason why God would do this. But Christians believe there is indeed reason for God to concern himself with the continued existence of rational souls.

And if survival is possible, then so is resurrection. If God can sustain the field of consciousness absent any material "base" whatsoever, then God can also provide a new base in the form of a resurrection body. This body, to be sure, would have to be crafted specifically to support and energize the particular conscious field in question; in view of the intimate dependence of mind on brain discussed earlier, not just any body and brain would do. And this means that the ordinary, prince-and-pauper type of body-switching thought-experiments really are not possible on this view. But the modal arguments for dualism supported by such thought-experiments are much less helpful than has been supposed.

I have spoken at length of the advantages of emergent dualism, but what of the costs? So far as I can tell, there is only one major cost involved in the theory, but some will find it to be pretty steep. The theory requires us to maintain, along with the materialists, that the potentiality for conscious life and experience really does exist in the nature of matter itself. And at the same time we have to admit, as McGinn has pointed out, that we have no insight whatever into how this is the case. I do not necessarily endorse McGinn's assertion that the brain-mind link is "cognitively closed" to us, though that possibility deserves serious consideration. And yet, in purely physiological terms, what is required for consciousness—or at least, some kind of sentience—to exist must not be all that complex, since the requirements are apparently satisfied in relatively simple forms of life. As McGinn puts it, "In the manual that God consulted when he made the earth and all the beasts that dwell thereon the chapter about how to engineer consciousness from matter occurs fairly early on, well before the really difficult later chapters on mammalian reproduction and speech."[13]

[13] McGinn, *Problem of Consciousness*, 19. Unfortunately, McGinn's fairly frequent references to God have to be taken heuristically and not as expressions of actual belief.

But if the price seems high, it may still be worth paying. As I've pointed out already, there just are no cheap and easy solutions to the mind-body problem, not unless we arbitrarily simplify it by throwing away some of the data. And if it strains our credulity to accept that we humans really are crafted from the dust of the earth, we ought to remember that this dust is itself the creation of the all-wise God, and rich with potentials beyond our imagining.

BRIAN LEFTOW

Souls Dipped in Dust

We have bodies, which are material things. We also have minds. If minds are immaterial things, it seems to follow that humans consist of two things, a material body and an immaterial mind. But there are alternatives. Aquinas believes that humans are material things and that humans have souls, which are immaterial things. Yet he is no dualist. For Aquinas, though a human soul is an immaterial thing, each human is one material thing, not a complex of a soul and a material thing.[1] And yet that material thing is just a soul draped in primary matter; if Thomas is not a dualist, this is because the body does not count for him as a "thing" in our makeup in addition to the soul. Thus for Aquinas, humans are material things, yet neither their souls nor their bodies as apart from their souls are.

The key to Thomas's position is his claim that the human soul is a human's substantial form. I now explain this claim and argue that Thomas's view is not as puzzling as it seems.

I. Emergence, Matter, and Form

To explain Thomas's view of body and soul, I must set out some of his metaphysics of material substances. Thomas is an emergentist. As he sees

My thanks to Eleonore Stump and Kevin Corcoran for comments on this paper.

[1] "Soul and body are not two actually existent substances. Rather, from the two come one actually existing substance" (S. Thomae Aquinatis, *Summa contra gentiles* [Turin: Marietti, 1909], I 69, 164).

it, just by coming to be in a new state, matter can constitute a new substance, distinct from any that has gone before. This state emerges naturally from matter's continuous evolution. So then does the new thing the matter constitutes.

Consider embryonic development. Once sperm and egg join, we have a zygote, alive, but able only to feed and grow, as plants do. For Thomas, if the zygote can do by nature only what plants do by nature, it is a plant: not only not human, but not even an animal.[2] But as the zygote grows, it gains a more complex shape and new qualities. By these continuous, gradual changes, some of its parts come to form a new thing, a sense organ. Once it has a sense organ, the fetus can sense. When the fetus can sense, it can do what animals do by nature. So it has a sensitive soul and is an animal, though not yet human.[3] Plant tissue becomes animal tissue, and a plant becomes an animal when the tissue, by continuous growth and alteration, comes to be in the right new state. Aquinas thinks this animal is not the plant in another form but a new individual.[4] There is a certain intuitive appeal to this: was your dog ever a plant? Were you?

As Thomas sees it, during the course of a pregnancy, the womb contains several nonhuman things—first semen, then a vegetable, then a nonrational animal. As semen changes to plant and plant to animal, new substances come to be because new "forms" are present: a plant soul, then a sensitive soul.[5] How do these "forms" come to be? Thomas writes that substantial forms preexist in the potency of matter: "The sensible and vegetable soul are drawn from the potency of matter, just like other forms whose production requires a power transforming matter."[6]

For Thomas, causes "draw" new forms from matter's resources. They alter the matter's quantity and qualities, shaping it, making it hotter, colder, wetter, dryer. Thus they bring it into new states (heat, moistness), which naturally emerge in it. These changes "dispose" matter for a new substantial form. Given the right quantities and qualities, the form

[2] S. Thomae Aquinatis, *Summa theologiae,* Ia 118, 2 *ad* 2.

[3] Ibid., Ia 76, 3 *ad* 3.

[4] Thomas writes that an individual's essence consists of designated matter and individuated form (Aquinatis, *Summa contra gentiles,* I 65). If it does, then if you have a new substantial form, new individua (see also Aquinatis, *Summa contra gentiles,* II 58). Now if the plant form continued "beneath" the animal form as a second, distinct substantial form, one could argue that the animal *is* the same individual as the plant (on Thomas's principles). But if the plant form were still there, the animal's tissue would also be plant tissue: what has a plant's form is a plant (on Thomas's principles).

[5] S. Thomae Aquinatis, *Quaestiones disputatae de potentia Dei,* in *Quaestiones disputatae,* vol. 1 (Turin: Marietti, 1931), 3, 9 *ad* 9.

[6] Ibid., 3, 11 *ad* 7, 81. See also *ad* 10.

supervenes. Thus someone wanting to turn one sort of matter, wood, into the element fire does so by heating that wood. This (thinks Thomas) brings it about eventually that the wood's matter has a pure quality of heat. Given the heat, the form of fire supervenes: the wood ignites. Again, for Thomas, one mixes elements—makes chemical compounds, which are new substances—by changing matter qualitatively:

> The active and passive qualities of the elements are contraries. They admit of more and less. From (such qualities) intermediate qualities can be constituted, which have a taste of the nature of the extremes, as . . . tepid between hot and cold. So by the abating of the elements' excelling qualities, an intermediate quality is constituted from them, which is the proper quality of a mixed body . . . and this quality is the proper disposition for the form of a mixed body, just as the simple quality is for the form of a simple body.[7]

Given a new quality, the form supervenes. Just as for a thing to be stably purely hot "makes" it fire, for a thing to be stably tepid "makes" it something else. The form is present just when the underlying quality is stably present. We may think that the qualities really do all the work here—that talk of a new form is just shorthand for talk of a quality that becomes stably present. But Thomas reverses this. As he sees it, a substance's underlying nature accounts for its qualities: the presence of the form of fire gives something the nature of fire, which accounts for the stable continuing presence of pure heat once prior heating of wood has brought it to the point of ignition. In the same way, given the right changes in the womb, a new soul supervenes. Some processes in the womb become self-sustaining, and so stably present. (For instance, the developing fetus gains a circulatory system of its own.) For them to start and continue is for live flesh to be ensouled.

As the zygote changes, it comes to form a plant. We can also say: the zygote's matter takes on the form of a plant. Thomas parses this as: there is an item, a form, such that the zygote's matter takes this item on. There is for Thomas an item such that when this item is present in what was the zygote's matter—that is, when this matter has taken this item on—a new substance has emerged. Thomas calls this substance-constituting item a substantial form.

[7] S. Thomae Aquinatis, *De mixtione elementorum,* in *S. Thomae Aquinatis opuscula omnia,* vol. 1, ed. R. Mandonnet (Paris: LeThielleux, 1927), 21.

II. Two Kinds of Matter

Let us now get more precise about Thomas's terms "matter" and "substantial form." Thomas distinguishes two sorts of matter:

> something is potentially human, namely sperm and menstrual blood . . . sperm which is potentially a human is made actually a human by the soul . . . that which is in potency to substantial being is called matter *from which*, [not] matter *in which*. . . . that is called matter which has existence from (the form) which comes to it, because of itself . . . it has no being. . . . Whence, simply speaking, (substantial) form gives existence to matter.[8]

No sperm is a human being, and sperm (thinks Thomas)[9] does not consist of human tissue. So what sperm consist of, sperm-stuff, is not the kind of matter of which humans consist. Sperm-stuff is matter *from which* a human comes. Matter *from which,* says Thomas, "of itself exists incompletely. . . . everything which is in potency can be called matter" from which.[10] "Matter," for Thomas, is actually shorthand for a relative term, *matter of x*.[11] And *x*'s matter from which is what is only potentially *x*, the stuff from which *x* is made or the parts from which *x* is immediately assembled. Save for prime matter (of which more anon), what is potentially *x* is actually something on its own. What is potentially human, in Thomas's example, is actually sperm. Sperm "exists incompletely" only in the sense that it is incompletely *human*. An item is matter from which insofar as it is *potentially* some thing or some way. To describe something as matter from which is to describe it as able to be or come to be of a different kind, or all or part of a different individual, than it actually is.

The matter *in which* a human exists is the matter of which he / she consists while he / she exists. This is of course human tissue. Nothing is human tissue until a human form, a soul, makes some matter human tissue. So while the matter which is to become human tissue exists before the soul arrives, the human tissue itself does not. Thus the matter *in which* a human exists has its existence from the form, the soul, which comes to the

[8] S. Thomae Aquinatis, *De principiis naturae,* in *S. Thomae Aquinatis opuscula omnia,* vol. 1, ed. R. Mandonnet (Paris: LeThielleux, 1927), c. 1, p. 8.

[9] Aquinatis, *Quaestiones disputatae de potentia Dei,* 3, 12.

[10] Aquinatis, *De principiis naturae,* c. 1, p. 8.

[11] This is so even for prime matter, which cannot exist save as some substance's prime matter (Aquinatis, *Summa theologiae,* Ia 66, 1c *et ad* 3).

matter *from which*. The matter from which, what was potentially *x*, does not survive *x*'s coming to be.[12] No bit of flesh *is* a bit of sperm, and beyond this, for Thomas, no bit of flesh *was* a bit of sperm. Perhaps some path through space and time begins with a bit of sperm, ends in a bit of flesh, and is continuously filled with matter belonging to one or the other. Even so, for Thomas, the flesh-bit and the sperm-bit are distinct individuals which never coexist, whose portions of the path do not overlap.

Some might disagree with Thomas and say: some tissue first was sperm-stuff, then was flesh. Some bits were first bits of sperm, then bits of flesh. As this is so, the human tissue—the very stuff, or bits, to which this term now refers—was there all along. But it actually became human tissue only when ensouled. So the same matter in one state is matter *from which* and in another is matter *in which*. Thomas's reply, I think, would be that there *is* matter which in one state is matter from which and in another is matter in which, but it is not any bit of any stuff-kind. If it were a bit of some kind of stuff, the substantial form of that kind of stuff, K, would be the bit's only real substantial form. For as Thomas sees it, substantial forms confer natures.[13] Natures are permanent attributes: a thing has its nature as long as it exists. But if a bit of K first is not, then is human tissue, being human tissue is not a permanent attribute of the bit. And if being human tissue replaced some attribute, that attribute was not permanent either.

Thomas claims that the *same* matter is first sperm, then (say) plant tissue, yet is not of itself any bit of any stuff-kind. One wants to know: if it is not of the same kind throughout the change, what makes it the same matter? For Thomas, again, qualitative and quantitative change underlies substantial change. The change from sperm to plant follows upon continuous alteration of the sperm's matter. Let's suppose that being sperm-stuff supervenes on having a heat of *m* degrees, and being plant tissue supervenes on a heat of *n* degrees. We can make sense of saying that the same stuff was first hotter, then colder. What stuff got colder? The hot stuff. We needn't call it sperm- or plant-stuff to talk about this sort of change; we can pick out a body of matter as hotter or colder than its surrounding matter without knowing what kind of stuff it is. Once we have done so, we can reidentify it by its original boundaries while its temperature changes, as long as it doesn't move.[14] This is easy if to be in place is to

[12] Save for prime matter—which does not affect the points I want to make.

[13] Aquinatis, *Summa contra gentiles*, IV 35.

[14] That last clause raises an interesting question. Consider some hot stuff changing its place. How does the world differ if, instead, the hot stuff stays in place and cools off, and some neighboring stuff heats up? Thomas is an Aristotelian, and so for him hot or cold stuff

have surfaces and edges in contact with the innermost surfaces / edges of the surrounding bodies, as Aristotle has it.[15] For on this view a quantity of matter in place has boundaries in direct contact with the innermost surfaces of the bodies containing it, and so if the latter don't move, neither does what they contain.

The matter which is first sperm, then plant, is the hot stuff in a certain place that got colder. "Hot" and "cold" aren't *kinds* of matter. Calling some stuff hot does not state its nature. Substantial forms give things their natures. So, hot and cold are qualities, not substantial forms, and picking out the matter that remains constant beneath substantial change as the hot stuff in a certain place lets Thomas keep his claim that the matter which continues beneath a substantial change does not belong to a kind of itself and has no substantial form of itself.

III. Substantial Forms

Let us turn now to substantial form. Aquinas explains the terms "matter" and "form" this way: "matter . . . of itself exists incompletely. . . . form gives existence to matter. . . . just as everything which is in potency can be called matter, so everything by which a thing has (substantial) being . . . can be called (a substantial) form."[16] Thomas defines substantial form by what it does: *x*'s form is that, intrinsic to *x*, which "makes" *x*'s matter constitute *x*—that is, makes that matter actually what it could have been or had been merely potentially.[17] If *x* is a substance composed of matter, *x*'s existing consists in or supervenes on that matter's being in a particular state—call it state F. The substantial form of *x* is that, intrinsic to *x*, by which *x*'s matter is F. For Aquinas, "a substantial form perfects not only a whole but each of its parts, and is whole in any of the parts."[18] So the substantial form of *x* is that *y* such that *y* is present as a whole in each part of *x*,[19] and for *y* to be so is for all of *x*'s matter to be F. Often *y* is a state (say,

is always in fact the matter of some substance. So Thomas can answer this way: if the hot stuff changes its place, some substance moves. In the second case no substance moves, but it is left open that at least one substance may undergo substantial change.

[15] Cf. Aristotle, *Physics* 4, 4, 212a5–7, 20–21.

[16] Aquinatis, *De principiis naturae*, c. 1, p. 8.

[17] Efficient and final causes also "give existence" to matter in their own way. Thomas rules them out by saying "by which": efficient and final causes are causes from which, not by which—extrinsic, not intrinsic causes.

[18] Aquinatis, *Summa theologiae*, Ia 76, 8, 461b.

[19] Ibid.; Aquinatis, *Summa contra gentiles*, II 72.

being animal) and for y to be present as a whole in each part of x (an animal) is for each part of x to be in that state (be animal). But Thomas's account of form is abstract enough to leave room for a y which is not a state. Where y is a human soul, the matter of x being live human tissue consists in y's being wholly present in each part of x.[20] Thus y is x's form, on Thomas's account: for Aquinas, the human soul is a human being's substantial form.[21] But (again) this does not entail that the soul is a state of the body.

Thomas holds that each material substance has just one substantial form.[22] This general feature of his metaphysics shapes his understanding of the from-which / in-which distinction. Our bodies consist of human tissue. We think they also consist of many things *other* than human tissue—quarks, electrons, protons, hydrogen, oxygen, water, hydrocarbons, and so forth. But on Thomas's terms, all these are matter from which we exist, not matter in which we exist. For quarks, electrons, and so on are presumably substances, each with their own forms. So if I existed in—as well as from—electrons and water, the same matter would exemplify the substantial forms of electron, water, and flesh. So for Thomas, the matter *in which* I exist is *just* human flesh and bone. In current terms, Thomas is an eliminativist about the matter from which substances come, or the parts from which they are assembled.[23]

Is Thomas's eliminativism plausible? The key to making sense of his view, I think, lies in noting that forms are, include, or subvene clusters of causal powers. Artifacts provide clear examples of this, and while Thomas denies artifacts the title "substance," he is at the same time clear that they do have their own "accidental" forms.[24] Consider chairs. Thrones, beanbags, and the strange products of avant-garde home design all count as chairs. But they have no shape in common. What makes them chairs is that they are able to (or perhaps are designed to) support humans in a roughly seated position. That is, they are chairs because they have a set of causal powers (or perhaps a function which involves these). Suppose then that a form is actually present only if the relevant causal powers are present. Then is the form of oxygen present in a water molecule? Oxygen bound in water cannot act as free oxygen does. We cannot breathe water.

[20] Aquinatis, *Summa theologiae,* Ia 76, 8; Aquinatis, *Summa contra gentiles,* II 72.

[21] Aquinatis, *Summa theologiae,* Ia 76, 1.

[22] So, e.g., Aquinatis, *Summa theologiae,* Ia 76, 4: the argument concerns substantial forms quite generally, though the stated topic is the soul.

[23] See Michael Rea, ed., *Material Constitution* (New York: Rowman and Littlefield, 1997).

[24] For both, see Aquinatis, *De principiis naturae,* c. 2.

Perhaps water has its distinctive chemical nature because hydrogen and oxygen combine to form it, and some matter in the water molecule is *shaped* like an oxygen atom, and were it broken free of its chemical bonds would *be* an oxygen atom.[25] If these things are true, oxygen is "virtually" present.[26] But what cannot act like oxygen isn't then actually oxygen: the form of oxygen is lacking.

Grant this much, and suddenly the forms of particles, atoms, and subcompounds fall away. Though what fills space in a certain region is *shaped* like all of these, it will not count as any of them. Let a general commitment to ontological simplicity shave the number of souls in a human to one.[27] And then you are left with two questions. One is of how the advent of a human soul can "make" a parcel of matter human flesh. I address this in sections 4 and 5. Part of this (I suggest) is just an ordinary case of emergence; the rest involves a perhaps primitive metaphysical concept the use of which is defensible. The second question is of what the soul is "paired with" in a human being if the soul is a human's only substantial form. I address this in section 6.

IV. Soul and Life

The soul "makes" our bodies alive. Its "union" with the body consists in its enlivening the body.[28] Its enlivening the body makes it the body's form:

> That by which something becomes a being in act from a being in potency is its form. . . . the (live) body becomes a being in act from being potentially existent through the soul, for in living things, to live is to be (and) through the soul, it lives in act. So the soul is the form of the ensouled, living body.[29]

> The soul is what enlivens the body. For living things, to live is to exist. So the soul is that by which the human body actually exists. Now a form is a this sort of thing. So the human soul is the form of the body.[30]

[25] And perhaps not. Here I am simply making the assumption least favorable to Thomas.

[26] On which concept see Aquinatis, *De mixtione elementorum.*

[27] From the three that some of Thomas's contemporaries believed in (Aquinatis, *Summa theologiae,* Ia 76, 3).

[28] Aquinatis, *Summa contra gentiles,* II 57.

[29] Ibid.

[30] S. Thomae Aquinatis, *De anima,* in Quaestiones disputatae, vol. 2 (Turin: Marietti, 1931), a. 1, p. 369.

ı Aquinas traces human life to the human soul, he is not saying that .. an life has no biological explanation, or that biology is incomplete without reference to souls. As he sees it, biology does not deal with souls because it presupposes what souls do: the presence of souls gives biology its subject matter. Biology deals with how bits of live tissue interact. The soul's arrival accounts for live tissue's existence, rather than for any particular event in or act by the tissue. What a soul "does" for a body by informing or enlivening it is more like creating its tissue *ex nihilo* than like the sort of interplay of causes in which biology deals. For the arrival of the human soul "turns" the matter from which a human would come into matter in which a human exists, nonhuman tissue into human, and as Thomas sees it, not one bit of that human tissue had been there before the soul arrived. Of course, this "creation" is not *ex nihilo,* but *ex* matter from which. All the same, if the soul's arrival accounts for the tissue's very existence, its arrival looks a lot *like* theistic creation—and its continued presence in that tissue, preserving its humanity (and so its existence), looks a lot like theistic conservation.

The soul's "turning" nonhuman into human matter is not a case of "metaphysical magic." It is (in the respect we're now discussing) one more case of emergence. The metaphysics of the nonhuman / human transformation is mostly that of the plant / animal transformation. By a continuous rearranging of live matter, the fetus's matter is prepared for a new form. It becomes able to host the human soul, and then this form appears. The new form brings with it the individual(s) its presence entails.[31] All this happens in so lawlike a way as to count as one more case of natural emergence and supervenience. Thomas also insists that the soul is a direct divine creation.[32] But these features of Thomas's account are compatible. For what is lawlike and natural in Thomas's account of human development is the occurrence of a divine act. The lawlike way fetal development leads to souls' appearance may make it look like the fetus's development causally accounts for the soul's appearance, but in this one case Thomas is (as it were) an occasionalist. Those who want to charge "magic" might point to God's role in ensoulment. But God's role is beside the point at present. Our topic is how the soul "turns" nonhuman into human matter upon arrival, not whence the soul arrives. This "turning," I claim, is not

[31] The Thomist soul is an individual, as I read Thomas. And when it becomes present, by its union with the body it constitutes a second new individual, the human being, whose thoughts the soul enables.

[32] Aquinatis, *Summa theologiae,* Ia 118, 2.

magic but just one more case of a form supervening on appropriate quantities and qualities and constituting a new substance.

The charge of magic might again light on the claim that the zygote is a nonhuman which eventually turns human. But any believer in evolution holds that this has occurred, and it is not odd to claim that ontogeny recapitulates phylogeny. Must we countenance emergence in this case? There are only three ways to deal with the zygote-to-baby transition.

1. One can say that there was no nonhuman-to-human change: what was in the womb was always human.

Thomas explicitly rejects this. As he sees it, there is no human without a human soul, and "since the soul is the act of an organic body, it cannot exist before there is any kind of organization of a body able to receive the soul."[33] The soul is the form of the *human* body, and a zygote is no human body. Some might rejoin that while the zygote is not a human body, it *is* a bit of human tissue, and becomes a human body merely by cell division and addition. But for Thomas, only the presence of the human form—the soul—makes tissue human, and so he would reject this. In so doing, he is not setting himself at odds with cell biology. The issue is not what happens in the womb, but at what point (and why) what is in the womb *counts as* human tissue. Thomas can agree that what is in the womb has human DNA, divides into further such cells, and gradually forms a human-shaped body. His position is that having human DNA does not suffice for being human tissue—that something is human tissue only if it has at some time been part of a whole, ensouled human body. This is a philosophical claim, not a biological one. It is not obviously wrong.

2. One can say that the womb's contents become human gradually, by degrees.

Thomas also explicitly rejects this.[34] Thomas just does not see being human as a matter of degree. Here common sense is surely on his side. If what is in the womb does not begin as human and does not become human by degrees, yet ends up human, then

3. At some point in gestation, what was nonhuman tissue turns into human tissue.

[33] Aquinatis, *Quaestiones disputatae de potentia Dei*, 3, 12, 83.
[34] Ibid., 3, 12, 84.

But on Thomas's account of things, if tissue turns human, there begins to be a form in the tissue which constitutes it as human tissue—that is, a human soul begins to be present. Thus, Thomas at least has arguments that we must accept a case of emergence here.

We want to ask just what the soul "does" to the body to enliven it. For Thomas, this is the wrong question. Thomas likens the way a plant soul "causes" in a plant the changes in which its being alive consists to the way the form of fire "causes" fire to rise.[35] All the form of fire "does" for fires is confer the nature due to which they naturally rise unless impeded. Fire rises by its nature. The form of fire's being "in" the fire is just fire's having this nature. So too, plants by nature grow, feed, and reproduce—the changes in which their being alive consists. The plant soul's being present in them just is their having such natures as to do all this naturally. Thomas insists that the one human soul does the jobs of plant, sensitive, and rational souls.[36] Presumably, then, it does the plant soul's job as the plant soul does it. That is, its "making" us alive just is our having such natures as to do naturally what live things do naturally. The difference in our case is that the life we live by nature (and so the life the soul "produces" in us) uses rational powers as well as those to feed, grow, and reproduce.

V. Thing and Form

For Thomas, the soul is a form, but it is also a particular in the same sense a hand or an eye is,[37] a sense which "excludes the inherence . . . of a material form."[38] This makes the soul an exception in his metaphysics. Every other form Thomas recognizes either is a "material form" and "inheres" like one or is an immaterial particular not naturally embodied.[39] There are three basic ways to understand the Thomist soul's being both a form and a particular thing. One way takes as given that the soul is an immaterial particular and then tries to show how such a thing can be a substantial form:

[35] *In II De anima,* lect. 7, no. 323.

[36] Aquinatis, *Summa theologiae,* Ia 76, 4.

[37] Ibid., Ia 75, 2 *ad* 1 *et* 2.

[38] S. Thomae de Aquino, *Summa theologiae* (Ottawa: Studii Generalis, 1941), Ia 75, 2 *ad* 1, 441a.

[39] God has a body only in the Incarnation, and could have refrained from Incarnation (Aquinatis, *Summa theologiae,* IIIa 1, 3). Angels can "assume" bodies, but have none by nature (Ia 51, 1). For the claim that God and angels are "forms," see *De ente et essentia,* c. 4, in Mandonnet, *S. Thomae Aquinatis opuscula omnia.*

call this a Platonic or Augustinian reading of Thomas. Another takes it as primitive that the soul is a substantial form and then tries to show how a substantial form can be an immaterial thing: call this an Aristotelian approach. A third would take it as primitive that the soul has some other unitary nature and would try to show how this nature allows it to be both: call this a "neutral monist" reading of Thomas.[40] I now offer a Platonic reading of Thomas.

For Aquinas, my soul's most basic relation to me is that it "informs" my body.[41] Thomas's account of this (say I) makes my Thomist soul something like a Platonic Form of Leftowhood. A Platonic Form is both an independent immaterial object and the form of a material object which instances it. It is not in itself a state. (For it to exist uninstanced is not for anything to be in a state, nor is it for there to be an unowned state.) And when Thomas denies his soul the "inherence of a material form," he is (I think) denying precisely that his soul is a state of the human body. But though a Form is not a state, a Form's bearer is in a certain state, and its being in that state is the Form's being present in it, or its "participating" in the Form: whatever Platonic "participation" comes to, it is at least clear that the dogwise arrangement of Fido's matter is by definition the presence of The Dog in Fido. Thomas actually uses the language of participation to speak of the soul-body relation:

> "The body participates in the soul's being."
>
> "While the soul's being is in some way the body's being, nevertheless the body does not manage to participate in the soul's being according to its whole nobility and power."[42]

For living things, to live is to be: so Thomas's point here is that the body participates in the soul's life. The Thomist soul is like natural-kind Forms in being present whole in every part of the informed matter.[43] Both Platonic Forms and Thomist souls are in space and (ordinary) time only *per*

[40] The term is of course Russell's. A fourth approach would simply take as primitive the conjunction of substantial form and particular thing—i.e., not attempt at all to explain how the two roles can be conjoined. But as I see it, this would not be an attempt to *understand* the view, or show how it could possibly be true.

[41] My body is the matter *in* which, not *from* which. And Thomas insists that we can even treat the body as a "partner" for the soul, present for it to inform, only because in so speaking we treat the soul as already there, informing the body (Aquinatis, *De anima,* 1 *ad* 15).

[42] Ibid., 1 *ad* 17, 371; 1 *ad* 17 *et* 18, p. 371.

[43] Aquinatis, *Summa theologiae,* Ia 76, 8.

accidens and because they are "conjoined" with clumps of matter.[44] If some matter ceases to belong to a natural kind, this does not destroy the Platonic Form itself: the Form continues to exist in a mode that is neither spatial nor in the ordinary sense temporal. So too Thomas's soul.[45] There are of course limits to this likeness: Thomas would not say that a body exemplifies or is a case of its soul.

A Form, informing something, does not act on it, as an efficient cause. All a Form "does" to its bearer is *be* there. For Thomas too, all my soul "does" to me, in enlivening me, is be there—in other words, it is just what Thomas thinks is present to account for my having certain powers.[46] Thomas does speak of the soul as doing certain things—understanding, moving the body, and so forth—but he does so only because he has a paraphrase to hand: "the eye . . . cannot be said . . . to act through itself. . . . the parts' acts are ascribed to the whole *through* the parts: we say that the human sees through the eye. . . . So it can be said that the soul understands, as that the eye sees, but it is more properly said that the human understands through the soul."[47]

The soul is that by which *we* do certain things. When Aquinas says that "the intellective soul acts through itself, seeing as it has a proper operation in which the body has no share,"[48] his point is that by having the sort of souls we do, *we* have an activity which we do not do by means of any body part.[49] To read Thomas's talk of the soul's activity aright, we must recall that he sees the soul as in a broad sense part of us,[50] and Thomas's part-whole metaphysic is strongly Aristotelian. As Aristotle sees it, "of the things that are thought to be substances, most are only potencies—(even) the parts of animals. For none of them exists separately. And when they are separated, then they too exist, all of them, merely as matter."[51] For Aristotle, my hands do not "exist separately." That is, "my hand" does

[44] For the soul's odd relation to time, see ibid., Ia 85, 4 *ad* 1. Thomas's point is that the soul is intrinsically "aeviternal," like angels (Aquinatis, *Quaestiones disputatae de potentia Dei,* 3, 10 *ad* 8).

[45] Aquinatis, *Summa theologiae,* Ia 75, 6.

[46] This is one difference between the soul-body relation and that between an angel and an "assumed" body (ibid., Ia 51, 2 *ad* 1, 2).

[47] Ibid., Ia 75, 2 *ad* 2.

[48] Aquinatis, *De anima,* 1, 369.

[49] At least, this account suffices for an incarnate soul. Discarnate souls act through themselves in a stronger sense (Aquinatis, *Summa theologiae,* Ia 89). A still-living severed hand, twitching, would act in the same way. Platonic Forms are not the kind of things to act under any circumstances—but I am not claiming that Aquinas's soul *is* a Form, only that it is *like* one.

[50] As form and matter are, cf. Aquinatis, *Summa theologiae,* Ia 3, 2.

[51] Aristotle, *Metaphysics* Z 16, 1040b5–8, trans. W. D. Ross.

not pick out any discrete thing. Still, I do have hands—or, perhaps better, I am handed. For my body is articulated handedly, that is, into the distinctive shapes which make someone handed. Further, my body is hand-divisible. Its matter can be parted in such a way that it ceases to have any matter where hands go. Aristotle defines hands functionally. For him, to have a hand is just to have certain powers to act, sited in an appropriate articulation of one's body, and "a hand exists" really asserts that someone has, by virtue of appropriate body shape, the powers to grasp, throw, and so forth.[52] That hands are "only potencies" means inter alia that "hand" picks out the material locations of distinct powers of the animal, to act or to be divided in some way.[53]

For Thomas as for Aristotle, undetached parts are just primary loci of powers of the whole. The hand is where, for example, my power to grip is.[54] To say that I grip with my hand is to say that I grip where I have the power to grip, and refer to the articulation where and due to which I have that power. For Thomas, while we live, our souls too are undetached parts of us (though not in quite the same sense of "part"). So for Thomas, to say that I think intellectually with my soul is to say that I so think "where" I have the power to think and point to the part of me "where" and due to which I have the power. For Thomas, such thinking has no organ.[55] This means that no body part is to such thinking as the hand is to gripping—that is, we do not have the power so to think due to any particular body part. And the claim that the soul thinks may be just a shorthand for such claims as that such thinking has no organ or that we think intellectually only due to having the souls we do.

If we read Thomas in the Platonist way, we see him as claiming that soul and body—concreta—stand in relations (formal causality and its converse, participation) which in all other cases link abstracta to concreta. But Thomas does argue this, *after* asserting that the soul is a particular as hand and eye are. The metaphysical "job" of a substantial form, its "formal causality," is to give its bearer the power to do the acts characteristic of members of a particular natural kind.[56] Thomas argues: the human soul

[52] I fill out this schematic account at length and back it exegetically in chapter 3 of my *Aquinas on Metaphysics: Matter, Parts and Number* (New York: Oxford University Press, forthcoming).

[53] And that because the whole has the potency to be divided in this way at this point, there "exists potentially" a detached mass of hand-shaped flesh that we call a hand equivocally.

[54] Thomas says at one point that even if I lose my eye, the power to see remains located in the socket.

[55] Aquinatis, *Summa theologiae*, Ia 75, 2.

[56] Ibid., Ia 76, 1.

does this. For our natural kind is rational animal, and our souls make us rational.[57] Thus the soul is our form.[58] Thus Thomas's case that the particular which is the soul is also our form *rests* on a claim that it exercises formal causality. And it is not just Thomas who thinks the soul our formal cause. Any dualist holding that our souls give us the powers which make us the kind of thing we are thinks this too.

But (we protest) how can pairs of particulars stand in relations which otherwise link only properties and particulars? The short answer is: within Platonism, at least, these relations *do not* link properties and particulars. They link pairs of particulars, for Platonic Forms (say I) *are* immaterial particulars. Multiply exemplified forms are present "by participation" in many places at once—present just because and in the sense that particulars are in certain states. They are not present *propria persona* anywhere in space. And so they are not universals, for multiply exemplified universals are wholly present in many places at once *propria persona.* Nor are Forms attributes. Having a property, within Platonism, really analyzes as having a particular *relation* of dependence on a Form: Fido's being a dog just is some matter's having the participation relation to The Dog. So for Platonists, participation is *not* the relation particulars have to properties. It is the relation particulars have to Forms, which generates their properties: the property of being a dog is really a relation of dependence on The Dog. It is this relation which is strictly speaking a universal; if, speaking more loosely, The Dog is a universal, this is because The Dog is a constituent of this relation. If all this is correct, there is nothing unusual in one particular thing's being another's "formal cause." Forms are particulars, and being a "formal cause" is just being the Formlike term of the participation relation.

Within Platonism, "participation" is the distinctive primitive relation linking Forms to particulars. Realists about universals substitute exemplification or inherence, equally primitive. Some forms of nominalism have their own primitives in (say) relations of natural likeness or other relations which group certain particulars, or the primitive existence of natural classes (class membership itself being a further and mysterious primitive, whether or not the classes are natural). Some nominalists do without any of these. As they see it, the only relation a theory of attributes need invoke is that of satisfaction, which links linguistic predicates or concepts to

[57] It is an open question just how Thomas would adjust this claim in light of what we now know about dolphins, chimpanzees, etc.

[58] Aquinatis, *Summa Theologiae,* Ia 76, 1.

particulars.[59] But satisfaction is equally a primitive, and current work in the philosophy of mind and language (for example, the "rule following considerations" of Wittgenstein and their elaboration by Kripke) does much to make it as mysterious and "metaphysical" (in the old pejorative sense) as exemplification, class membership, participation, and the rest. So it seems to me that any theory of attributes will include a primitive relation due to whose obtaining particulars have attributes.

Any ontology must include a theory of attributes. And any approach to mind and body must be set within an overall ontology. Thus whoever who speaks to the mind-body problem will have some primitive such as participation in his or her repertory. Now Thomas does not hold a Platonist theory of universals.[60] But he does use a lot of participation talk, particularly in causal contexts.[61] So Thomas has the concept of participation available to him generally. He may take it as a primitive. But Thomas does say a lot about the relation, and perhaps these glosses define rather than explicate participation.[62] Either way, it is in participation's favor that it can do work in many contexts (as in Thomas's account of creation *ex nihilo*, particularly if it *is* a primitive concept):[63] as long as you're going to have some such primitive, why not one that will do more work for you? Thomas's body / soul theory is just one more use for this concept.

There *is* no form / thing problem, on the reading of Thomas that I propose. There is instead the need to recognize that Thomas's view of the soul has a Platonist component, and that for Platonists, Forms in general *are* particular things. Nor is there even a problem of trying to explicate the soul-body relation more than we have. Suppose as a worst case that, for Thomas, participation *is* a primitive. If so, we can try to grasp it by analogies, but we cannot give an account of it. And this is fine. This is what primitives in the theory of attributes are like in general, and everybody has at least one such primitive. Thus Thomas's position on the soul-body relation (I claim) is no worse off than Platonism's view of the Form-instance

[59] See on these D. M. Armstrong, *Nominalism and Realism* (New York: Cambridge University Press, 1978), 11–27.

[60] See, e.g., *De ente et essentia*, c. 3.

[61] For a good example, see Aquinatis, *Summa theologiae*, Ia 44, 1. For massive treatment, see Cornelio Fabro, *Participation et causalité selon S. Thomas d'Aquin* (Louvain: Publications Universitaires de Louvain, 1961); Andre de Muralt, *Néoplatonisme et aristotelisme dans la métaphysique médiévale: Analogie, causalité, participation* (Paris, 1995); Louis Geiger, *La participation dans la philosophie de S. Thomas d'Aquin*, 2d ed. (Paris:, J. Vrin., 1953).

[62] This is Eleonore Stump's view.

[63] See again Aquinatis, *Summa theologiae*, Ia 44.

relation, and Platonism's primitive may be no worse than those of other theories of attributes.

One question left unanswered in section 3 was, How can the advent of a human soul "make" a parcel of animal flesh into human flesh? On my account of Thomas, this occurs when matter comes into a new substance-constituting state, and its being in that state is the soul's presence by participation in the body's matter. Now here an objection looms. We said above that Thomas means a human being to be one material substance. For Thomas, "matter joined to form is the same as matter actually existing."[64] For the form of water to be joined to some matter is just for that matter to be water: to actually be what it is, to have its nature. The form is just that by which the matter is itself. Now for Thomas, "the human body is the matter proportionate to the human soul. It is compared to the soul as potency to act."[65] So for Thomas, soul joined to live body is the same as live body actually existing. The soul is just that by which the live body is itself. Soul joined to live body adds up to or composes one material thing, the live body. But the Platonist reading seems not to allow this, for Forms and their participants do not add up to single substances: Fido and The Dog are two substances, not one.

I reply that this is true but irrelevant. Fido is the result of a relation between the The Dog and what in a different sense participates in The Dog—Fido's matter. One substance is the product of a relation between matter and Form. And so too, for Thomas, one human substance is the product of a relation between its matter and its form.

VI. The Soul's Complement

For Thomas, every substance has just one substantial form: any substance's stuff belongs to just one stuff-kind. So while human flesh comes *from* all sorts of other matter, the human form exists *in* just human flesh and bone. And *in* human flesh and bone, the form's—that is, the soul's—metaphysical complement is matter stripped of all substantial forms.[66] If the soul is the sole substantial form of a human being, there is no other form there for the matter to have, and so what the soul informs must be formless or "prime" matter: "because the soul is a substantial form . . . there is not some other substantial form mediating between the soul and

[64] *In II de anima,* lect. 1.

[65] Aquinatis, *De anima,* 1 *ad* 5.

[66] For a brief treatment of prime matter see Aquinatis, *De principiis naturae,* c. 2.

prime matter. . . . the soul, inasmuch as it is the form giving existence, does not have some other medium between it and prime matter."[67] Because the soul is present, the matter in which it exists is human flesh. But flesh is the *product* of the union of soul and prime matter, metaphysically speaking, not an intermediary by which the soul is united to prime matter.

To say that prime matter has no substantial form of its own is not to say that it has no attributes. For one thing, Thomas thinks that the prime matter of the elements and of the heavens differs by being "directed to different acts": elemental prime matter is such as to host elemental forms but not those of heavenly bodies, heavenly prime matter is such as to host forms of heavenly bodies but not those of elements.[68] Again, when the soul comes to the fetus, the matter which undergirds this change is (say) the hot stuff over here: which is extended, qualitied matter "disposed for" the presence of a substantial form. That there is no continuing *substance* at both ends of a substantial change does not entail that *nothing* continues beneath it. But prime matter is not a substance.[69] And while one can see prime matter as qualitied and extended in a way that does not depend conceptually on hosting a substantial form, prime matter, having no such form of its own, has no nature of its own, save that of a power to receive some rather than other forms.

For Thomas, if we refer to something as a human body, we refer to it as already including the soul, not as paired with a soul externally.[70] So Thomas is no soul-body dualist, for on his account body *includes* soul: soul-body dualism would be soul-soul dualism. For Thomas, the soul's metaphysical complement is not a body but prime matter; a human being is a soul in prime matter. If this is so, Thomas is no substance dualist, for what there is in us apart from the soul is not a substance. Nor is Thomas any other sort of dualist, because what there is to the body if it is abstracted from the soul—prime matter—hasn't the stature to be a partner in any sort of dualism. It cannot even exist on its own.[71] Now the soul's complement is not wholly unextended and unqualitied. It is instead the matter

[67] Aquinatis, *De anima,* a. 9, 407.

[68] Aquinatis, *Summa theologiae,* Ia 66, 2 *et ad* 4.

[69] For Thomas, "a substance is a thing suited not to exist in a subject. . . . in the notion of substance is understood, that it has a nature to which existence not in another is suited" (Aquinatis, *Summa contra gentiles,* I 25, p. 27). Prime matter can only exist "in another." Prime matter cannot exist save under some substantial form or other, and so as part of some substance (Aquinatis, *Summa theologiae,* Ia 66, 1).

[70] Aquinatis, *De anima,* 1 *ad* 15.

[71] See again Aquinatis, *Quaestiones disputatae de potentia Dei,* 2.

which receives first the brute and then the human soul in the womb, whose continuity makes passage from the one to the other a change in something rather than simple replacement of matter: the warm moist stuff in this place, prime matter with physical traits but viewed in abstraction from the stuff-kind in which the soul puts it. So on Thomas's account a human being is just a soul clothed in extended qualitied stuff: a soul dipped in dust and rendered visible. We might picture a human as a dust-coated light: the dust glows because it coats a soul, and the dust's glowing is the light's way of being in it.

E. J. LOWE

Identity, Composition, and the Simplicity of the Self

I believe that I am an altogether simple entity, lacking any proper parts. This is not to say that I believe that I am an immaterial soul or Cartesian ego, although that possibility is consistent with what I believe. In defense of my belief, I shall advance an argument which I shall call the "Simplicity Argument."[1] This argument, I contend, is demonstrably valid, so that its conclusion can be rejected only on pain of rejecting one or more of its premises. Some of its premises are indeed contestable, but I shall try to show that considerable difficulties face those who wish to reject them. Later, I shall consider some of the implications—and some of the non-implications—of accepting the conclusion of the Simplicity Argument.

The premises of the Simplicity Argument are eight in number, and they divide into two classes: the first four premises are principles concerning myself and my body—what I shall call "self / body principles"—and the second four premises are general mereological principles. Here are the premises, beginning with the four self / body principles:

1. I exist, as does my body.
2. I am not identical with my body.
3. I am not identical with any proper part of my body.
4. I do not have any proper part which is not a proper part of my body.

[1] I first advanced a version of this argument in my *Subjects of Experience* (Cambridge: Cambridge University Press, 1996), 39–40. The argument was dubbed "the Simplicity Argument" by Eric Olson in his "Human Atoms," *Australasian Journal of Philosophy* 76 (1998): 400. For my reply to his criticisms, see my "In Defense of the Simplicity Argument," *Australasian Journal of Philosophy* 78 (2000): 105–12.

Now for the four mereological principles, each of which I have given a name which follows its statement:[2]

5. If an object has some proper parts, then the mereological sum of those parts exists and is a proper or improper part of that object. ("Fusion")
6. If an object has a proper part, then it has another proper part which is not a proper part of that first part. ("Weak Supplementation")
7. No two objects which have proper parts have exactly the same proper parts at the same time. ("Weak Extensionality")
8. The relation of proper parthood is transitive. ("Transitivity")

The conclusion of the Simplicity Argument is this:

9. I have no proper parts: I am an altogether simple entity.

I leave to an appendix a formal demonstration of the validity of the Simplicity Argument, but an informal demonstration can be given now. Suppose, for reductio, that I have some proper parts, which are all the proper parts I have. By premise 4, these could only be parts of my body. That being so, these parts have, by premise 5 (Fusion), a mereological sum which is itself a part, either proper or improper, of my body. Since, by hypothesis, these are the only proper parts I have, that mereological sum and I have exactly the same proper parts, so that, by premise 7 (Weak Extensionality), it and I are identical. But since that mereological sum either is a proper part of my body or else, if it is an improper part of it, is identical with my body, it follows that either I am a proper part of my body or else I am identical with my body. But the first possibility is incompatible with premise 3 and the second possibility is incompatible with premise 2. Hence we must reject the hypothesis that I have some proper parts and conclude that I am an altogether simple entity, assuming that I and my body do indeed exist, as premise 1 maintains.

Two of the premises listed earlier, 6 and 8—Weak Supplementation and Transitivity—have not been explicitly appealed to in this informal version of the Simplicity Argument, although the need to include them is manifest in the formal version presented in the appendix. Weak Supplementation is

[2] Each of these principles is endorsed by classical extensional mereology. For details, see Peter M. Simons, *Parts: A Study in Ontology* (Oxford: Clarendon, 1987), chap. 1, esp. 37–41. I do not exactly duplicate Simons's terminology nor, in the appendix to this essay, his symbolism.

needed to exclude the possibility that I have just one proper part, which is a proper part of my body, whereas my body has many proper parts. If that were possible, I would not be identical with my body—because it and I would have different proper parts—but nor would I be identical with my supposed single proper part, since nothing can be identical with a proper part of itself. Hence, I would not lack proper parts altogether, and so would not be a simple entity in that sense, and yet I would not be identical either with my body or with any proper part of it, as premises 2 and 3 of the Simplicity Argument require. Moreover, I would not have any proper part which was not a proper part of my body, as premise 4 requires. (I leave to the formal version of the Simplicity Argument, in the appendix, the reason for including premise 8, Transitivity.)

As I remarked earlier; those who wish to reject the conclusion of the Simplicity Argument—and I imagine that they will constitute the vast majority of philosophers who hold any opinion on the matter—must reject one or more of its premises. Let us then see what the prospects are for doing this with any plausibility. Take premise 1 first. Some philosophers have indeed held that "the self" does not exist, some of them on the grounds that "I" is not a referring expression.[3] But rather few are prepared to defend that heroic and literally self-denying position, so I shall ignore it here. Similarly, I shall ignore the view that premise 1 is false because there is no such thing as my body, which idealist philosophers may contend on the wider ground that there are no material things at all.

What about premise 2, that I am not identical with my body? I hold this to be true on the familiar grounds that I and my body have different persistence-conditions. There are, plausibly, changes which my body could survive but which I could not survive, and vice versa. This, at bottom, is because it is a necessary condition of my continuing to exist that I should have a capacity for conscious thought—even if I need not always be exercising that capacity throughout my existence—whereas this is not a necessary condition of my body's continuing to exist. Of course, some philosophers strongly resist this contention that I am not identical with my body, most interestingly those who subscribe to the position known as "animalism."[4] These philosophers acknowledge the distinction between a person, such as myself, and a mere lump of matter, but

[3] For the view that 'I' is not a referring expression, see G. E. M. Anscombe, "The First Person," in *Mind and Language*, ed. S. Guttenplan (Oxford: Clarendon, 1975).

[4] For a recent defense of animalism, see Eric Olson, *The Human Animal: Personal Identity without Psychology* (New York: Oxford University Press, 1997).

emphasize that the human body is not a mere lump of matter: rather, it is a living organism and one which, they contend, is identical with the human person whose body it is. According to animalism, then, when I have a conscious thought, it is the living organism which is my body that has that thought, since it and I are identical.

Animalism, it seems to me, is subject to the following difficulty, among others: it is liable to collapse into the view that I am identical *not* with my whole body but only with a proper part of it, most plausibly my brain. For consider this: it seems perfectly conceivable that, following a dreadful accident, all of my body apart from my brain should cease to function, even though my brain remains capable of functioning normally and sustaining all the processes of conscious thought necessary for my survival. In such a case, it may be quite possible in principle for my brain to be kept alive and functioning by means of a life-support system, while the rest of my body is destroyed. In these circumstances, it seems plausible to say, I would continue to exist and have conscious thoughts, even though the only remaining part of my body would be my brain (including, of course, all of my brain's own proper parts). What should the animalist say about me in such circumstances, though? I think he would have to say that in those circumstances I would be identical with my brain. But if I would be identical with my brain in those circumstances, it seems that I must be identical with my brain even in normal circumstances, that is, even when my whole body exists rather than just my brain. For if the thing which has survived the accident and thereafter has my conscious thoughts is *my brain,* then it was my brain which had my conscious thoughts before the accident, not my whole body. But it is I who have my conscious thoughts, so it follows that I was my brain before the accident.

Let us then consider the possibility of denying premise 3 and maintaining that I am indeed identical with a proper part of my body, the most plausible candidate being my brain. My reason for rejecting this possibility is, once again, that it seems to me that I and my brain have different persistence-conditions—indeed, that I have different persistence-conditions from those of *any* proper part of my body. It seems perfectly conceivable, for instance, that I could go on having conscious thoughts throughout a process in which the organic matter of my brain was systematically replaced by inorganic matter, in which case my brain would eventually cease to exist but I would not. Of course, it may be remarked that in these circumstances there would be no time at which I would lack a brain. But the significant point is that the brain I would end up with would not be identical with the brain I started with, which is enough to show that I could not be identical with either of them. Some philosophers might, I suppose, dispute this point, urging that what makes a brain one and the same brain is the identity of the person whose brain it is. However, not only is such a claim implausible in itself, it is also useless for the purposes of anyone who wishes to identify a person with his or her brain, because it presupposes, on the contrary, that a person's identity is independent of that of his or her brain.

What about premise 4, that I do not have any proper part which is not a proper part of my body? It is not clear to me how this could be denied by anyone but a dualist. Historically, some dualists have indeed maintained that a person is some sort of combination of material body and immaterial soul. In that case, even if my supposed soul were a simple entity, altogether lacking proper parts, I myself would not be a simple entity, since my body and my soul would be distinct proper parts of me. But I take it that the evidence for the existence of immaterial souls is slim at best. That being so, I cannot see what proper parts I could have apart from parts of my body. Perhaps it may be urged that my conscious thoughts are parts of me but not of my body, but that would seem to involve a category mistake. I, if I am anything, am a persisting thing—a "continuant" or "substance"—whereas my thoughts are events or happenings.[5] Although an event may have other events as proper parts—as, for example, a battle has various skirmishes among its proper parts—it seems impossible for a continuant or substance to have events as proper parts, just as it is impossible for an event to have continuants or substances as proper parts. A continuant or substance may *participate* in various events—as, for example, a soldier may participate in a battle—but that is quite a different matter. A soldier cannot be a part of a battle, though he may be a part of an army engaging in a battle.

Having explored, albeit rather cursorily, the prospects for denying one or more of the self / body principles invoked in the Simplicity Argument, let us look next at the prospects for denying one or more of the mereological principles which that argument involves—beginning with the Fusion principle, premise 5. Some philosophers may, I think, be inclined to urge that this principle is indeed too strong, on the grounds that not just any objects whatever can be taken to be proper parts of some one further object, their supposed "mereological sum." For instance, it is perhaps not plausible to maintain that there is an object which is the mereological sum of the Eiffel Tower and my left foot and which consequently has the latter two objects

[5] I argue that I am a substance or continuant in my *Subjects of Experience,* chap. 2. Thus, I reject "bundle" theories of the self, which identify it with the sum of its thoughts or perceptions.

as proper parts. Why not? Presumably, because those two objects seem to be quite unrelated to one another. Of course, they cannot really be quite unrelated, since they inevitably stand in certain spatiotemporal and causal relations to one another. However, it might appear that these relations do not suffice to warrant our calling them parts of a single object. I am not sure about that. It is true that the ways in which the Eiffel Tower and my left foot are related to one another are not much like the ways in which my left and right feet are related to one another, since the latter are in close proximity and causally influence each other's activities. But so what?

In any case, even if the foregoing doubts are legitimate, they do not in fact threaten the Fusion principle, premise 5, because that principle does not imply that *any two objects whatever* have a mereological sum—only that any two objects *which are proper parts of some other object* have a mereological sum. Moreover, even if the Fusion principle is rejected in its full generality, all that the Simplicity Argument strictly needs is the following pair of much weaker premises:

5a. If *my body* has some proper parts, then the mereological sum of those parts exists and is a proper or improper part of my body.

and

5b. If *I* have some proper parts, then the mereological sum of those parts exists and is a proper or improper part of me.

Now, the proper parts of any human body obviously *are* in close proximity to one another and causally influence each other's activities in numerous ways, so that there are not the same grounds for denying that any number of them have a mereological sum as there are for denying that the Eiffel Tower and my left foot have a mereological sum. So premise 5a is immune to this line of objection. And I assume that 5b is likewise immune to it.

Let us turn next to premise 6, the Weak Supplementation principle, which states that if an object has a proper part, then it has another proper part which is not a proper part of that first part. Why might this be challenged? One possible reason for challenging it arises as follows. Suppose, as was envisaged earlier, that a dreadful accident befalls me, leaving me with my brain and its proper parts as the sole remaining parts of my body. Would my body still exist in these circumstances, and if so, would it now be identical with my brain? In my earlier response to the animalist, I implicitly assumed that in these circumstances my body would have ceased to exist. But that might possibly be questioned. What we may seem to be faced with here is a version of the ancient problem of Dion and Theon, more recently presented as the problem of Tibbles and his tail.[6] So let us look briefly at that problem.

Let us denominate "Tib" that object, if there is one, which includes every proper part of Tibbles except his tail and its proper parts. And suppose that Tibbles's tail is destroyed. Tib, it would seem, continues to exist in these circumstances, as does Tibbles, but they become indiscernible from one another, at least in respect of their nonmodal and nonhistorical properties. Do they therefore become identical with one another? That seems to be a suggestion of doubtful intelligibility, unless one can make sense of what André Gallois calls the "Occasional Identity Thesis," maintaining that things which are numerically distinct at one time can be numerically identical at another.[7] I am not inclined to accept that thesis, and I imagine that most philosophers will agree with me in this. Another possible solution to the problem about Tibbles is to deny that any such object as Tib exists, at least so long as Tibbles retains his tail. Peter van Inwagen would favor this verdict, rejecting as he does what he calls the Doctrine of Arbitrary Undetached Parts.[8] But, again, this is not a popular solution, since it is hard to believe that Tib does not exist.

However, more germane to our own concerns, yet another possible solution to the problem of Tibbles and his tail might be to reject the Weak Supplementation principle: this would allow us to say that Tib does indeed exist prior to Tibbles's loss of his tail and continues to exist thereafter, but remains only a proper part of Tibbles and consequently cannot ever be identical with Tibbles, despite their becoming "indiscernible." Now, in like manner, it might be maintained that, after my dreadful accident, my brain remains only a proper part of my body, which itself continues to exist, even though my body then has no other proper part disjoint from my brain. I concede that this suggestion may have some superficial appeal. However, it is not clear, on reflection, that it really has any explanatory power as far as problems like that of Tibbles are concerned. If the suggestion is correct, it

[6] See, e.g., Michael B. Burke, "Dion and Theon: An Essentialist Solution to an Ancient Puzzle," *Journal of Philosophy* 91 (1994): 129–39. I discuss the case of Tibbles in *Kinds of Being: A Study of Identity, Individuation and the Logic of Sortal Terms* (Oxford: Blackwell, 1989), chap. 6.

[7] See André Gallois, *Occasions of Identity: The Metaphysics of Persistence, Change, and Sameness* (Oxford: Clarendon, 1998). I raise some objections to Gallois's theory in my review of his book, in *Mind* 109 (2000): 354–57.

[8] See Peter van Inwagen, "The Doctrine of Arbitrary Undetached Parts," Pacific *Philosophical Quarterly* 62 (1981): 123–37.

follows, of course, that two numerically distinct objects can exactly coincide spatially, that is, can exist in exactly the same place at the same time. However, the latter possibility is one which it is already plausible to acknowledge on quite other grounds: on the sort of grounds, for instance, that we may judge a bronze statue and the lump of bronze composing it to be numerically distinct objects which exist in exactly the same place at the same time. The distinctness of the statue and the bronze follows from the differences which obtain between their respective persistence-conditions. So why not similarly say, in the case of Tibbles and Tib, or in the case of my body and my brain, that these objects are distinct from one another, even when they allegedly coincide, simply in virtue of the differences which obtain between their respective persistence-conditions? What is added to the explanation of their nonidentity by saying that one is a proper part of the other? Nothing, as far as I can see.

My own intuitions concerning the puzzle cases now before us lead me to say that, in fact, the case of Tibbles and Tib should not be assimilated to that of me and my brain. I am inclined to say that Tib ceases to exist upon the destruction of Tibbles's tail, while on the other hand I am inclined to say that the body of which my brain was formerly a proper part no longer exists once I have nothing left of it but my brain. In neither case, then, am I inclined to say that two formerly distinct things both continue to exist but exactly coincide. Hence, I certainly have no need to deny the Weak Supplementation principle in order to account for these cases. The relevant difference between Tib and my brain, it seems to me, is that Tib is not an ontologically independent object in its own right, since it is only introduced to us as what is "left over" when we "subtract" (in thought) Tibbles's tail from Tibbles. And once Tibbles's tail no longer exists, there is no such thing to "subtract" from Tibbles, so that nothing any longer supports the putative reference to the object we elected to call "Tib." In short, no such thing as Tib was conceived to be any longer exists. I grant that this line of reasoning may not convince everyone, but I shall pursue the issue no further here as it does not impinge directly upon my main theme.

Before looking at premise 7 of the Simplicity Argument, the Weak Extensionality principle, I shall briefly consider the prospects for denying premise 8, the Transitivity principle. It may be conceded that there are senses of "part" in which the parthood relation is not transitive. For instance, we could define the notion of an *immediate proper part* as follows: *a* is an immediate proper part of *b* if and only if *a* is a proper part of *b* and there is no proper part of *b* of which *a* is a proper part. Immediate proper parts are possible. For instance, taking an atom to be an object which has no proper parts, the mereological sum of two atoms has each of those atoms as an immediate proper part, in the sense just defined. Immediate proper parthood is not a transitive relation. Indeed, it is an intransitive relation: if *a* is an immediate proper part of *b* and *b* is an immediate proper part of *c*, then *a* is not an immediate proper part of *c*. So, if by "part" one meant, in a certain context, "immediate proper part," then parthood in that sense would not be a transitive relation. But this obviously does not undermine the thought that there is a basic notion of parthood which does rightly treat it as a transitive relation. And that that thought is correct seems to me pretty well incontestable.

Perhaps the most promising premise of the Simplicity Argument to challenge, if one wants to resist its conclusion, is premise 7, the Weak Extensionality principle, which states that no two objects which have proper parts have exactly the same proper parts at the same time. Notice that we have to express the principle this way rather than saying, more simply, that no two objects have exactly the same proper parts at the same time, because the latter version would imply, implausibly, that there is no more than one atom—that is, no more than one object lacking proper parts. For, trivially, any two objects which lack proper parts have exactly the same proper parts, namely, none. Since I believe that atoms exist, holding myself to be one and any other person to be another, it is particularly important for me to express the Weak Extensionality principle in the way I have done. For I do not want to be forced into saying that you and I are identical.

If the Weak Extensionality principle is rejected, then it must be conceded that two different objects can exist in exactly the same place at the same time, because if two different objects have exactly the same proper parts at a certain time, they cannot occupy different regions of space at that time (unless, trivially, they have the same proper parts because they have no proper parts at all). Now, many philosophers are reluctant to admit that two different objects can exist in exactly the same place at the same time, so that these philosophers cannot afford to reject the Weak Extensionality principle.[9] However, I myself, as I have already indicated, am prepared to allow that two different objects can exist in exactly the same place at the same time—for example, a bronze statue and the lump of bronze composing it—so it may be wondered why I am willing to endorse

[9] See, e.g., Michael B. Burke, "Preserving the Principle of One Object to a Place: A Novel Account of the Relations among Objects, Sorts, Sortals, and Persistence Conditions," *Philosophy and Phenomenological Research* 54 (1994): 591–624.

the Weak Extensionality principle.[10] The reason, of course, is that I do not believe that objects which stand in the composition relation to one another have exactly the same proper parts. Consider, thus, the bronze statue and the lump of bronze composing it. The statue, I hold, is numerically distinct from the lump, because they have different persistence-conditions: there are changes which the statue can survive but not the lump, and vice versa. But, for the same reason, a proper part of the statue such as its head is numerically distinct from the mass of bronze composing the head. Now, the mass of bronze composing the head is certainly a proper part of the lump of bronze composing the whole statue but, given that the head is not identical with that mass of bronze, it does not follow that the head is a proper part of the lump of bronze composing the whole statue. And, indeed, I want to deny that the head of the statue is a proper part of the lump of bronze composing the whole statue. A lump of bronze cannot, I think, have something like the head of a statue as one of its proper parts, for a reason which I shall explain in a moment. Similarly, I do not think that the mass of organic matter composing a living animal can have one of that animal's organs, such as its heart, as a proper part. So, if I am right, and the statue and the lump of bronze composing it do not have exactly the same proper parts, I can quite consistently endorse the Weak Extensionality principle. Notice, though, that I only want to deny that every proper part of the statue is a proper part of the lump of bronze composing it, not that every proper part of the latter is a proper part of the former.

Here is an argument for denying that the head of a bronze statue is a proper part of the lump of bronze composing the whole statue. Call the statue S, the head H, and the whole lump of bronze B. And let B_h be the mass of bronze composing H. Then suppose, for reductio, that H is a proper part of B. Now, if H is a proper part of B, it is surely also a part of any lesser mass of bronze B*, such that B* is a proper part of B and B_h is a part of B*. But then it follows that H is a part of B_h, the mass of bronze composing H. For B_h itself is a proper part of B and B_h is a part of B_h. However, H clearly cannot be a proper part of B_h, so H must be an improper part of B_h and thus identical with B_h. But H is not identical with B_h, for the same reason that S is not identical with B. Put more intuitively, the reasoning here is that if we successively pare away parts of B outside H, we shall eventually reduce B to B_h, the mass of bronze composing H; but if H is a part of every reduced mass in the series of ever decreasing masses

[10] I defend the possibility of coinciding objects in "Coinciding Objects: In Defense of the Standard Account," *Analysis* 55 (1995): 171–78. See also my *The Possibility of Metaphysics: Substance, Identity, and Time* (Oxford: Clarendon, 1998), 198–99.

thus generated, H ought to be a part of B_h itself, the last member of this series—and yet it cannot be. Anyone who wants to resist the conclusion of this argument must find a principled and non-question-begging reason for excluding B_h from the series while including other masses of bronze which differ only minimally from B_h.

However, it may be surmised that there is a problem lurking for me here. I am able to insist on the numerical distinctness of the statue and the lump of bronze composing it, while endorsing the Weak Extensionality principle, because I contend that the statue has proper parts, such as its head, which are not numerically identical with the masses of bronze composing them. But if I urge that the head, say, and the mass of bronze composing it have different proper parts for the same sort of reason, I have obviously set out upon a regress which cannot plausibly be supposed to be infinite. If the regress is not infinite, however, then I can only maintain my allegiance to the Weak Extensionality principle if I can find another sort of reason for denying that objects which stand in the composition relation to one another have exactly the same proper parts. It cannot always be the case that the only way in which two such objects differ in respect of their proper parts is inasmuch as the composed object has proper parts which are composed by, but not identical with, proper parts of the composing object. But my belief is that there are indeed other ways in which two such objects can differ in respect of their proper parts.

Consider, for example, an organic molecule and the various atomic and subatomic particles which compose it. There are parts of such a molecule, namely, the various valence bonds that give it its structure, which are not composed by any of the objects that compose the molecule. Those valence bonds are real parts of the molecule, which would have to be represented as such in any adequate model or diagram of the molecule. Two different kinds of molecule can have the same kinds of objects composing them, but differ in their structure as a consequence of having different kinds of valence bonds. A valence bond, I shall say, is a *structural* part of a molecule, whereas the various particles composing it are *component* parts of it. And my contention is that when one object composes another, they differ at least in their structural parts.

Notice that I do not say that when one object is composed by another, as the statue is composed by the lump of bronze, none of the structural parts of the former are composed by proper parts of the latter. Indeed, I would describe the head of a statue as being one of its structural parts, while acknowledging that the head is composed by a mass of bronze which is a proper part of the lump of bronze composing the whole statue. My claim is only that when one object is composed by another object, or by a plurality of other objects, the former *can* have structural parts which are not composed by any of the objects which are parts of the composing object or objects, this possibility being illustrated by the valence bonds of an organic molecule. Once it is recognized that parts of a statue such as its head and arms are structural rather than component parts of the statue, we can more easily understand why the destruction of those parts should lead to the destruction of the statue, whereas it can easily survive the destruction of many of its component parts.

Our present concern, recall, is with the acceptability of premise 7 of the Simplicity Argument, the Weak Extensionality principle. I have been trying to explain why I am happy to endorse that principle, even though I believe that two distinct things can exist in exactly the same place at the same time. A mere acceptance of the latter possibility does not by any means commit one to rejecting the Weak Extensionality principle. Nor, however, can that principle be rejected by those who deny that two distinct things can exist in exactly the same place at the same time—as we remarked earlier. So why should anyone at all want to reject the Weak Extensionality principle? I can think of no good reason.

Now, however, we have surveyed all of the premises of the Simplicity Argument and, I suggest, found all of them to be, on reflection, rather plausible—certainly, more plausible than their respective negations. But in that case we ought to accept the conclusion of the Simplicity Argument, that I have no proper parts: I am an altogether simple entity. Now, of course, it is rightly said that one philosopher's modus ponens is another's modus tollens. There are those who may find the conclusion of the Simplicity Argument so intuitively unacceptable that they are persuaded that one or more of its premises must be false, even if they are not sure which. For the benefit of these philosophers, I must say something about the conclusion of the Simplicity Argument which may help them to find it more acceptable. But before I do so, I want briefly to discuss a view about persons which might seem to be a more plausible rival to my own.

The view I have in mind is one which maintains that while, indeed, I am not identical with my body or any proper part of it, as I also maintain, I am in fact *composed* (or "constituted") by my body, rather in the way in which the bronze statue is composed by the lump of bronze.[11] The trouble

[11] For recent versions of this view, see Lynne Rudder Baker, "Need a Christian be a Mind-Body Dualist?" *Faith and Philosophy* 12 (1995): 489–504; and Kevin J. Corcoran, "Persons and Bodies," *Faith and Philosophy* 15 (1998): 324–40. Of course, some philosophers believe—mistakenly, in my view—that composition is identity: see, e.g., Harold Noonan, "Constitution Is Identity," *Mind* 102 (1993): 133–46. But any such philosopher who holds that I am composed by my body or any proper part of it must, obviously, argue against either premise 2 or premise 3 of the Simplicity Argument.

with this view, of course, is that it conflicts with the Simplicity Argument. For if I am composed by my body, then proper parts of my body are proper parts of me—and yet, by premise 4 of the Simplicity Argument, I have no proper parts which are not proper parts of my body. How, then, can I fail to be identical with my body or some proper part of it, as the Simplicity Argument implies? In the case of the statue, it was possible to maintain that the statue has proper parts which are not parts of the lump of bronze composing it but, as we have seen, there is no corresponding reason to maintain that I have proper parts which are not proper parts of my body. So the purported analogy breaks down. The only remotely plausible means of escape, for someone wishing to insist that I am composed by my body, is to reject the Weak Extensionality principle and contend that I am composed by, but not identical with, my body, and yet have exactly the same proper parts as it has. But I can see no independent motivation for this contention, which seems to be driven by the conviction that I must have bodily proper parts and yet am not identical with my body.

Now let me return to my own view and its defense. One reason why some philosophers may reject the conclusion of the Simplicity Argument is that they may suppose that it implies the truth of a doctrine that is often vulgarly called "Cartesian dualism," namely, the doctrine that I am an immaterial, nonextended substance only contingently related to my physical body. Now, certainly, the Simplicity Argument implies the truth of a form of substance dualism, for its implication is that I and my body are two numerically distinct substances, or continuants. But it is not at all obvious that it implies that I am an immaterial and nonextended substance. By an "immaterial" substance I understand one which has no physical properties and by a "nonextended" substance I understand one which occupies no finite part of space. Must I have no physical properties and occupy no finite part of space, if I am a simple substance, altogether lacking proper parts? By no means, surely, since the fundamental particles of physics—things like quarks and electrons—are, it seems, simple substances and yet have physical properties and occupy finite parts of space. (I set aside here considerations which might lead us to favor a field interpretation of quantum physics over a particle interpretation, since the latter is at least intelligible. I also ignore, for present purposes, complications arising from the Heisenberg Uncertainty Principle, which implies that quantum particles have "fuzzy" boundaries.)

To this it may be objected that if an object occupies a finite part of space—by which I mean a three-dimensional region of space of finite extent—then it must have distinct proper parts and hence be nonsimple. For, it may be said, such an object must have a left and a right half, or a top and a bottom half, or some other such pair of proper parts, however one chooses to describe them. But this claim may certainly be challenged. What entitles one to assume that the left and right "halves" of a spatially extended object must be *proper parts* of that object? Let us recall our earlier distinction between component parts and structural parts. Now, a fundamental physical particle, such as an electron, has no component parts: it is not composed of anything, since all that it could be composed of would be other particles, but in describing it as a "fundamental" particle one is precisely denying that it is composed of other particles.[12] If electrons are some day discovered to be composed of other particles, this will simply imply that we should no longer regard them as *fundamental* particles. It may be—though this seems unlikely—that there are in fact *no* fundamental particles, because *every* physical particle is composed of others. Even if that is in fact so, however, it is still perfectly conceivable that there should be fundamental physical particles and that electrons are precisely that. If that is what they are, then electrons have no component parts. But do they perhaps have structural parts—and might not the putative left and right "halves" of an electron qualify as structural parts of it? I do not think so, because I do not believe that an object can have structural parts unless it has component parts. The structural parts of an object serve to *relate* its component parts in certain appropriate ways: thus, the valence bonds of an organic molecule serve to relate its component atoms in such a way as to give the molecule its characteristic overall structure. But where an object has no component parts, there is nothing for structural parts to relate.

Perhaps it may be suggested, however, that the putative left and right halves of an electron are neither component nor structural, but *spatial* parts of it—and thus still proper parts of that object. But what do we, or should we, mean by a "spatial part" of a spatially extended object? If all we mean is a part of that object which is itself spatially extended, then what I have been calling component parts and structural parts will qualify as spatial parts, since they are spatially extended. And an electron, we have concluded, has no such parts. On the other hand, if what we mean by an expression such as "the left half of this electron" is something like "this electron from its midpoint to its leftmost extremity," then it is not clear, I suggest, that we are referring to a distinct entity at all. Rather, it seems to me, talk of the left and right "halves" of the electron is just a potentially misleading way of talking about the electron—the *whole* electron—insofar as it extends

[12] See further my "Form without Matter," *Ratio* 11 (1998): 214–34, or my *Possibility of Metaphysics*, chap. 9.

leftward or rightward. In other words, I am not at all convinced that there really are any such things as "spatial parts" of objects in the intended sense.

The upshot of this discussion is that I see no reason to infer, from the premises of the Simplicity Argument, that I am an object possessing no physical properties and altogether lacking spatial extension—that is, something immaterial and either punctiform or else spatially unlocated. That I should have the latter characteristics is perfectly compatible with the premises of the Simplicity Argument, but it is not implied by them. And, indeed, I am quite strongly inclined to hold a contrary view, namely, that I do have some physical properties and am spatially extended. In particular, I believe that I have the same weight as my body and occupy the same space that it occupies.

It may be objected now that if I have the same weight as my body, and yet am neither identical with it nor composed by it, then the combined weight of me and my body must be twice the weight of either of us.[13] And yet if, grotesquely, I were to die while weighing myself, one would not expect the pointer of the weighing machine suddenly to register half the weight which it registered when I was alive. I am inclined to dismiss this sort of objection as being as fatuous as it is tasteless. When I say that I have the same weight as my body, I mean the "same" not just quantitatively, but numerically. The term "the weight of my body" may be taken, in this context, to refer to something like a *trope,* or *property-instance*—that is, a so-called abstract particular.[14] And the suggestion is that *my* weight, in this sense, just is (identical with) the weight of my body: in other words, that I inherit my weight from my body.[15] Likewise, I inherit my size and shape from my body. I do not think that the notion of such property inheritance can be charged with being inherently mysterious, since it is clearly exemplified in cases in which one thing is composed by another: the statue inherits its weight, size, and shape from the weight, size, and shape of the lump of bronze which composes it. All I am suggesting is that property inheritance is not restricted solely to cases in which the inheritor is *composed* by the object from which it inherits.

I have claimed that I inherit my weight, size, and shape from my body. But other things I do not inherit from my body, most notably my con-

[13] See, e.g., Dean W. Zimmerman, "Criteria of Identity and the 'Identity Mystics,'" *Erkenntnis* 48 (1998): 281–301, esp. 293–94.

[14] See Keith Campbell, *Abstract Particulars* (Oxford: Blackwell, 1990).

[15] More cautiously, perhaps, it should be said that my weight is not determinably distinct from the weight of my body, in view of certain difficulties—which I cannot go into here—concerning the identity-conditions of tropes. See further my "Entity, Identity, and Unity," *Erkenntnis* 48 (1998): 191–208, or my *Possibility of Metaphysics,* chap. 3.

scious thoughts. If my body has these at all—and I am inclined to say that it does not—then it inherits them from me. I concede that much more needs to be said about the inheritance relation than I have said here and, indeed, that much more needs to be said about self-body relations more generally. But I hope I have said enough to show that an acceptance of the Simplicity Argument is quite compatible with a rejection of so-called Cartesian dualism.

One further question I might raise is this. If the conclusion of the Simplicity Argument is true, what are the implications, if any, for the prospects of a person surviving the destruction of his or her body, without replacement? My own view is that we cannot answer this question either way without information which we presently lack. Even if, as I believe, an embodied person is a physical, spatially extended object, inheriting his or her physical and spatial properties from his or her body, I have no argument for the claim that a person is an essentially embodied object, even though there may be grounds for thinking that a person must begin his or her existence in an embodied condition. The only properties of a person that I can confidently claim to be essential are psychological ones, such as the property of possessing a capacity for conscious thought. Whether that capacity could be possessed by a disembodied person I do not know.

Appendix: A Formal Version of the Simplicity Argument

To conclude the paper, I shall now present, as promised earlier, a formal version of the Simplicity Argument. Let 'I' denote me and 'B' denote my body. Let '<' express the relation of proper parthood, and let '$[x_1 + x_2 + \ldots x_n]$' denote the mereological sum of $x_1, x_2, \ldots$ and x_n. Then the eight premises of the Simplicity Argument listed at the beginning of the paper may be expressed formally as follows:

1. $(\exists x)(x = \mathrm{I})\ \&\ (\exists x)(x = \mathrm{B})$
2. $\sim(\mathrm{I} = \mathrm{B})$
3. $(\forall x)(x < \mathrm{B} \supset \sim(\mathrm{I} = x))$
4. $(\forall x)(x < \mathrm{I} \supset x < \mathrm{B})$
5. $(\forall x)(\forall y_1)(\forall y_2) \ldots (\forall y_n)((y_1 < x\ \&\ y_2 < x\ \&\ \ldots y_n < x) \supset (\exists z)$ $(z = [y_1 + y_2 + \ldots y_n]\ \&\ (z < x \lor z = x)))$
6. $(\forall x)(\forall y)(y < x \supset (\exists z)(z < x\ \&\ \sim(z = y)\ \&\ \sim(z < y)))$
7. $(\forall x)(\forall y)(((\exists z)(z < x)\ \&\ (\exists z)(z < y)) \supset (x = y \equiv (\forall z)(z < x \equiv z < y)))$
8. $(\forall x)(\forall y)(\forall z)((x < y\ \&\ y < z) \supset x < z)$

The conclusion of the Simplicity Argument may be expressed thus:

9. $\sim(\exists x)(x < \mathrm{I})$

Since premise 1 is formally redundant, it will not figure in the proof that follows. What I shall in fact prove is not that premises 2–8 together entail proposition 9, for they do not: rather, I shall show that premises 2–8 together entail either that proposition 9 is true or else that I have infinitely many proper parts. This limitation arises from the fact that premise 5, as I have formalized it here, only caters for a finite number of proper parts and is thus weaker than the informal version of 5 stated at the beginning of the paper.

Suppose, for reductio, that I have some proper parts, a_1, a_2, . . . and a_n and that these are all the proper parts that I have:

10. $a_1 < \mathrm{I}\ \&\ a_2 < \mathrm{I}\ \&\ \ldots a_n < \mathrm{I}\ \&\ (\forall x)(x < \mathrm{I} \supset (x = a_1 \vee x = a_2 \vee \ldots x = a_n))$

From (10) we can immediately infer

11. $a_1 < \mathrm{I}\ \&\ a_2 < \mathrm{I}\ \&\ \ldots a_n < \mathrm{I}$

and from (11) and (4) we can infer

12. $a_1 < \mathrm{B}\ \&\ a_2 < \mathrm{B}\ \&\ \ldots a_n < \mathrm{B}$

From (12) and the Fusion principle (5) we can infer

13. $(\exists z)(z = [a_1 + a_2 + \ldots a_n]\ \&\ (z < \mathrm{B} \vee z = \mathrm{B}))$

Instantiating for '*z*' in (13), we get

14. $r = [a_1 + a_2 + \ldots a_n]\ \&\ (r < \mathrm{B} \vee r = \mathrm{B})$

From (14) we can immediately infer

15. $r = [a_1 + a_2 + \ldots a_n]$

However, we can also prove

16. $\sim(r = a_1)\ \&\ \sim(r = a_2)\ \&\ \ldots \sim(r = a_n)$

The proof of (16) is as follows. Suppose, for reductio, that for some i between 1 and n inclusive, $r = a_i$. By (11), $a_i < I$. That being so we have, by the Weak Supplementation principle (6), that $(\exists z)(z < I \mathbin{\&} {\sim}(z = a_i) \mathbin{\&} {\sim}(z < a_i))$. Instantiating for '$z$' here, we get: $s < I \mathbin{\&} {\sim}(s = a_i) \mathbin{\&} {\sim}(s < a_i)$. But, given that $s < I$, we have, by (10): $s = a_1 \vee s = a_2 \vee \ldots s = a_n$. So let $s = a_j$, for some j between 1 and n inclusive. Then we have, from above: ${\sim}(a_j = a_i) \mathbin{\&} {\sim}(a_j < a_i)$. Hence, on the hypothesis that $r = a_i$, we have: ${\sim}(a_j = r) \mathbin{\&} {\sim}(a_j < r)$. However, contradicting this, we have from (15), by the definition of 'sum': $a_j = r \vee a_j < r$. This completes the reductio in proof of (16), and we can now proceed with the main proof.

From (15) and (16), by the definition of 'sum', we can infer

17. $a_1 < r \mathbin{\&} a_2 < r \mathbin{\&} \ldots a_n < r$

And from (10) we can immediately infer

18. $(\forall x)(x < I \supset (x = a_1 \vee x = a_2 \vee \ldots x = a_n))$

From (17) and (18) we can infer

19. $(\forall x)(x < I \supset x < r)$

From (11) and the Fusion principle (5) we can infer

20. $(\exists z)(z = [a_1 + a_2 + \ldots a_n] \mathbin{\&} (z < I \vee z = I))$

Instantiating for 'z' in (20), we get

21. $t = [a_1 + a_2 + \ldots a_n] \mathbin{\&} (t < I \vee t = I)$

From (21) we can immediately infer

22. $t = [a_1 + a_2 + \ldots a_n]$

From (15) and (22) we can infer

23. $r = t$

From (21) and (23) we can infer

24. $r < I \vee r = I$

From (24), by the Transitivity principle (8), we can infer

25. $(\forall x)(x < r \supset x < I)$

From (19) and (25) we can infer

26. $(\forall x)(x < I \equiv x < r)$

From (11) and (17) we can infer

27. $(\exists x)(x < I)\ \&\ (\exists x)(x < r)$

From (27) and the Weak Extensionality principle (7) we can infer

28. $I = r \equiv (\forall x)(x < I \equiv x < r))$

From (26) and (28) we can infer

29. $I = r$

From (14) we can immediately infer

30. $r < B \vee r = B$

Suppose, taking the first disjunct of (30)

31. $r < B$

From (3) we can infer

32. $r < B \supset {\sim}(I = r)$

And from (31) and (32) we can infer

33. ${\sim}(I = r)$

This contradicts (29). Suppose instead, taking the second disjunct of (30)

34. $r = B$

From (2) and (34) we can infer

35. $\sim(I = r)$

This again contradicts (29). Q.E.D.

What we have proved here is that if premises 2–8 are true, then (10) is false. The negation of (10) does not entail (9), the proposition that I do not have any proper parts, but it does entail the proposition that if I have any proper parts, I have infinitely many. On the reasonable assumption, then, that I do not have infinitely many proper parts, we may conclude that I have none. This assumption is not needed, however, if *a* stronger (infinitary) version of premise 5 is employed, as is implicitly done in the informal version of the Simplicity Argument stated at the beginning of the paper.

LYNNE BAKER

Materialism with a Human Face

My overall aim in philosophy is to understand the common world that we all share—the world in which we have friends and pay our bills and go on vacations and negotiate bureaucratic red tape, the world in which others do or don't return our phone calls, the world in which we are happy or frustrated. This world, Husserl's *Lebenswelt,* is populated with many different kinds of things: not only with cabbages and kings, but also with rocks, dogs, genes, teapots, birth certificates, statues, and flags. Prominent among the things that we encounter in the *Lebenswelt* are people, human persons like ourselves.

I approach this shared world assuming commonsense materialism: each of the concrete things in it is ultimately constituted by aggregates of fundamental particles. But, as I formulate the idea of constitution, constitution is not identity. It would be a mistake to suppose that ordinary things are identical to, or are reducible to, aggregates of fundamental particles. For there are many different primary kinds of things, and things of one primary kind have different persistence conditions from things of another primary kind. This is my general outlook; it is not specific to the question of what a human person is, but it is applicable to that question.

A human person is a material object in the same way that a statue or a carburetor is a material object. A statue is constituted by, say, a piece of marble; but it is not identical to the piece of marble that constitutes it. The piece of marble could exist in a world in which it was the only occupant, but no statue could. Nothing that is a statue could exist in a world without artists or institutions of art. A human person is constituted by an organism, a member of the species *Homo sapiens,* but is not identical to the organism that constitutes her. The human organism could exist in a world in which no psychological properties whatever were exemplified, but no person could. Nothing that is a person could exist in a world without first-person perspectives. A human organism that develops a first-person perspective comes to constitute a new thing: a person. I'll call this 'the Constitution View' of human persons.

Just as different statues are constituted by different kinds of things (pieces of marble, pieces of bronze), so too different persons are (or may be) constituted by different kinds of things (human organisms, pieces of plastic, Martian matter). What makes something a person (no matter what it is "made of") is a first-person perspective; what makes something a piece of sculpture (no matter what it is "made of") is its relation to an art world. What makes a person a *human* person is that he or she is constituted by a human organism. But a person could start out as a human person and have organic parts replaced by synthetic parts until she was no longer a human person. With the persistence of her first-person perspective, she would still exist and still be a person, even with a synthetic body. If she ceased to have a human body but retained a first-person perspective, she would still exist, but not as a human. If she ceased to be a person (that is, ceased to have a first-person perspective), however, she would cease to exist altogether.

On the Constitution View, a human person and the animal that constitutes her differ in persistence conditions without there being any actual physical intrinsic difference between them. The persistence conditions of animals—all animals, human or not—are biological; and the persistence conditions of persons—all persons, human or not—are not biological.[1] On my view, what makes a human person a *person* is what I am calling a 'first-person perspective'. What makes a human person a *human* is being constituted by a human organism. (I do not distinguish between human organisms and human bodies; my body now is identical to a human organism. But it does not follow that I am identical to a human organism; I am merely constituted by a human organism.) So, there are two theoretical ideas—the notion of constitution and the notion of a first-person perspective—that need explication.

I. The First-Person Perspective

A first-person perspective is the defining characteristic of all persons, human or not.[2] From a first-person point of view, one can think about

[1] For an extended defense of this claim, see my *Persons and Bodies: A Constitution View* (Cambridge: Cambridge University Press, 2000).

[2] For a more detailed account, see *Persons and Bodies*, chap. 3, and my "The First-Person Perspective: A Test for Naturalism," *American Philosophical Quarterly* 35 (1998): 327–48.

oneself as oneself and think about one's thoughts as one's own. In English, the ability to conceive of oneself as oneself is marked grammatically by a sentence with a first-person subject of a psychological or linguistic verb and an embedded first-person reference.[3] We English speakers not only use first-person pronouns to refer to ourselves ("I'm happy"), but also to attribute to ourselves first-person reference ("I wonder whether I'll be happy in ten years"). The second occurrence of 'I' in "I wonder whether I'll be happy in ten years" directs attention to the person per se, without recourse to any name, description, or third-person referential device to identify who is being thought about. When I wonder whether I'll be happy in ten years, I am wondering about myself as myself; from a first-person perspective, I do not need to pick myself out as one object among many. I could still have this thought even if I had total amnesia. The first-person perspective opens up a distinction between thinking of myself as myself, on the one hand, and thinking of myself as Lynne Baker, or as the person who is reading this paper, on the other. Once someone can make this conceptual distinction, she can think of herself in the first person as a subject in a world of things different from herself. The first-person perspective is the ability to consider oneself as oneself in this way. This is the basis of all forms of self-consciousness.

A being can be conscious without having a first-person perspective. Dogs and other mammals are conscious; they have psychological states like beliefs and desires (simple ones, anyway); they can engage in practical reasoning using these simple beliefs and desires. Such animals have points of view; but their points of view are not conceptions of themselves as themselves. If a dog could talk, it could say, "I'm hungry"; but the dog could not have the thought expressible by "I'm sure that I'm hungry." The simple first-person in "I'm hungry" may be, as Peter Geach and Bertrand Russell argued, eliminable. The embedded first-person reference in "I'm sure that I'm hungry" is, as I have argued elsewhere, not eliminable.[4] It is the ability to entertain the latter kind of thought that manifests the first-person perspective. There are many kinds of intentional states that only a being with a first-person perspective can have—namely, those that require one as the thinker to conceive

[3] See Hector-Neri Castañeda, "He: A Study in the Logic of Self-Consciousness," *Ratio* 8 (1966): 130–57, and "Indicators and Quasi-Indicators," *American Philosophical Quarterly* 4 (1967): 85–100. For a study of philosophy from a first-person point of view, see Gareth B. Matthews, *Thought's Ego in Augustine and Descartes* (Ithaca: Cornell University Press, 1992).

[4] See Baker, *Persons and Bodies*, chap. 3, and "First-Person Perspective."

of oneself as oneself. If a dog, *per impossibile,* came to have a first-person perspective, then the dog would come to constitute a canine person. If a gorilla were taught a language sufficiently close to English that we could recognize embedded first-person references, then that gorilla would come to constitute an ape person. Anything that has a first-person perspective is a person.

So, what distinguishes human persons from animals is not consciousness; nor is it the ability to have intentional states like fearing or desiring. The ability to have intentional states is a necessary, but not a sufficient, condition for being a person. To be a person—whether God, an angel, a human person, a Martian person, an artificial person—one must be capable of having a first-person perspective.

Our first-person perspectives may well be the product of natural selection. But whether they are or not, the appearance of a first-person perspective makes an ontological difference in the world. Human animals are continuous with nonhuman animals in every way but one: only human animals (as far as we know) constitute persons. If biologists do not recognize a first-person perspective as biologically significant, then . . . well, it just goes to show that ontology does not recapitulate biology.

II. Constitution

What distinguishes human persons—who, like all persons, have first-person perspectives—from other kinds of persons is that human persons are constituted by human bodies. The relation of constitution itself is a perfectly general one: U.S. dollar bills are constituted by pieces of paper; genes are constituted by DNA molecules; diplomas are constituted by pieces of parchment or by pieces of paper. Constitution is thus a very general relation, not a relation peculiar to persons and bodies.[5]

Nor is constitution an obscure relation. Not only is it very familiar to everyone, but also the term 'constitution' is susceptible of explicit definition in terms of ordinary logical and modal ideas. Since I have presented a detailed exposition of the idea of constitution elsewhere, here I want to describe constitution more informally.[6]

[5] See Baker, "Unity without Identity: A New Look at Material Constitution," in *New Directions in Philosophy*, Midwest Studies in Philosophy, vol. 23, ed. Howard Wettstein (Malden, Mass.: Blackwell Publishers, 1999), 144–65; and Baker, "Why Constitution Is Not Identity," *Journal of Philosophy* 94 (1997): 599–621.

[6] Baker, *Persons and Bodies*, chap. 2, and "Unity without Identity."

The basic idea of constitution is this: when certain kinds of things are in certain kinds of circumstances, things of new kinds, with new kinds of causal powers, come into existence. For example, when a certain combination of chemicals is in a certain environment, a thing of a new kind—an organism—comes into existence. A world without organisms, even if it contained the "right" combination of chemicals but in the "wrong" environment, would not have the same things in it as a world with organisms. So, constitution makes an ontological difference. Call the answer to the question, "What most fundamentally is *x*?" *x*'s 'primary kind'. If *x* constitutes *y*, then *x* and *y* are of different primary kinds. Each thing has its primary-kind property essentially.

The notion of constitution can be explicated in terms of familiar logical and modal ideas. Using 'primary kind' for what a thing most fundamentally is, Michelangelo's *David* is of the primary kind *statue*, and its primary-kind property is the property of being a statue. Let the term 'circumstances' stand for all the background conditions that are necessary but not sufficient for something to be of a certain primary kind. For example, the circumstances for something to be a statue (that is, statue-favorable circumstances) include an art world; the circumstances for something to be a gene (gene-favorable circumstances) include processes of reproduction of organisms. Now let F be *x*'s primary-kind property and G be *y*'s primary-kind property. Then, *x* constitutes *y* at *t* if and only if

(a) *x* and *y* are spatially coincident at *t*.
(b) *x* is in G-favorable circumstances at *t*.
(c) Necessarily, if anything that has F as its primary-kind property is in G-favorable circumstances at *t*, then there exists some spatially coincident thing at *t* that has G as its primary-kind property.
(d) Possibly, *x* exists at *t* and there is no spatially coincident thing at *t* that has G as its primary-kind property.
(e) If *y* is immaterial, then *x* is also immaterial.

The point of the last clause is to insure that materiality is not lost by constitution. If something is material (a piece or marble, a piece of cloth), then what it constitutes (a statue, a flag) is also material. These conditions demonstrate the coherence of the idea of constitution.

Constitution is not identity, understood in the strict, Leibnizian sense, but constitution is nevertheless a genuine relation of unity. Constitution is as intimate as a relation can be short of identity; it is not just spatial co-location. If *x* constitutes *y*, then *y* inherits many of *x*'s properties and *x* inherits many of *y*'s properties. Elsewhere, I have spelled out this inheriting in detail, in terms of borrowing properties, or of having properties derivatively.[7] If *x* constitutes *y*, then *x* has some properties in virtue of constituting *y*, and *y* has some properties in virtue of being constituted by *x*. For example, my driver's license is constituted by a piece of plastic. The piece of plastic borrows the property of allowing me to check in for an airline flight from the driver's license that it constitutes; the driver's license borrows the property of marking my place in a novel from the piece of plastic that constitutes it. Similarly, a person, Sam, is constituted by a human body. Sam derives the property of being able to reach the light bulb from his body's being six feet tall; and Sam's body derives the property of having a right to be in a reserved seat from Sam's having purchased a reserved-seat ticket.

There are two ways for an object to have a property: derivatively or nonderivatively. Say that *x* has constitution relations to *y*, or is constitutionally related to *y* if and only if either *x* constitutes *y* or *y* constitutes *x*. Then, roughly, to have a property nonderivatively is to have it independently of constitution relations; to have a property derivatively is to have it in virtue of being constitutionally related to something that has it independently of constitution relations.[8] Betsy Ross's first U.S. flag had the property of being rectangular derivatively; it borrowed that property from the piece of cloth that constituted it. The constituting cloth had the property of being rectangular nonderivatively—the piece of cloth could have been rectangular without constituting anything. On the other hand, the flag had the property of being revered nonderivatively; the constituting cloth had the property of being revered derivatively. In the given background in which flags are revered, but pieces of cloth are not, the cloth would not have been revered if it had not constituted something that was revered. Not all properties are subject to being had derivatively—for instance, the property of being identical to a person is not.[9] But what we

[7] Some properties are excluded from the definition of 'having properties derivatively'. I identify four kinds of properties that cannot be had derivatively: alethic properties, "identity / constitution / existence" properties, properties rooted outside the times at which they are had, and hybrid properties. For detailed exposition of 'having properties derivatively', see Baker, *Persons and Bodies*, chap. 2, and "Unity without Identity."

[8] The actual definition has the odd consequence that your body nonderivatively has the ability to survive loss of the first-person perspective. (Since your body has that property, but you do not, your body does not have that property derivatively.) I could add a clause to the definition of '*x* has H nonderivatively' to prevent the definition's having the odd consequence: e.g., "*x*'s having H does not entail instantiation of any property that *x* has derivatively." Since I do not think that this odd consequence has serious repercussions, I won't add a clause to the definition to prevent its having the odd consequence.

[9] No properties of any of the following types may be had derivatively: *(a)* properties expressed in English by the locutions 'essentially' or 'necessarily' or 'primary kind' (as in 'has F

might call "ordinary" properties—properties like being red, or having the genes for blue eyes or even being tax-exempt, properties that do not entail the existence of things in other times or worlds—may be had derivatively. If x has a property F derivatively, then there is some y such that y has F nonderivatively, and x is constitutionally related to y.[10] The idea of having properties derivatively explains how x and y have so many properties in common when x constitutes y.

Constitution, as I construe it, shows how there can be a relation of unity that is not identity, a relation that is intermediate between identity and separate existence. It is not surprising that constitution is like identity in some ways and unlike identity in other ways. We have seen how constitution differs from identity: if x constitutes y, x and y are of different kinds and have different persistence conditions. Now we see how constitution is similar to identity: if x constitutes y, x and y each inherit properties from the other and hence have many of their properties—size, location, color, texture, and others—in common.

III. Persons and Bodies

Human persons differ from nonbodily or immaterial persons (if there are any) in that human persons are not just pure subjects, but are necessarily embodied. They are constituted by bodies. And their bodies are the objects

---

as its primary-kind property'), or variants of such terms ("alethic properties"); *(b)* properties expressed in English by the locutions 'is identical to' or 'constitutes' or 'exists' or variants of such terms ("identity / constitution / existence properties"); *(c)* properties of any sort such that necessarily, x has it at t only if x exists at some time other than t ("properties rooted outside the times at which they are had"—Roderick Chisholm's idea); *(d)* properties that are conjunctions of two or more properties that either entail or are entailed by two or more primary-kind properties ("hybrid properties").

[10] We could turn this into a sufficient condition, as well as a necessary condition, for 'having F derivatively' as follows: Say that x has F *supernonderivatively* iff *(a)* x has F nonderivatively, and *(b)* x's having F does not entail instantiation of any property such that x has it derivatively. Then, the following schema is true: 'The fact that x has F derivatively = the fact that x is constitutionally related to y and y has F supernonderivatively.'

In general, x has property F iff there is some y such that *(a)* either $x = y$ or x is constitutionally related to y, and *(b)* y has F nonderivatively, and *(c)* y's having F nonderivatively does not entail instantiation of any property such that y has it derivatively. (Without clause *c*, from the facts that I am constitutionally related to my body and my body has the property of being able to survive loss of a first-person perspective nonderivatively, it would follow that I have the property of being able to survive loss of a first-person perspective. Since this consequence would be inconsistent with the Constitution View of human persons, it must be avoided. Hence, clause *c*.) This note and note 8 were prompted by correspondence with Tom Senor.

of first-person reference. If Smith wonders whether she has cancer, she is wondering about her body from a first-person point of view. She is not wondering whether there is a malignant tumor in some particular body identified by a third-person demonstrative pronoun or description; she is wondering whether there is a malignant tumor in her own body, considered as herself. This is different from wondering about a material possession, say. If Smith wonders whether there is a dead battery in her car, she wonders whether there is a dead battery in a particular car, which she identifies by a description or a third-person demonstrative reference. Without a third-person way to think about the car, she could not wonder about its battery. But if Smith is wondering how she will die, she can think of her body as her own without recourse to any name or description or second- or third-person demonstrative pronoun. And reference without recourse to the familiar third-person devices is the mark of first-person reference.

What distinguishes human persons—who, like all persons, have first-person perspectives—from other kinds of persons is that human persons are constituted by human bodies that are the objects of their first-person reference. Part of the relation between a human person—Jones, say—and her body is that Jones can think of her body and refer to it, and to no other, in the first-person way, "from the inside." The body with respect to which Jones has a first-person relation is the body that she (normally) can move without moving anything else, the body that she tends when she is in pain, and the body that expresses intentional states that are hers. States like pain, longing, sadness, hope, fear, frustration, worry, effort, and joy as well as states like believing, desiring, and intending are expressed through posture, facial expression, sounds, and other bodily motions. The body that expresses Jones's intentional states is the body to which Jones has a first-person relation. Jones's first-person relation to her body at t does not imply that Jones thinks of her body at t; indeed, Jones may believe at t that she is disembodied. The body to which Jones has a first-person relation is the body which would sweat if Jones were in a sauna, and so too is the body that would cringe if Jones were threatened, or the body that would move if Jones decided to leave the room. Jones's body at time t distinguishes Jones from all other persons at t. What distinguishes me now from all other coexisting persons—even physical and psychological replicas of me, if there are any—is that at this time, I have a first-person relation to this body and to no other; and any replica of me at this time has a first-person relation to some other body.

Let me show how the idea of constitution-without-identity, defined above, applies to persons and bodies.[11] Name the human animal that

[11] For a more detailed exposition of the Constitution View, see *Persons and Bodies*, chap. 4.

constitutes Jones "Body." Jones's primary-kind property is the property of being a person; Body's primary-kind property is the property of being a human body. Person-favorable circumstances are the organismic and environmental conditions conducive to development and maintenance of a first-person perspective. To say that Jones is constituted by Body at *t* is to say the following:

(a′) Body and Jones are spatially coincident at *t*.
(b′) Body is in organismic and environmental conditions at *t* conducive to development and maintenance of a first-person perspective; and
(c′) It is necessary that: for anything that has the property of being a human body as its primary-kind property at *t* and that is in organismic and environmental conditions at *t* conducive to development and maintenance of a first-person perspective, there is some spatially coincident thing that the property of being a person as its primary-kind property at *t;* and
(d′) It is possible that: Body exists at *t* and there is no spatially coincident thing that has the property of being a person as its primary-kind property at *t;* and
(e′) If Jones is immaterial, then Body is immaterial.

Let me make three brief comments. The first concerns the organismic and environmental conditions conducive to development and maintenance of a first-person perspective at *t*, as cited in (b′) and (c′). The relevant organismic conditions are that the organism, particularly the brain, is developed to the extent that a normal baby's brain is developed at birth. The relevant environmental conditions include those in which the infant naturally develops various senses of 'self', as described by developmental psychologists.[12] The first-person perspective, on my account, fits easily into the framework of developmental psychology. The second comment concerns (d′) It is possible that: Body exists at *t* and there is no spatially coincident thing that has the property of being a person as its primary-kind property at *t*. Body could exist at *t* but be dead; in that case, Body would not be in the relevant organismic conditions conducive to development and maintenance of a first-person perspective, and so would not constitute a person. The third comment concerns (e′) Biologists, and most everybody else, would agree that Body is not immaterial. Hence, by modus tollens, we conclude that Jones is not immaterial. (The reason for this last clause is to

[12] For example, see Daniel N. Stern, *The Interpersonal World of the Infant* (New York: Basic Books, 1985), and Jerome Kagan, *Unstable Ideas: Temperament, Cognition, and Self* (Cambridge: Harvard University Press, 1989).

rule out the possibility that Body could constitute a Cartesian person that had an immaterial soul.)

Now let me make some contrasts between persons and higher animals. Although dogs and other higher animals are subjects of mental states, they do not have first-person perspectives. Dogs are conscious; they have beliefs and desires (in a severely limited range); and they have points of view.[13] But, as we have seen, a first-person perspective requires more. A first-person perspective requires that one can *conceive* of oneself in a uniquely first-personal way. Both a dog and I can believe that there's food behind the rock; but only I can conceive of myself as believing that there's food behind the rock. There is a sense in which a dog has a "first-person relation" to its body, but it is not the same sense in which I have a first-person relation to my body. Both the dog and I can move our bodies without moving anything else. But, unlike the dog, I can think about my body in a way that only a person can: I can wonder whether I'm shrinking. To wonder about my body is to wonder about myself. (I can also think about myself in ways that have nothing to do with my being embodied: I can wonder whether I'll still be happy next year.) So, although I am not identical to my body, the constitution relation is a unity relation—tight enough so that I myself am (derivatively) an animal without being identical to an animal.

In short, I am constituted now by a body that is essentially an animal. On the one hand, because constitution is not identity, it does not follow that I am essentially an animal. On the other hand, because constitution is a relation of genuine unity, I inherit many of my body's properties, in particular its physical and biological properties. I have the property of having a liver derivatively—in virtue of being constituted by something (an animal) that has a liver independently of its constituting anything. The result is this: The body that constitutes me now is essentially (and nonderivatively) an animal, and it is contingently (and derivatively) a person; I am essentially (and nonderivatively) a person, and I am contingently (and derivatively) an animal.[14]

The idea of having properties derivatively also applies to mental properties. For example, many of my mental states—like wanting food—are shared with higher animals like dogs. If my mental state is of a type that a dog could have, then I have it derivatively. (If a dog could have it, then so could a human animal that did not constitute anything have it.) In that

[13] See Baker, "First-Person Perspective."

[14] I am not claiming that all essential properties are nonderivative. Although a (nonderivative) statue has its shape solely in virtue of being constituted by something of that shape, it is plausible to suppose that something that is a statue nonderivatively has its shape essentially.

case, my body has the mental state nonderivatively. This does not imply that the organism that constitutes me has one desire for food, and I have another. Rather it implies that my desire for food depends on my being constituted by an animal.

On the other hand, the property of hoping that I will not be in debt next year is one that I have nonderivatively. I have that property independently of my constitution-relations to my body, since my having it does not entail that I am constituted by something that could have had it without constituting anything. Indeed, since I am constituted by my body, and only something with a first-person perspective could have that hope, my body could not have that property without constituting a person, according to the Constitution View. Therefore, some of my mental states (such as wanting food) I have derivatively; other of my mental states (such as hoping that I will not be in debt next year) I have nonderivatively.

In each case, there is just one desire and one hope. The Constitution View is not subject to a charge of duplicating mental states (or anything else). I have the thought nonderivatively; the animal that constitutes me has it derivatively—solely in virtue of constituting something that has the thought nonderivatively. The account of 'having a property derivatively' makes it perfectly clear what it means to say that there is a single thought that I have nonderivatively and the animal that constitutes me has derivatively.

IV. Replies to Some Objections

Although not identity, constitution makes for real unity. As such, it has been caricatured by those who cannot imagine a relation of unity that is intermediate between identity and separate existence. The idea of such an intermediate position strikes some philosophers as incoherent.[15] As we have seen, however, the notion of constitution-without-identity is demonstrably coherent. Since I reply in detail to numerous objections to the Constitution View elsewhere, here I'll respond to what seem to me the main worries of the critics.[16]

[15] Anyone who believes in the Christian doctrine of the Trinity is committed to there being a relation (besides proper parthood) between strict identity and separateness. So, an orthodox Christian believer is in no position to declare the claim that there is an intermediate relation between identity and separateness to be incoherent. An orthodox Christian believer should look for fault in my specific account of constitution, not in the general idea of constitution-without-identity.

[16] See Baker, *Persons and Bodies*, chaps. 7, 8.

1. Some philosophers do not see how things that are exactly alike in microstructure can be of different kinds or can have different persistence conditions. For example, Michael Burke asks how a statue and a piece of copper that makes it up can belong to different kinds. They are "qualitatively identical. Indeed, they consist of the very same atoms. What, then, could *make* them different in sort?"[17]

This question is a worry only on the assumption that the nature and identity of a thing are determined by its actual intrinsic physical properties. But we have independent reason to think that ordinary things—like statues, flags, carburetors, and passports—have relational properties essentially. (Nothing that is a statue could exist in the absence of an art world.) As I have argued at length elsewhere, it is an error to assume that difference in essential properties is ipso facto a difference in intrinsic properties.[18] And without the assumption that all essential properties are intrinsic properties, the worry about how *x* and *y* can have all the same actual intrinsic properties and yet differ in kind or in persistence conditions disappears.

Once we see that a thing can have relational properties essentially, we are freed from supposing that if *x* and *y* differ in primary kind, then there must be an actual physical intrinsic difference between *x* and *y*. And being freed from that supposition, we can see how an animal can have certain biological properties essentially, and a person can have those same biological properties contingently. Difference in primary kind and difference in essential properties go together, whether the essential properties are intrinsic or relational. And to ask why something has the essential properties that it has is to ask a nonsensical question. (Why is it essential to the number four that it is even? Why is it essential to organisms that they have cells?)

2. Some critics think that the Constitution View forces one to posit linguistic ambiguities. For example, Eric Olson makes a number of assumptions about my view that simply are in error. He says that although I (Baker) take the sentence 'Human animals are primates' at face value (as I do), he thinks that I claim that the sentence 'Human animals are sentient' "must be understood differently" from 'Human animals are primates'.[19] I make no such claim. Indeed, I think that dogs, human animals, and

[17] Michael B. Burke, "Copper Statues and Pieces of Copper: A Challenge to the Standard Account," *Analysis* 52 (1992): 14.

[18] Baker, "Why Constitution Is Not Identity."

[19] Eric T. Olson, "Reply to Lynne Rudder Baker," *Philosophy and Phenomenological Research* 59 (1999): 163.

human persons are sentient in exactly the same way: they are conscious; they have various conscious states (like feeling pain). What sets human persons apart from dogs and human animals that do not constitute persons is that human persons have first-person perspectives, not that they are sentient.

In general, I take the predicate 'is an H' to be univocal, but not to be identical to either of the predicates 'is constitutionally related to an H' or 'is identical to an H'. Here are truth conditions for 'is an H' used predicatively, where 'H' can be instantiated by any of a broad range of properties:[20]

> 'x is an H' is true iff either *(a)* *x* is constitutionally related to an H, or *(b)* *x* is identical to an H.

'I am an animal' used predicatively is true in exactly the same sense as 'Fido is an animal'. 'Human animals are sentient' is true in exactly the same sense as both 'Dogs are sentient' and 'Human persons are sentient'. The difference between human persons on the one hand and dogs and human animals on the other does not lie in what it means to be sentient, but rather lies in the source of sentience. Dogs and persons differ in that in virtue of which they are sentient: Dogs and human animals are sentient in virtue of being identical to animals of a certain sort; human persons are sentient in virtue of being constituted by animals of a certain sort. But 'is sentient' is univocal: the same property is being attributed in all three cases. So, the Constitution View does not lead to positing ambiguities in predicates.

3. A related criticism concerns the use of the personal pronoun 'I'. The criticism (this one by Paul Snowden) runs like this: Animals have evolved to use 'I'. So, if a person is not identical to an animal, then when the sentence "I am identical to an animal" comes out of the animal's mouth, there are two statements—a true one by the constituting animal and a false one by the person. But that's absurd. Therefore, the objection goes, the person is identical to the animal.[21]

[20] 'H' cannot be instantiated here by *(a)* an alethic property (any property expressed in English by the locutions 'essentially' or 'primary kind' (as in 'has F as its primary-kind property'), or by 'possibly' or 'necessarily' or variants of such terms); or *(b)* an "identity / constitution / existence" property (any property expressed in English by the locutions 'is identical to' or 'constitutes' or 'exists' or variants of such terms); or *(c)* a property rooted outside the times at which it is had (any property such that necessarily, *x* has it at *t* only if *x* exists at some time other than *t*). For greater detail, see *Persons and Bodies*, chap. 2.

[21] Paul F. Snowden, "Persons, Animals, and Ourselves" in *The Person and the Human Mind*, ed. Christopher Gill (Oxford: Clarendon, 1990): 83–107.

This argument is specious. We can agree that animals evolved to use 'I'. But when animals evolved to the point of being able to use 'I' in a way that manifests a first-person perspective, they came to constitute persons. According to the Constitution View, the pronoun 'I', when used sincerely and literally by a human person, always refers nonderivatively to the person—the person constituted by an animal. When "I am identical to an animal" issues from the mouth of the animal that constitutes me, I refer to myself (the person) nonderivatively, and say of myself that I am identical to an animal. What I say is false since, although constituted by an animal, I am not identical to an animal. (If I had simply said, predicatively, "I am an animal," then what I said would have been true, since on the Constitution View I have the property of being an animal derivatively.)

There are not two referents of 'I'—any more than there are two persons or two animals—where I am. So, when "I am identical to an animal" issues from an animal's mouth, there are not two statements—a true one by the animal and a false one by the person. There is only one statement (a false one) made nonderivatively by the person. If the sentence had been, "The thing that constitutes me is identical to an animal," it would have been true.

On the Constitution View, 'I' always refers nonderivatively to the person using it. If a person is constituted at *t* by a particular animal, and the person uses 'I' at *t*, then the person refers at *t* to a person constituted by the animal. This is so even if the person is attributing to herself a property that an animal could have without constituting anything. For example, if Jones says, "I am hungry," Jones refers to herself nonderivatively by means of 'I' and attributes to herself the property of being hungry, a property that she has derivatively in virtue of being constituted by an animal. When a person refers to herself, she does not fail to refer to the constituting animal: she refers to an embodied being constituted by that animal. Since you are constituted by a body, you refer to yourself, an embodied being, when you say, "I generally have good digestion." There are not two referents of 'I', nor are there two digestive systems. There is a single digestive system that you have derivatively and the animal that constitutes you has nonderivatively. The Constitution View simply does not result in linguistic incoherence.

4. Some criticisms simply do not apply to my view. For example, consider this one, by Olson again. "I found it hard to understand how, despite having all the right biological features, I could fail to be an organism; or how, despite having all the right psychological features, or at any rate all the right physical features, the organism that 'constitutes' me

could fail to be a person."[22] But I do not "fail to be an organism." I most assuredly am an organism. But I have the property of being an organism, not in virtue of being identical to an organism but in virtue of being constituted by an organism. Nor does the organism that constitutes me "fail to be a person." It most assuredly is a person: me. Again, according to the Constitution View, the organism has this property, not in virtue of being identical to a person but in virtue of constituting a person. Of course, I think that anything that has all the right biological features is an organism, and anything that has all the right psychological features is a person.

Still, one might press the complaint by saying that on the Constitution View, a human person is not *strictly speaking* an animal. Consider Olson again: "Baker's view still entails that there are beings physically indistinguishable from human animals that are *strictly speaking* not animals (even if they 'are' animals in the sense of being constituted by animals); and it entails that there are beings physically indistinguishable from human people that are *strictly speaking* not people."[23] What does "strictly speaking" mean here? On the one hand, suppose that "*strictly speaking* not animals" means "not identical to animals." In that case, we should interpret the charge that "there are beings physically indistinguishable from human animals that are *strictly speaking* not animals" like this: "there are beings physically indistinguishable from human animals that are not identical to animals." No quarrel there. That's just my view. I have explained in significant detail how there can be beings physically indistinguishable from human animals that are constituted by human animals, but are not identical to the animals that constitute them. It is no criticism of my view to point out what I insist upon (and what I have shown to be coherent). To suppose otherwise is just to beg the question.

On the other hand, suppose that "strictly speaking" means "speaking seriously and literally." In that case, the criticism just misfires. For I am not committed to the existence of beings that are physically indistinguishable from human animals but that, speaking seriously and literally, are not animals. Speaking seriously and literally, I think that human persons are human animals derivatively, in virtue of being constituted by animals. In neither case—whatever "strictly speaking" means—does the criticism have any purchase on the Constitution View.

[22] Olson, "Reply to Baker," 163.

[23] Ibid., 163–64; Olson's emphases.

5. Then there is a criticism from the opposite quarter. Several philosophers charge that if I am a person and the animal that constitutes me is a person, then we have duplication of persons. Variations of this line worry about how many persons, how many speakers, how many thinkers, how many mental states there are.[24] Here is a sharpened version of the argument:

(i) If I am not identical to my body and my body is a person and I am a person, then where I am there are two persons.
(ii) It is false that where I am there are two persons.
(iii) I am a person, and my body is a person.
(iv) ∴I am identical to my body.

The first premise clearly begs the question against the Constitution View. For it presupposes what the Constitution View explicitly denies—namely, that if x is not identical to y, then x is not the same F as y. However, according to the Constitution View, we count, not by identity, but by identity-or-constitution.[25] Where F is a property that can be borrowed,[26]

$$x \text{ is the same F as } y = [(x = y \text{ or } x \text{ is constitutionally related to } y) \ \& \ x \text{ is F}]$$

According to the Constitution View, the constitution relation yields a unity: if x is constitutionally related to y, and x has F nonderivatively and y has F derivatively, it does not follow that there are two F's. And an argument against the Constitution View that employs an unargued-for premise that supposes otherwise just begs the question against the Constitution View.

Since my body is a person solely in virtue of constituting me, my body is not a different person from me. Again: I have the property of being a person nonderivatively (and essentially), and my body has the property of being a person derivatively (and contingently). So, the Constitution View neither denies that my body is a person nor implies that wherever I am, there are two persons—my body and I. My body and I are the same person.

[24] Snowden, "Persons, Animals, and Ourselves," and Eric T. Olson, *The Human Animal: Personal Identity without Psychology* (New York: Oxford University Press, 1997).

[25] Philosophers who would oppose the Constitution View also allow that we do not count by identity. See, for example, David Lewis, "Survival and Identity," in *The Identities of Persons,* ed. Amelie Oksenberg Rorty (Berkeley: University of California Press, 1976), 26–28; and Harold Noonan, "Constitution Is Identity," *Mind* 102 (1993): 133–46.

[26] That is, F is not an alethic property, nor an "identity / constitution / existence" property, nor a property rooted outside the times it is had, nor a hybrid property. For details, see Baker, *Persons and Bodies,* 48–49.

Similarly, there are not two animals where I am. Since I am an animal in virtue of being constituted by something that is nonderivatively an animal, I am an animal derivatively. Since the animal that constitutes me is a person only because it constitutes something that is a person nonderivatively, it is a person derivatively. As we have seen, since I am an animal derivatively, I am not a *different* animal from the animal that constitutes me; and since the constituting animal is a person derivatively, she is not a *different* person from me. This is why it is not the case that wherever I am there are two persons or two animals.

6. Here is one last criticism advanced by those who do not think that the Constitution View is really a materialist account of persons:[27]

(i) If a human person x is a material being, then there is some material object to which x is identical.
(ii) x is not identical to x's body (or any part of it). [the Constitution View]
(iii) If x is not identical to x's body (or any part of it), then there is no material object to which x is identical.
(iv) ∴There is no material object to which x is identical. ((ii) & (iii), modus ponens)
(v) ∴Human person x is not a material thing. ((i) & (iv), modus tollens)

Premise (iii) is false. It would just beg the question against the Constitution View to suppose that if human person x is identical to a material object, then she is identical to her body or some part of it. She is identical to herself and not another thing. This is true whether she is a material being or not. Whether the *only* way for me to be a material being is for me to be identical to my body or some part of it is what is at issue and cannot be assumed in a premise against the Constitution View. For if the Constitution View is correct, then I am a material being and I am not identical with my body or with any part of my body.

Of course, a human person is strictly identical to some material thing: himself or herself. It would be nonsensical to require that there be *something else* to which a human person is strictly identical; and it would beg the question against the Constitution View to disallow that *human*

[27] Alvin Plantinga offered this argument (or something like it) at the Notre Dame Conference on the Mind / Body Problem in 1994. See also Peter van Inwagen, "Materialism and the Psychological-Continuity Account of Personal Identity," in *Mind, Causation, and World,* Philosophical Perspectives, no. 11, ed. James E. Tomberlin (Malden, Mass.: Blackwell Publishers, 1997), 312.

person is a material-object category. For according to the Constitution View, *human person* has as great a claim to be a material-object category as *marble statue* does. So, the claim that a human person is a material being is not ad hoc. The Constitution View, as I have developed it, is decidedly not ontologically neutral about persons: it takes *human person* to be a material-object category.

Indeed, if the argument just given—for the conclusion that on the Constitution View a human person is not a material object—were sound, a parallel argument would show that Smith's body is not a material object. Smith's body has existed over forty years, and it is constituted by aggregates of cells—different aggregates of cells at different times. Therefore, Smith's body is not identical to any particular aggregate of cells. One cannot say that at any given time, there is some aggregate of cells that is identical to Smith's body unless one says that Smith has as many different bodies as she has aggregates of cells. But that's not how bodies are individuated: Smith has a single body, constituted at different times by different aggregates of cells. Nor can one say that Smith's body is identical to a disjunction of all the aggregates of cells that make up the body throughout its existence. Assuming, as I do, that identity is a necessary relation, the view that Smith's body is identical to a disjunction of all the aggregates of cells that make it up would have an untoward consequence: If Smith's barber on some occasion of haircutting had cut one strand of Smith's hair one millimeter shorter, Smith's body would no longer have existed. For if Smith's body were identical to a certain disjunction of aggregates of cells, then with the subtraction of even one cell, Smith's body would no longer have existed.[28] Here's an argument that is parallel to the argument that on the Constitution View a human person, Smith, is not a material object. This parallel argument would show that Smith's body is not a material object:

(i′) If Smith's body is a material being, then there is some material object to which Smith's body is identical.

(ii′) Smith's body is not identical to any aggregate of cells (or to any disjunction of aggregates of cells).

[28] Here is the argument: Suppose that Smith's body = A (a disjunction of certain aggregates of cells). Take away one of the cells in one of the aggregates; then one of the original aggregates is replaced by a new aggregate. So the disjunction is replaced by a new disjunction, just like the old but minus one cell. Call the new disjunction of aggregates 'A-'. Obviously, A-≠A. Now if Smith's body = A, and A≠A-, then Smith's body≠A-. So, if A had been replaced A-, Smith's body would have ceased to exist.

(iii′) If Smith's body is not identical to any aggregate of cells (or to any disjunction of aggregates of cells), then there is no material object to which Smith's body is identical.
(iv′) ∴There is no material object to which Smith's body is identical. ((ii′) & (iii′), modus ponens)
(v′) ∴Smith's body is not a material thing. ((i′) & (iv′), modus tollens)

Since even substance dualists would agree that Smith's body is a material thing, something is wrong with this parallel argument. It seems clear that what is wrong with the argument is premise (iii′). Of course, Smith's body is a material thing, even though it is not identical to any aggregate of cells or to any disjunction of aggregates of cells. So, (iii′) is false. Similarly, in the original argument, Smith is a material thing, even though she is not identical to any human or other body. So, (iii) is false as well.[29]

In short, neither the linguistic nor the metaphysical objections that I have seen hold water. Each one either attributes to the Constitution View some consequence that it does not have (as in claiming that it denies that I am an animal) or blatantly begs the question with a premise that presupposes that the Constitution View is false (as in the assumption that if I am a material object, then I must be identical to my body, or to some part of it).

V. Why Accept the Constitution View?

I have set out the Constitution View of human persons in some detail; I have tried to deflect objections to it, and I have shown that the general idea of constitution-without-identity is coherent. But are there any positive reasons to accept the Constitution View? To my mind, the answer is a resounding yes. First, without any special pleading for persons, the Constitution View of human persons shows exactly how human persons are like and unlike other material things—from genes to statues and passports. That is, the Constitution View shows how human persons are part of the material world without reducing personal to something nonpersonal. Indeed, as I have shown elsewhere, the Constitution View brings with it a general account of material beings.[30]

Let me compare the Constitution View to its rivals—Substance Dualism and Animalism. I'll deal with Substance Dualism briefly. The main advantage

[29] Such considerations might drive some to four-dimensionalism; I think that that would be a mistake, but discussing why is beyond the scope of this paper.

[30] Baker, *Persons and Bodies*, chap. 9.

of the Constitution View over Substance Dualism is that the Constitution View achieves almost everything that a Dualist wants without postulating any immaterial substances. For example, the Constitutionalist agrees with the Dualist on all the following points: *(a)* A human person is not identical to her body. A human person can survive complete change of body. *(b)* Not all truths about human persons are truths about bodies. *(c)* A person has causal powers that a body would not have if it did not constitute a person. *(d)* Most important, persons have ontological significance: being a person is not just a contingent and temporary property of some fundamentally nonpersonal thing.[31] It seems to me that if these and other desiderata can be satisfied by both a materialist view (like the Constitution View) and an immaterialist view (like Substance Dualism), the materialist view is preferable. The Constitutionalist can give the Dualist what she wants while avoiding the well-known and long-discussed problems of Substance Dualism.

The other main rival to the Constitution View is Animalism. Animalism is the view that we persons have the persistence conditions of animals. It is the view that persons are identical to human animals.[32] The Animalist View has two important consequences (that discredit it to me). First, unlike both Substance Dualism and the Constitution View, the Animalist View entails that bodily transfer, or replacement of body, is metaphysically impossible. Indeed, on the Animalist View, it is metaphysically impossible that I should have had a different body from the one that I actually have. Second, on the Animalist View, being a person is irrelevant to the kind of individual that one fundamentally is. Indeed, as one Animalist has put it, perhaps we cannot properly call that vegetating animal a *person* since it has none of those psychological features that distinguish people from non-people (rationality, the capacity for self-consciousness, or what have you). If so, that simply shows that you can continue to exist without being a person, just as you could continue to exist without being a philosopher, or a student or a fancier of fast cars.[33] On the Animalist View, my being a person is metaphysically on a par with my "being a philosopher, or a student or a fancier of fast cars."

Since I have argued against Animalism at great length in *Persons and Bodies*, here I just want to pose a dilemma for anyone who holds that persons are

[31] For greater detail, see ibid.

[32] Even though David Wiggins is well known for developing a view of constitution-without-identity, he does not apply that view to persons and animals. He takes persons to be identical to animals, but animals not to be identical to their bodies. (By contrast, the Constitution View takes persons not to be identical to animals, but animals to be identical to their bodies.)

[33] Olson, *Human Animal*, 17.

identical to human animals. What is the status of human animals? Are they continuous with the rest of the animal kingdom or do they differ in some fundamental way from, say, apes? To hold that human animals are fundamentally different from other kinds of animals is to posit a biologically unmotivated gap in the animal kingdom. Biologists emphasize the continuity between human and nonhuman animals; they see rather small differences in degree not in kind. Hence, it would seem that we should not suppose that human animals are fundamentally different from other kinds of animals.

So, suppose that, according to the Animalist View, human animals are not fundamentally different from other kinds of animals. Then, how can such an Animalist account for the vast differences between nonhuman animals and human animals that are or constitute persons—who have art, science, literature, philosophy, government, religion, and so on; who have discovered evolution and intervene in evolutionary processes, clone mammals, devise medical treatments, stop epidemics, and so on? If such Animalists are right, a complete inventory of what's in the world need not mention persons at all; the property of being a person is just a temporary and contingent property of animals that are ontologically level with animals that do not constitute persons. Such an Animalist just has to deny the ontological significance of data like these: We alone among animals have the capacity to assess and modify our goals, to own up to what we do, to hold each other responsible for what we do. We alone are moral agents. We alone can wonder what kind of beings we are. (The list could go on indefinitely.) None of these things, on the Animalist View, has any ontological significance whatever. So, an Animalist must either posit a biologically unmotivated gap between human and nonhuman animals or deny the ontological significance of what is distinctive about human persons.

According to the Constitution View, the most significant fact about us ontologically is that we are persons (that is, we have first-person perspectives). Since our being persons (having first-person perspectives) underwrites the possibility of moral and rational agency, the Constitution View ties what is morally and rationally important about us, and what matters to us, directly to what we basically are. (Contrast the Animalist, according to whom our existence and persistence are independent of having mental states whatever, and who has no way to connect what is unique about us to what we basically are.) The fact, if it is a fact, that the first-person perspective evolved naturally does not diminish its ontological significance: Beings with a capacity for a first-person perspective are fundamentally different from other beings.

There would be no "us" at all if we were not persons. If there were no persons, there would be no *me* to consider my own persistence conditions.

Our abilities to ask "What am I?" and to make life plans and wonder how we'll die (and all the other things that require a first-person perspective) are indicative, according to the Constitution View, of the kind of beings that we are. Let me conclude by reiterating three features of the Constitution View that I take to recommend it over both Substance Dualism and the Animalist View:

1. The Constitution View situates human persons firmly in the material world, without reducing them to something essentially nonpersonal.
2. The Constitution View allows for the possibility that a human person could have a different body from the one that she actually has.
3. The Constitution View ties what is distinctive about us—our ability to care about our long-term future, to try to change our habits in light of rational assessment of our goals—to what we are most fundamentally: persons. The existence of persons makes an ontological difference in the world.

PART III

Does Life after Death Require Dualism?

TRENTON MERRICKS

How to Live Forever without Saving Your Soul

Physicalism and Immortality

I. Temporal Gaps

The claim that human persons are physical things does not, of necessity and all by itself, render personal immortality problematic.[1] After all, there doesn't seem to be a problem with the mere idea of a physical thing, even a living physical thing, that lasts forever. Nevertheless, the physicalist who believes in immortality has a worry that her dualist counterpart does not. This worry is grounded in a bit of empirical, contingent fact: If human persons are physical objects, then they die and, as a result, cease to exist.

Exactly *how* death results in a physical person's ceasing to exist does not matter for our purposes. It could be that everyone ceases to exist immediately upon dying, because the atoms they comprise cease to be caught up in a life and so cease to compose anything at all. Or perhaps the mummified linger longer than the cremated. Or perhaps there is some other story to be told here. The details about how and when death results in ceasing to exist are not important for our purposes. All that matters here is that human persons, if physical, cease to exist as a result of dying. (If, on the other hand, human persons are substantial souls, then presumably death brings mere disembodiment rather than nonexistence.)

Thanks to Michael Bergmann, Anthony Ellis, Daniel Howard-Snyder, Eugene Mills, Mark Murphy, Eric Olson, Alvin Plantinga, Michael Rea, Theodore Sider, and Dean Zimmerman for helpful comments and suggestions.

[1] Stipulations: 'Physicalism' means that human persons are physical and substance dualism is false; it does not mean that everything is physical. 'Immortality' and 'everlasting life' are interchangeable, as are 'human body' and 'human organism'.

Now there is (presumably) a possible world in which human persons don't die and so, even if physical, don't cease to exist. Maybe there is another possible world in which humans do die but, immediately upon death, are whisked away while a duplicate decays in their stead; and maybe in that world the deceased does not cease, but continues to exist as a corpse until, at some later time, she comes back to life.[2] And maybe there is a world in which, upon death, each person's memories, personality, and so on are immediately "realized" in a new organism; and, one might argue, that means that at death each person jumps to (and becomes co-located with?) a new organism, never ceasing to exist. Nevertheless, I submit that these worlds are not actual. I submit that if persons are physical things, then—in the actual world—they die and their death results in their ceasing to exist.

And this creates the worry. For if a person dies and ceases to exist, then her enjoying everlasting life implies that that very person will come back into existence. Thus, given the fact that persons die and—if physicalism is true—cease to exist sometime after death, personal immortality, for the physicalist, implies a dreaded "temporal gap" in a person's life.

II. Criteria and Explanation

Imagine that you build a time machine that can "take you to the future." You push the Start button. You (and the machine) disappear. You then reappear at some later date. Now there are easier ways to travel to the future. Just sit there for a minute, and you'll move ahead a minute in time. The whole purpose of the time machine, of course, is to get you to some future time while "skipping" all the times between now and then. In other words, the time machine causes a temporal gap in your life.

The idea of a *future*-traveling time machine doesn't seem incoherent or contradictory. We have no trouble making sense of a person's "jumping ahead" in time. That is, a person's jumping ahead in time and experiencing a temporal gap is not obviously incoherent in the way that, for example, a person's being simultaneously under five feet tall and over six feet tall is.

If you find time machines too fantastic, consider instead a watch that is disassembled, perhaps for cleaning. Suppose that, as a result, it ceases

[2] Cf. Peter Van Inwagen, "The Possibility of Resurrection," *International Journal for the Philosophy of Religion* 9 (1978): 114–21.

to exist.[3] Suppose further that when its parts are reassembled, that watch comes back into existence. The watch thus traverses a temporal gap. Of course, the watch example is controversial. But the claim that the watch jumps through time via disassembly and reassembly—even if it makes questionable assumptions here and there—is at least coherent. It is not contradictory or obviously absurd. It is not, for example, like the claim that one has found a round square in one's pocket, next to the number seven.

So the worry is *not* that asserting the occurrence of a temporal gap in a person's life, between death and glory, makes no sense or is obviously absurd or is clearly incoherent. The worry, instead, is that such a gap—which in some sense certainly *seems* possible enough—might not *really* be possible.

We can begin to see why one might worry that gaps are not really possible by noting the stock example of a *criterion of identity over time:* spatiotemporal continuity. If spatiotemporal continuity were the true criterion of identity over time, temporal gaps—that is, temporal *dis*continuities—would be impossible. And even if one has doubts about spatiotemporal continuity as a criterion of personal identity over time, one might worry that whatever the true criterion is, it will preclude gaps.

To better see the issues surrounding criterion-based worries about temporal gaps, we need to say a bit more about criteria of identity over time. Criteria of identity over time are metaphysically necessary and sufficient conditions for identity over time. But not just any such condition is a criterion. A criterion must also be *informative.* Conditions of identity over time are informative only if one can, at least in principle, assert that they are satisfied without presupposing the identity for which they are said to be criteria.[4]

[3] Some will object that the watch doesn't cease to exist after disassembly, but—because it leaves all of its parts (at one level of decomposition) behind—persists as a "scattered object." Note that in this respect, in the leaving behind of all of its parts at one level of decomposition, the disassembled watch is analogous to the dead and decayed in a way that the time traveler is not.

[4] Criteria of personal identity over time as I have defined them—informative metaphysically necessary and sufficient conditions for identity—are not "epistemic criteria." That is, they are not the grounds or evidence which guide and justify our beliefs about particular instances of personal identity over time (Trenton Merricks, "There Are No Criteria of Identity over Time," *Noûs* 32 (1998): 106–24). This needs to be emphasized, because the expression 'criteria of identity over time' is ambiguous, sometimes meaning criteria as I have defined them, sometimes meaning grounds or evidence for a judgment of identity. In philosophical contexts, the way I am using that expression is now standard (Derek Parfit, *Reasons and Persons* [Oxford: Clarendon, 1984], 202; Harold Noonan, *Personal Identity* [New York: Routledge, 1989], 2).

Because criteria must be informative, criterion-based worries about temporal gaps are closely related to the suspicion that nothing could *explain* what makes a person in the distant future identical with a person who, long before, died, decayed, and disintegrated. To get a feel for why one might suspect this, imagine two people who come into existence ten thousand years from now, alike in all their intrinsic qualitative features. What could *explain* the fact that one of them, but not the other, is (identical with) the long-gone Napoleon? One might suspect that nothing could. Certainly claims like "One of them, but not the other, exemplifies Napoleon's haecceity" or "One of them, but not the other, was conceived of the very sperm and egg as was the Little General himself" don't satisfy. They seem to presuppose the identity in question rather than explain it.

Now note that if there were an informative necessary and sufficient condition for one, but not the other, of these future persons being identical with the bygone Bonaparte, that condition would explain that identity. By contraposition, if there is no explanation of identity across a temporal gap, then there is no criterion that sanctions that identity. Moreover, if we assume that all instances of identity over time must hold in virtue of satisfying some criterion or other, the worry that there could be no explanation of personal identity across a gap returns us to the charge that identity across a temporal gap is precluded by the relevant criteria of identity.

III. Alleged Explanation I: Reassembly

Christian philosophers and theologians have, historically, been concerned with the *resurrection of the body*, concerned with how a human body could jump the temporal chasm between the time of its ceasing to exist and Resurrection Day. For a very long time, the dominant view was that resurrection was akin to the reassembly of a watch.[5] "Resurrection as reassembly" involves Resurrection Day reassembly of all the parts at a certain level of decomposition—such as all the atoms—that composed the person at the time of her death.[6] For those physicalists who (like me)

[5] See Caroline Walker Bynum, *The Resurrection of the Body in Western Christianity, 200–1336* (New York: Columbia University Press, 1995).

[6] The relevant level of decomposition presumably involves very small parts, for clearly the bigger parts of many dead people (e.g., their organs) are simply not available for future reassembly. So I'll focus my discussion on the reassembly of atoms, although, of course, one could choose to focus on quarks or something else suitably tiny. The unavailability of organs immediately suggests an objection to resurrection as reassembly. Perhaps some of even the smallest

believe that human persons are identical with "their" bodies or organisms, resurrection as reassembly purports to offer a venerable and straightforward *explanation* of how personal identity could bridge a temporal gap.

But there are problems with resurrection as reassembly. The most striking, and one that has vexed resurrection's apologists since at least the second century, involves cannibalism. Suppose a cannibal eats you; some of the atoms of your flesh go on to compose the cannibal; and the cannibal then dies. Resurrection Day comes and God sets out to reassemble both your body and the cannibal's body from the atoms that composed each at its last moment. But some of the atoms that composed your body at your death also composed the cannibal's body at her death. God cannot, therefore, reassemble both your body *and* the body of the cannibal.

One might try to defend resurrection as reassembly from the "cannibal objection." For example, Athenagoras tried to block that objection by asserting that human flesh was not digestible; it passes right through the cannibal (yucky) to await the resurrection of the eaten.[7] Or, to take a second example, one could insist that, in a case of cannibalism, either the dinner or the diner cannot rise again. But these defenses fail. The first fails because, of course, human flesh *is* digestible. The second is unacceptable because it renders resurrection unavailable both to (some) bodies involved in cannibalism and also to (some) bodies of, among others, organ donors and / or recipients. Cannibalism, postmortem organ donation, and the many other ways that one body's parts are passed to another show us that resurrection as reassembly is untenable.

Another objection to resurrection as reassembly is suggested by the fact that if I were, right now, to reassemble the atoms that composed my body when I was five years old, I might thereby get *some* body, but obviously I wouldn't get *mine*.[8] But then it seems objectionably arbitrary to suppose that the atoms that compose a body at death have the "ability" to bring it back by reassembly, when we know this "power" is denied to the atoms that compose a body at other times during its existence.[9] This sort of

---

parts that compose a person's body at death will cease to exist before Resurrection Day—who says atoms or even quarks are everlasting?—and so won't be available for reassembly.

[7] Bynum, *Resurrection*, 33.

[8] Van Inwagen, "The Possibility of Resurrection," 120.

[9] This is not to say that it is arbitrary to accord *some* special status, with regard to resurrection, to the parts that compose a body at death. One might think, for example, that identity over time implies *some* kind of material continuity. If so, then perhaps the resurrected body must be composed of some of the atoms that composed it at death. But this suggestion does not imply resurrection as reassembly. Note also that neither cannibalism nor organ donation nor any known facts preclude resurrection bodies having *some* of the parts they had at death.

objection to resurrection as reassembly is an old one, defended as far back as Origen.[10]

Note that the objection from arbitrariness works only because *having all the same atoms (arranged in the same ways)* is not a sufficient condition of bodily identity. Nor is it a necessary condition, else my body, which is constantly shedding atoms, would not persist for any appreciable duration. So having all the same atoms (arranged in the same ways), being neither necessary nor sufficient for sameness of body, fails twice over to be a criterion of bodily identity over time. This failure shows that even if there were no other problems with resurrection as reassembly, it would still be an inadequate response to the *criterion-based* challenge to temporal gaps. For even if persons are identical with "their" bodies, resurrection as reassembly does not offer a *plausible general criterion* of personal / bodily identity that would render resurrection possible. Nor does it even purport to show that the criterion of personal identity fails to preclude resurrection. Nor does it suggest any reason why resurrection's defenders need not respond to the criterion-based challenge to personal identity across a temporal gap. If we want to address that challenge directly, we must look elsewhere.

IV. Alleged Explanation II: Psychological Continuity

Some physicalist believers in immortality won't be bothered by the failure of resurrection as reassembly to provide an unproblematic, criterion-based account of how a body that died can come back into existence on Resurrection Day. For they will insist that worries about reassembly or about any other process that allegedly secures the resurrection of the *body* across a temporal gap is, insofar as *personal* immortality is concerned, beside the point. For these physicalists hold that the body—that is, the human organism—is one thing, the person another.

The first philosopher clearly to insist on a distinction between persons and their associated organisms / bodies, and to do so in a way that did not presuppose any kind of dualism, was John Locke. This distinction was tied directly to Locke's views on the criteria of identity over time for persons and organisms.[11] Locke thought, very roughly, that a person's—but

[10] Bynum, *Resurrection*, 64.

[11] Locke contrasted persons and "men." But 'men', in Locke's idiolect, means human organisms. According to Locke, the persistence conditions of "men" are just like the persistence conditions of other organisms such as "Oaks" and "brutes" (John Locke, *An Essay concerning Human Understanding*, ed. P. H. Nidditch [Oxford: Clarendon, 1975], 330–35).

not a human organism's—persistence amounts to the persistence of her psychology and "consciousness."[12]

Given the context of this chapter, it is worth taking note of one of the considerations that might have led Locke to a psychological criterion of personal identity, and so, as a result, led him to distinguish persons from their bodies. According to Harold Noonan,[13] one of Locke's "most obvious and important motives" for embracing that criterion was to allow for life after death even if substance dualism turned out to be false. If Noonan is right, the psychological criterion, in its earliest incarnation at least, was tailor-made to explain the resurrection of a physical *person* (if not a body) across a temporal gap.[14]

So imagine I die and then cease to exist. Imagine also that, a thousand years hence, God creates a person who has all the beliefs and desires I had at death and has seeming memories or quasi-memories of my experiences in this life. On the most straightforward version of the psychological theory—perhaps Locke's version—this person would be me. Because the possibility of identity across a thousand-year gap is thus implied by a Lockean criterion of personal identity over time, Locke can directly counter the charge that a temporal gap is inconsistent with the criterion of personal identity over time.

But the most straightforward version of the psychological criterion seems to have unpalatable consequences, the most familiar being that one person could be identical with two or more future persons. In his notes on Locke's *Essay*, Jonathan Edwards develops this charge. I quote Edwards's remarks on this in full, not because they are particularly new, but rather because—being written when Edwards was a college student in the 1720s—they are particularly old. I suspect they constitute the earliest explicit presentation of this now very familiar charge, including even what appears to be a characterization of quasi-memory:

> Identity of person is what seems never yet to have been explained. It is a mistake, that it consists in sameness, or identity, of consciousness—if, by sameness of consciousness, be meant, having the same ideas hereafter,

[12] Locke, *Human Understanding*, 328–48.

[13] Noonan, *Personal Identity*, 30–31.

[14] This is evidence that Locke's prohibition of one thing's having "two beginnings of Existence" (Locke, *Human Understanding*, 328) is not a prohibition of temporal gaps. Rather, it implies only that if *a* is identical with *b*, then the very first moment at which *a* exists, that is, the moment at which *a* exists and it is true that at no earlier time did *a* exist, is also the very first moment at which *b* exists.

And don't miss the irony: The most popular criterion of personal identity over time—one in terms of psychology—was suggested, in part, to make gaps possible; so the most popular

that I have now, with a notion or apprehension that I had had them before; just in the same manner as I now have the same ideas, that I had in time past, by memory. It is possible, without doubt, in the nature of things, for God to annihilate me, and after my annihilation to create another being that shall have the same ideas in his mind that I have, and with the like apprehension that he had had them before, in like manner as a person has by memory; and yet I be in no way concerned in it, having no reason to fear what that being shall suffer, or to hope for what he shall enjoy. —Can anyone deny, that it is possible, after my annihilation, to create two beings in the Universe, both of them having my ideas communicated to them, with such a notion of their having had them before, after the manner of memory, and yet be ignorant one of another; and, in such case, will any one say, that both these are one and the same person, as they must be, if they are both the same person with me. It is possible there may be two such beings, each having all the ideas that are now in my mind, in the same manner that I should have by memory, if my own being were continued; and yet these two beings not only be ignorant one of another, but also be in a very different state, one in a state of enjoyment and pleasure, and the other in a state of great suffering and torment. Yea, there seems to be nothing of impossibility in the Nature of things, but that the Most High could, if he saw fit, cause there to be another being, who should begin to exist in some distant part of the Universe, with the same ideas I now have, after manner of memory: and should henceforward coexist with me; we both retaining a consciousness of what was before the moment of his first existence, in like manner; but thenceforward should have a different train of ideas. Will any one say, that he, in such a case, is the same person with me, when I know nothing of his sufferings, and am never the better for his joys.[15]

I don't expect Edwards's prescient comments to convert the diehard devotee of the psychological criterion; they are merely the first (the very first) volley in a still ongoing battle. But they do point to the following serious worry about the psychological criterion, given the topic of this paper. The psychological criterion—if it is to secure resurrection of the person—must be "liberal" enough to cover thousand-year gaps which contain no persisting brain or other "realizer" of mental states. Yet it must also be

objection to temporal gaps—that they are precluded by any plausible criterion of personal identity—is in tension with the most popular criterion of personal identity over time.

[15] Jonathan Edwards, *The Works of Jonathan Edwards,* vol. 1., ed. Edward Hickman (Carlisle, Pa.: The Banner of Truth Trust, 1974), ccxxii.

"conservative" enough to preclude the possibility of one pre-resurrection person's being identical with more than one post-resurrection person.

It would not help to guarantee the needed elements of conservatism by defining 'memory' in such a way that to remember someone's experiences *just means,* among other things, being the person who had those experiences. For then one could not claim that a resurrected person has memories of a deceased's experiences without presupposing that the resurrected is identical with the deceased. And so the fact that the resurrected person has those memories could not be a criterion of her identity with the deceased. Nor could it explain that identity. But it was, in part, the hope of finding just such an explanation that led Locke to his approach to personal identity in the first place.

V. There Are No Criteria of Personal Identity

We have examined—and I have raised some prima facie objections to—the two classic and most familiar alleged *explanations* of how personal identity could span the temporal gap between death and Resurrection Day.[16] I now want to offer my own response to the worry about explanation, a response that departs in a fundamental way from all of its predecessors (except for that of Mavrodes).[17] My response will involve the claim that identity can hold across a temporal gap even if there is no explanation of that identity's holding. My defense of this claim builds on the thesis that there are no criteria of personal identity over time. So my defense of this claim, as we shall see, will also issue in a response to the worry that no plausible criterion of identity over time could sanction identity across a temporal gap.

A full-dress defense of the claim that there are no criteria of personal identity over time is beyond the scope of this paper. I have offered such a defense elsewhere.[18] Here I shall simply present an outline of the main

[16] A third "classic" explanation is the rabbinical view according to which having the same allegedly indestructible bone from the spinal cord accounts for the identity of the resurrected with the deceased (Bynum, *Resurrection,* 54; Philip Quinn, "Personal Identity, Bodily Continuity, and Resurrection," *International Journal for Philosophy of Religion* 9 [1978]: 111).

[17] George Mavrodes, "The Life Everlasting and the Bodily Criteria of Identity," *Noûs* 11 (1977): 27–39.

[18] Merricks, "No Criteria of Identity," 106–24; Merricks, "Endurance, Psychological Continuity, and the Importance of Personal Identity," *Philosophy and Phenomenological Research* 59 (1999): 983–97, is also relevant.

argument. So suppose, as I believe, that personal identity over time just is—is analyzed as—the relation of numerical identity holding between a person existing at one time and a person existing at another.[19] What then differentiates *personal* identity over time from, say, *tree* identity over time are the *relata;* the *relation*—numerical identity—is the same. Suppose also, as is very plausible, that that relation is itself primitive, unanalyzable.

Given these suppositions, an earlier person's being identical with a later person cannot be *analyzed as* her satisfying the criterion of identity over time with a later person. Thus, an earlier person's being identical with a later person is a state of affairs *distinct from* the state of affairs of the earlier person's satisfying the criterion of identity over time with the later person. But—as I argue at length elsewhere[20]—there is no good reason to think that the obtaining of one of these states of affairs is necessary and sufficient for the obtaining of the other. So there is reason to deny that the alleged criterion's being satisfied is necessary and sufficient for the identity's holding. That is, there is reason to reject *criterialism,* the claim that there really is a criterion of identity over time, about persons.

Note that I am not suggesting that *any* unmotivated position ought to be rejected. That would have absurd results, such as our rejecting a claim and rejecting its denial, if both the claim and its denial were unmotivated. I am suggesting something much more plausible. I am suggesting that we ought to assume, for any distinct and contingent states of affairs S and S*, either that S can obtain in some possible world where S* does not obtain or vice versa, unless there is *some* reason to think otherwise. (And just *seeing* that it must be otherwise counts as a reason in the sense at issue here.) This is a reasonable assumption. I think it is presupposed by a great deal of our reasoning about what is broadly logically possible.

VI. An Objection and a Reply

As noted above, my argument against criterialism builds on the point, also defended by argument, that there is no good reason to think there are any such criteria. I would like to supplement the argument for this point by responding to the following objection: Necessarily, for every macrophysical

[19] I assume that persons last over time by *enduring,* not by way of having "temporal parts" at various times. For accounts of endurance, see Trenton Merricks, "Endurance and Indiscernibility," *Journal of Philosophy* 91 (1994): 165–84; Merricks, "Persistence, Parts and Presentism," *Noûs* 33 (1999): 421–38.

[20] Merricks, "No Criteria of Identity."

occurrence there are microphysical occurrences upon which that macrophysical occurrence supervenes;[21] thus a physical human person's enjoying identity over time, being macrophysical, has a microphysical supervenience base in every possible world, and the disjunction of those supervenience bases—being both necessary and sufficient for personal identity over time—constitutes a criterion of personal identity over time.

I have argued elsewhere[22] that the doctrine of "microphysical supervenience" is false. Not all macrophysical occurrences supervene on the microphysical. This does not imply, all by itself, that a human's identity over time does not supervene on the microphysical. It could be that although microphysical supervenience in full generality is false, the doctrine restricted to personal identity is true. Nevertheless, the restricted claim loses much (or all) of its intuitive motivation once we see that the general claim is false.

And we have further reason to resist the claim that a human's identity over time supervenes on the features and doings of the microphysical. As I have argued elsewhere,[23] plausible and familiar assumptions about half-brain transplant and human fission imply that there could be a diachronic process comprising all and only a person's atoms being interrelated (and having intrinsic features) that is only *contingently* correlated with her identity over time.[24] This in turn implies that personal identity could fail to supervene on that diachronic process. Thus it follows that personal identity does not supervene (in every possible world) on processes involving the atoms (or, of course, other microscopica) that compose a person during the course of her life.

One might object that we have here a reason to deny only *local* supervenience. To deny local supervenience in this case is to deny only that a

[21] This claim is restricted only to worlds in which macrophysical entities have microphysical parts; it does not imply that events involving *macrophysical simples* supervene on the microphysical. Moreover, the "macrophysical occurrences" in question are restricted to those that are appropriately *qualitative* (see Trenton Merricks, "Against the Doctrine of Microphysical Supervenience," *Mind* 107 [1998]: 59–71). Occurrences of identity over time are appropriately qualitative. That is, the claim that *someone or other* enjoys identity over time is qualitative. But this is not so for claims about the identity of the person—P? P*? Kobe Bryant? —who enjoys this identity.

[22] Merricks, "Microphysical Supervenience."

[23] Trenton Merricks, "Fission and Personal Identity over Time," *Philosophical Studies* 88 (1997): 163–86.

[24] Those assumptions are, roughly: first, if half of my brain were transplanted (and the rest of my brain destroyed), I would be identical with the half-brain recipient; second, in a case of double half-brain transplant (a case of fission), it is false that I would be identical with both of the numerically distinct half-brain recipients.

person's identity over time supervenes on the intrinsic features of, and interrelations among, the atoms that compose him at the various times at which they compose him. And this denial is consistent with the claim that personal identity *globally* supervenes on the microphysical. This denial is consistent with the claim that whether one persists supervenes on the features and activity of *all the microscopica in the universe*. Crucially, global supervenience of this sort allows personal identity's supervenience base to include factors *extrinsic* to that person. (For example, that base could include relations to atoms that compose a brain hemisphere recently removed from one's skull).

Now many—myself included—want to resist the suggestion that whether one persists supervenes on extrinsic factors. Whether someone in the future is I should not be a matter of what atoms are like that neither compose that future person or me nor cause any intrinsic difference in that person or me. Moreover, we can argue that the failure of local supervenience in this case *entails* the failure of global supervenience.[25] If this argument works, then plausible assumptions about half-brain transplant and personal fission entail that personal identity supervenes neither locally nor globally on the microphysical. If this argument works, we have a good reason to dismiss the objection at the start of this section.

This argument will turn on a key assumption. That assumption is that the things that happen over a period of time and within a certain region of space in one world can, without any qualitative or intrinsic differences, be the *only things that happen* in some other world.[26] For example, if our world contains, among other things, a flea that dances for one hour, there is another world that lasts but an hour and contains nothing but a single dancing flea. Moreover, the flea and its parts in that short-lived world are intrinsically just like the flea and its parts in our world during its hour-long dance. (Of course, this principle allows extrinsic—or relational—differences between our two fleas; for example, the fleas could differ with respect to living on a dog. And it allows nonqualitative differences between our two fleas; for instance, they really could be *two* fleas, differing in their identity.)

Now consider a diachronic arrangement of microscopica on which personal identity over time fails to *locally* supervene. In some worlds the

[25] Cf. Merricks, "Microphysical Supervenience"; Cranston Paull and Theodore Sider, "In Defence of Global Supervenience," *Philosophy and Phenomenological Research* 52 (1992): 833–54.

[26] Something along these lines is defended by David Lewis, *On the Plurality of Worlds* (Oxford: Basil Blackwell, 1986), 86–92.

atoms in that arrangement compose a single person for whom personal identity holds throughout the duration of the arrangement. In some worlds they do not. Given the key assumption, there is a world whose only atoms are those in the diachronic arrangement and in that world they compose a person for whom personal identity holds.[27] There is also another world whose only atoms are those in the diachronic arrangement, and in that other world they do not compose a person for whom personal identity holds. We now have a failure of *global* supervenience.

Given the key assumption, the only way to block this argument is to insist that identity's holding between a person at one time and a person at another is not *intrinsic* to the person involved, but is rather analyzed as his or her being related to some other thing (or things). It is to insist that 'P = P*' is somehow incomplete, missing some crucial third term. But anyone who insists upon this is mistaken. And, needless to say, such insistence goes far beyond the idea, considered above, that whether a person enjoys personal identity could *supervene on* factors extrinsic to the person herself.

VII. No Explanation Necessary

Temporal gaps in a person's life, of the sort implied by death, decay, and resurrection, are not ruled out by the true criterion of personal identity over time, for—so I say—there *is no* true criterion of personal identity over time. Nor is it incumbent upon the defender of resurrection to offer a criterion of personal identity in virtue of which personal identity could straddle a temporal gap. After all, because there is no criterion of identity over time, personal identity never holds, across temporal gaps or otherwise, in virtue of satisfying a criterion of personal identity. Criterion-based worries about, and related criterion-based arguments against, resurrection dissipate once we reject criterialism itself.

Moreover, given the denial of criterialism, we can argue that there need be no explanation at all of the holding of identity across a temporal gap. The first step in this argument is to note that the claim that there are no criteria of identity does not imply that there are no informative sufficient conditions for identity. For example, it is consistent with the rejection of criterialism that an informative and metaphysically *sufficient* condition for P at *t* to be identical with P* at *t** is that laws of nature L hold and P at *t* is re-

[27] See note 21 for the sense in which a fact of identity over time is relevantly qualitative.

lated to P* at t^* by biological process B.[28] So suppose, for the sake of argument, that that condition really is a sufficient condition for P at *t*'s identity with P* at t^*. Then, if P at *t* satisfies this condition for being identical with P* at t^*, we thereby have an *explanation* of P at *t*'s identity with P* at t^*.

So the denial of criterialism is consistent with there possibly—or even actually—being an explanation of the holding of personal identity. However, the denial of criterialism is *not* consistent with there being some informative metaphysically sufficient condition or other for P at *t*'s identity with P* at t^* in *every possible* case of P at *t*'s identity with P* at t^*. To see this, assume, for *reductio,* that in every possible instance of P at *t*'s identity with P* at t^*, there is an informative sufficient condition for that identity. Now consider the disjunction of those informative sufficient conditions. That disjunction is an informative *necessary and sufficient* condition for P at *t*'s identity with P* at t^*.[29] But the existence of a condition like that is inconsistent with the denial of criterialism. RAA.

There must be some possible instance of P at *t*'s being identical with P* at t^* that does *not* hold in virtue of P at *t*'s satisfying some informative metaphysically sufficient condition of identity with P* at t^*. In other words, it is possible that P at *t* is identical with P* at t^* and there is *no explanation* of this fact.

Now it just might be that there is some yet-to-be-discovered explanation, some informative metaphysically sufficient condition, for resurrection's requisite transgap identities. But, for the sake of argument, let us grant to resurrection's detractors that this is not so. Let us grant that, in fact, there is *no possible explanation* of how personal identity could hold across a temporal gap. But this does not imply that temporal gaps are impossible. It implies only that identity across a temporal gap would be one of the cases—cases whose possibility follows from the rejection of criterialism—in which identity holds without explanation.

VIII. Intuitions Favoring Temporal Gaps

Given the coherence of the time machine and the watch that jumps temporal gaps by way of reassembly, it seems safe to say that temporal gaps as

[28] Merricks, "No Criteria of Identity," 118–19.

[29] *Being an informative condition of identity* is closed under disjunction. Suppose that *p* is an informative condition of identity; that is, *p does not presuppose* the identity for which it is a condition. Surely any claim weaker than *p*—such as *p* or *q*—will not presuppose more than *p* itself, and so will not presuppose that identity. So if *p* does not presuppose the identity in question, and *q* is a condition for that identity and also does not presuppose it, then *p* or *q* will not presuppose it and so will be informative.

such are not obviously impossible. And if we grant this about some temporal gaps, given the rejection of criterialism, it is hard to see why one should insist—without any argument—that temporal gaps in the case of human persons are impossible.

Moreover, once we reject criterialism, we can sidestep criterion-based arguments against the possibility of temporal gaps in a person's career. Once we reject criterialism, we can also conclude that the possibility of resurrection is not impugned even if identity across a temporal gap could not possibly be explained. Now these are purely defensive maneuvers, blocking criterion-based challenges to the possibility of temporal gaps and so to the possibility of our resurrection. Of course, that temporal gaps have not been shown to be impossible does not imply their possibility. But I do think we have *some* reason for thinking that such gaps are, in fact, possible. I think, for instance, that the case of the time traveler is not merely coherent but seems to be truly possible.

And consider this. It seems possible that, when God set about to create me, God was able to do just that: create *me,* not just somebody or other.[30] To do this, God didn't need to make use of matter that had previously been mine, for none had. To do this, God didn't need to secure my continuity, for any kind of continuity at all, with something I had previously been continuous with, because I hadn't previously been. And if God could see to it that I—not just somebody or other—came into existence the first time around, what's to preclude God from doing it again, years after my cremation?

IX. Intuitions Opposing Temporal Gaps

One might insist that, questions about criterialism and explanation aside, temporal gaps of the sort implied by resurrection are just plain *impossible.* In response, as noted above, temporal gaps of the relevant sort don't seem obviously impossible or incoherent. The dogmatic insistence on the outright impossibility of such gaps betrays, I think, an exaggerated and overweening confidence in one's modal intuition, in one's ability to peer into the space of possibility with a clear and unfaltering gaze and to see that what seems to be possible, in some sense and to at least some of us, is not really so. Modesty is more becoming.

[30] This presupposes that "essence precedes existence"; for a defense of that claim, see Alvin Plantinga, "On Existentialism," *Philosophical Studies* 44 (1983): 1–20.

And modesty is not preserved by repackaging. Suppose one argued against temporal gaps, starting with the premise that a *metaphysically necessary* condition of a person's persistence is that he or she experiences no temporal gaps. Or suppose one's argument began with the claim that "no gaps" is an *essential* property of each human person. These are just different ways to repackage what is, at bottom, the modal intuition that gaps are impossible. I think that the outright rejection of temporal gaps without any argument, based only on modal intuition, is unjustified.

Persons have essential properties. *Being no taller than oneself* and *possibly being conscious* are two trivial examples. And, necessarily, if one of my essential properties is not exemplified in the future, I will not persist in the future. So a human's essential properties generate necessary conditions for her persistence. Thus the foe of temporal gaps could argue that some of the necessary conditions for a human's persistence preclude gaps. (Once we reject criterialism, this seems to be the only plausible way left to argue against the possibility of temporal gaps and resurrection.)

Yet I don't think this line of argument, even if it avoids merely repackaging the "no gaps" intuition, will show that temporal gaps are impossible. After all, the obvious essential properties of human persons—such as *being no taller than oneself* or *being possibly conscious*—don't preclude gaps. Nor are gaps precluded by those properties which, while less obvious, are nevertheless widely presumed to be essential, properties like *being human* or *being the product of sperm S and egg E*. The essential property candidates that would allegedly threaten temporal gaps are, I suppose, properties that involve persisting by way of certain kinds of material or causal continuity. Whatever these candidate "gap blockers" turn out to be, I think that they will be suggested by our observations of how things in fact last over time.

And I think our observations justify the claim that certain conditions that always accompany our identity over time never span temporal gaps. Our observations might also justify us in holding that these conditions are both nomologically necessary for our persistence and also prevented from jumping gaps by the laws of nature. But it is hard to see what would justify one's asserting that these conditions are both *metaphysically* necessary for our persistence and such that they cannot *possibly* bridge temporal gaps. Perhaps modal intuition justifies it. But, as with the intuition that gaps are impossible, I think the wisest course here is modesty about the limits of modal intuition.

Indeed, perhaps we ought to recommend modesty all the way around. Perhaps I ought to withdraw even my cautious claims supporting the possibility of temporal gaps. Perhaps the most reasonable position is that—although we might have hunches one way or the other—our fairly feeble faculties for discerning what is possible deliver no clear and justified judgments about the possibility of temporal gaps and resurrection. If so, then we are left with the weaker conclusion that, *for all we know,* resurrection of the decayed human person is possible; that, *for all we know,* immortality is possibly available to a physical human being.

That is, we are left with this weaker conclusion if our only insight into this matter comes from modal intuition. But at least some religious believers think we have another source of information. They think that God has promised, by way of special revelation, resurrection of the body, a resurrection that has historically been interpreted—even by dualists—to imply a temporal gap.[31] Others might claim only that Scripture promises immortality, but being physicalists well aware of the facts of death and decay, they will conclude that personal identity across a temporal gap is thereby promised as well.[32] Of course, these believers could concede that modal intuition alone won't allow us to see whether temporal gaps in the life of a person are possible. But they will insist that revelation—not modal intuition—gives a good reason to think such gaps will actually occur, and so, of course, are possible.

It isn't surprising that certain religious beliefs offer support for the physicalist's belief in immortality, a support that would otherwise be lacking. For the belief in immortality is often wed to religious beliefs. But not necessarily, and not even always. Dualists as diverse as Socrates and J. M. E. McTaggart believed in personal immortality, but did not believe it was tied to divine intervention or in need of justification by way of special revelation.[33] And it does appear that dualism has this advantage, regarding immortality, over physicalism: The dualist without religious beliefs can much more reasonably believe in life after death than can the physicalist who is similarly secular. For the dualist can suggest that life after bodily death is a natural result of, say, the simplicity of the soul. Or she can argue

[31] Bynum provides a detailed account of Christian discussions of resurrection from 200 to 1336. Among the theologians she discusses, the nearly universal assumption was that the very body that dies is resurrected; the focus of their debates was not *whether* this will happen, but *how*—given decay, cannibalism, and all the rest—it will happen.

[32] Elsewhere (Trenton Merricks, "The Resurrection of the Body and the Life Everlasting," in *Reason for the Hope Within,* ed. Michael Murray [Grand Rapids, Mich.: Eerdmans Publishing, 1999], section 4) I argue that Christian creeds and Scripture support physicalism itself.

[33] See the *Phaedo*; J. M. E. McTaggart, *Some Dogmas of Religion* (New York: Krause Reprint, 1969); McTaggart, *Studies in Hegelian Cosmology* (New York: Garland Publishing, 1984).

that the belief in the persistence of the soul after the death of the body is justified by empirical evidence such as near-death experiences, séances, or some other such thing. Or she can simply note that since the person—a soul—is one thing, the body another, there is no reason to expect a person's existence to end at bodily death.

But for the physicalist, all hope of an afterlife resides only in the promises of God. For the physicalist believes that the death of her body is the death of her. And subsequent resurrection is surely not justified by any empirical evidence currently available. Moreover, while it might be "natural" for a simple soul to leave its body behind at death, it surely isn't "natural" for a decayed human person to rise again in glorious resurrection. Although resurrection may not be impossible, it will certainly take a miracle.

KEVIN CORCORAN

Physical Persons and Postmortem Survival without Temporal Gaps

There are at least two ways to be a physicalist about human persons. One could, like Eric Olson and Trenton Merricks,[1] believe that human persons are bodies, in the sense of being identical with bodies. Alternatively, one could believe, as I do, that human persons are essentially constituted by their bodies without being identical with the bodies that constitute them.[2]

On either of these *physicalist* accounts of human persons, as I understand them, it is not possible for a human person to continue to exist if that person's body does not continue to exist. Suppose then you are a physicalist of one of these two sorts. Suppose too that you believe that it is not possible for a human body to begin to exist more than once; that is, suppose you believe that once a human body ceases to exist *that* body cannot begin again to exist. Does the combination of these commitments rule out the possibility of physical persons persisting into an afterlife? In this paper I suggest that they do not. I sketch a view of survival that is consistent both with views of human persons according to which persons are physical (either in virtue of being identical with their physical organisms

[1] Olson, *The Human Animal: Personal Identity without Psychology* (Oxford University Press), 1997; Merricks, "A New Objection to Apriori Arguments for Dualism," *American Philosophical Quarterly* 31 (1994): 80–85; Merricks, "How to Live Forever without Saving Your Soul: Physicalism and Immortality," in this volume.

[2] For a constitution account of persons see Lynne Baker's contribution to this volume and her *Persons and Bodies: A Constitution View* (Cambridge: Cambridge University Press, 2000). See also my "Persons, Bodies and the Constitution Relation," *Southern Journal of Philosophy* 37 (1999): 1–20; and "Persons and Bodies," *Faith and Philosophy* 15 (1998): 324–40. My view of persons differs from Baker's insofar as, according to me, a human person is *essentially* human and *essentially* constituted by whatever body does constitute him or her.

or in virtue of being essentially constituted by them) and with the claim that human bodies cannot enjoy temporally gappy existence.

I. The Problem of Persistence

Orthodox Christians believe in the resurrection of the body and the life of the world to come. Such a commitment seems to present orthodox Christians who are also anthropological physicalists with formidable difficulties. For example, if a human person A who existed in 1770 exists in the hereafter, then a physical object numerically identical with A's body exists in the hereafter. But there appear to be good reasons for denying that (say) George Washington's body could exist in the hereafter. For starters, even if his body survived for sometime as a fairly well preserved corpse, chances are it has undergone radical decay over the years and has since passed out of existence. More disturbing, it seems that many bodies do not survive as well-preserved corpses, but are cremated, cannibalized, mutilated, or caused to pass out of existence in some other fashion. And this of course presents us with an apparent puzzle. How can a physical object that exists in the hereafter be numerically identical with a physical object that has either radically decayed or otherwise passed out of existence? It would seem that no human body in the afterlife could possibly be, say, George Washington's body or—to choose a more gruesome example—William Wallace's body.[3]

Though not all orthodox Christian theologians of the past have been anthropological physicalists, many have struggled in systematic ways to make sense out of the Christian doctrine of bodily resurrection in the face of puzzles much like these.[4] Their concern has not been with whether or not it is *possible* for the same numerical body that apparently suffered mutilation or decay to exist in an afterlife, but *how* it does so. It is worth pointing out, in fact, that since most orthodox Christian theologians have been dualists it has been the concern of *dualists* to understand how a body that apparently suffered a martyr's death can be numerically the same as a

[3] William Wallace, the famous liberator of Scotland whose life is dramatized in the film *Braveheart,* is reported to have been torn limb from limb and his entrails put on display in spatially diverse locations throughout Britain. I thank Kelly Clark for bringing this bit of history to my attention.

[4] For fascinating reading on the importance of bodily continuity and numerical sameness in patristic and medieval reflections on the resurrection, see Caroline Walker Bynum's *The Resurrection of the Body in Western Christianity, 200–1336* (New York: Columbia University Press, 1995).

body that enjoys resurrection life. Indeed it is a very recent phenomenon that numerical sameness of body is no longer considered an important feature of the Christian doctrine of resurrection.[5]

II. Resurrection and Reassembly

Historically, the most dominant view of resurrection of the body seems to be resurrection by reassembly.[6] On this view, what happens when God resurrects a human body is that God gathers together all of the smallest bits (the atoms, say) that compose a body at death, reassembles them, and causes them to be propertied and related in exactly the way those atoms were propertied and related at the time of death. The resulting object, it is believed on this view, is the previously existing body. Lest resurrection by reassembly be facilely rejected, it ought to be noted that there are analogies to this view in common experience. When my camera is taken in for repairs, thoroughly dismantled, cleaned, and later reassembled, what we are inclined to say, I think, is that the camera returned to me is numerically the same as the camera I took in for repairs. True, the camera did not persist through its disassembly and cleaning, but its constituent parts did. The camera received after repairs, on this view, is the same as the camera taken in for repairs because it has all the same parts propertied and related in exactly the same way. On the reassembly view of resurrection, so too with human bodies.

There are several objections to the view of resurrection by reassembly. I will mention two. First, suppose your body becomes the tasty hors d'oeuvre of a cannibal and that some of the atoms that once made up your body become part of his or her body. The cannibal, let us suppose,

[5] See, for example, Bruce Reichenbach, *Is Man the Phoenix?* (Grand Rapids, Mich.: Eerdmans, 1978): "The language of resurrection is misleading when it suggests that the very thing which died will be raised again. . . . [This] seem[s] generally contrary to any factual possibility, given the disintegration of bodies upon death and the dispersal of their constituent elements" (181). See also John Hick, *Death and Eternal Life* (San Francisco: Harper and Row, 1976): "A human being is by nature mortal and subject to annihilation at death. But in fact God, by an act of sovereign power, either sometimes or always resurrects or reconstitutes or recreates him—*not however as the identical physical organism that he was before death*" (279; my emphasis). And John Cooper, although he does not come right out and say it, seems to think that the resurrection bodies we human beings will enjoy in the afterlife are not the same numerical bodies we had in our pre-resurrection existence. See his *Body, Soul and Life Everlasting* (Grand Rapids, Mich.: Eerdmans, 1989), 185–95.

[6] See Bynum, *Resurrection of the Body.*

immediately dies. How can God see to it that *both* you *and* the cannibal get reassembled, since now the very atoms in question have two equal claimants? It would seem that God cannot resurrect both of you since some of the atoms that composed your body at death composed the cannibal's body at death, and in order for God to resurrect either of you God must reassemble *all* of the atoms that belonged to your respective bodies at death. So if God reassembles all of the atoms that composed your body at death, then the cannibal must forego resurrection. Likewise, if God reassembles all of the atoms that composed the cannibal's body at death, then you must forego resurrection. But the Christian Scriptures seem pretty clearly to teach, and the Christian church seems pretty clearly to believe, that resurrection is for everyone.[7] So the fact of cannibalism seems to tell against resurrection by reassembly.[8]

There is another problem with the reassembly view of resurrection. Consider once again our camera. I suggested earlier that gathering all of the camera's parts and reassembling them would result in numerically the same camera. But there is a very relevant disanalogy when it comes to the sorts of changes a human body can suffer without loss of identity and the sorts of changes a camera can suffer without loss of identity. For example, suppose you take your camera in for repairs and all or nearly all of the parts of the camera are replaced. Now surely the camera you receive after repairs is not the same as the camera you took in for repairs. The persistence conditions for cameras, we might say, do not tolerate complete or nearly complete part replacement. Such is not the case, however, with human bodies. Human bodies are constantly sloughing off old bits and taking on new ones. In fact the atoms that composed your body twenty years ago are not the same as the atoms that compose your body today.[9] And this presents a serious problem for the reassembly view of resurrection. For imagine that God were to take all of the atoms that composed your body at age ten and reassemble them, placing the living human body that results right next to you. Who has your body, you or the reassembled ten-year-old? The answer, I think, is that you have your body and that the body that results from reassembly is a numerically distinct body. What this seems to show is

[7] The teaching, of course, is that some are resurrected to a life of eternal happiness with God and others to eternal torment in hell. I shall not be interested in pursuing this topic here.

[8] See Bynum's discussion of undigestible bits in her *Resurrection of the Body*, chap. 1.

[9] If you are inclined to object to this comparison on the grounds that the example of the camera was an all-at-once replacement of parts, whereas the replacement of atoms in humans occurs over time, I later offer reasons for thinking that a human being *can* survive (where a camera *cannot*) an all-at-once replacement of parts.

that sameness of bits is not among the persistence conditions for human bodies. In other words, while it is plausible to believe that gathering all of the parts that composed your camera and reassembling them will result in numerically the same camera, such is not the case with human bodies. Gathering and reassembling all the atoms that composed your body at any stage of its past career will not result in numerically the *same* body. And if the defender of resurrection by reassembly insisted that what is required for resurrection are the atoms that compose the body *at death,* then there would seem to be no principled reason for privileging those atoms. Why not the atoms that composed one's body at age seventeen or thirty?

In short, given the fact that human bodies gain and lose bits of stuff throughout their careers without ceasing to exist, and given the fact that there is no principled way to settle on some particular batch of atoms as the atoms necessary for reassembly, I think the right conclusion to draw is that the reassembly view of resurrection ought to be rejected.

I have just given two reasons for rejecting the reassembly view of resurrection. Neither depends on the denial of the claim that human bodies can enjoy spatiotemporally gappy existence. Yet the reassembly view of resurrection does depend on the possibility of intermittent existence, while such a possibility has a long line of distinguished detractors, including, among others, John Locke and, recently, Peter van Inwagen.[10] In fact, it is van Inwagen's commitment to the impossibility of gappy existence that leads him to believe that the only way (conceivable to him at least) for God to resurrect our bodies is to prevent them from falling apart and decaying. And van Inwagen's theologically disturbing speculation is that God engages in a mass bait-and-switch operation at the point of each person's death: God whisks away corpses at the point of death and preserves them in some divine holding area while God simultaneously replaces the stolen corpses with simulacra that rot and pass out of existence in their stead.[11]

[10] Locke, *An Essay concerning Human Understanding,* ed. Peter H. Nidditch (Oxford: Clarendon, 1991), bk. 27, section I.1; Van Inwagen, "The Possibility of Resurrection," in *Immortality,* ed. Paul Edwards (New York: Macmillan, 1992), 242–46.

[11] So for van Inwagen, death is not the passing out of existence of a person since, according to van Inwagen, persons persist through death as corpses. Is death then not the cessation of a person's life? Van Inwagen thinks that a life can cease in two ways. One is for it to be *suspended.* When a life has ceased by being *suspended* the simples that were caught up in it at the moment of cessation retain their individual properties and relations to one another. Another way for a life to cease, however, is for it to be *disrupted.* The life of an organism that has been blown to bits by a bomb, or has undergone the normal processes of biological decay for (say) fifteen minutes, is a life that has been *disrupted.* A life that has ceased in the sense of

Let us suppose van Inwagen is right, at least about the impossibility of gappy existence. How then might persistence into an afterlife go if it doesn't go the way van Inwagen has suggested? Before we can answer that question it is important to get clear on both what a human body is and on what its persistence conditions are.

III. Bodies and Persistence

By the words *human body* I mean, for starters, to pick out that entity usually associated with the words *physical organism of the species Homo sapiens*. Thus understood, what the term *human body* picks out is to be distinguished from the mass of cell-stuff that constitutes it. One but not the other is a mere mass or aggregate. And a mass just is a mereological sum. Therefore, the one but not the other is able to survive material part replacement.

So by *body* I mean to refer to the same kind of object that Locke speaks of when he says that a "living animal is a living organized body"[12] and a "man" "nothing but a participation of the same continued Life by constantly fleeting particles of matter, in succession vitally united to the same organized Body."[13] Now by "Life" I take Locke to have meant an individual biological event of a very special sort, a sort that is remarkably stable, well individuated, self-directing, self-maintaining, and homeodynamic. The Lockean way of capturing what a living animal is finds expression in van Inwagen's description of an organism. Organisms, says van Inwagen, are "things that are composed of

---

being *suspended* can continue if energy is supplied to the simples whose activity has been suspended. Van Inwagen must be committed to the claim then that *human* lives are never disrupted but only cease by being suspended, since he believes that God whisks our corpses away and preserves them until the resurrection, when God, presumably, stimulates the simples back into action. (See van Inwagen's discussion in *Material Beings* [Ithaca: Cornell University Press, 1990], 145–48, and in his "Possibility of Resurrection." Van Inwagen says that he, being fond of oxymorons, likes to refer to an organism whose life has ceased by being suspended as a "living corpse" [*Material Beings,* 147].) In addition to the idiosyncratic nature of van Inwagen's gloss on the *cessation* of life, his view also entails the following highly controversial claim, namely, that consciousness is not an essential property of persons, that a person can exist and be completely lacking in consciousness. In other words, on his view, the very thing that is a person in this world could exist in another world without ever having been a conscious being.

[12] Locke, *Essay concerning Human Understanding,* bk. 27, section 5.

[13] Ibid., section 6.

objects whose activities constitute lives,"[14] where once again by "life" van Inwagen means the special sort of self-directing biological event just mentioned.

This view of physical organisms suggests the following criterion of identity:

> If x and y are physical organisms, then x is identical with y if and only if x and y are constituted by (sets of) physical simples whose activities constitute the same continued life.

This view of human bodies entails that, strictly speaking, human corpses are not human bodies. The activities of the simples constitutive of a corpse are not caught up in a life. Human corpses are merely masses of dead cell-stuff. Thus the phrase "dead body" literally expresses nonsense, just as the phrases "artificial intelligence" and "plastic wood" do. In garden variety discourse, however, we use the phrase "dead body" to successfully refer to heaps of dead cell-stuff.

So much for bodies. What of their conditions for persistence? There are good reasons for denying that spatiotemporal continuity is sufficient for the survival of physical organisms. For it seems possible that an evil genius could totally annihilate a body at, say, t_2 and that God could replace it with a newly created molecular duplicate at precisely the same time, and in precisely the same place as the place occupied by the original body at the time of its annihilation. Time t_2 would thus mark the end of one body's existence and the beginning of a duplicate's existence, while the spatial region originally filled by the annihilated body would come to be wholly filled by a body numerically distinct from it. This seamless replacement of one body with another seems to suggest that spatiotemporal continuity is not sufficient for the persistence of bodies.[15]

If spatiotemporal continuity is not sufficient for the persistence of bodies, is it nevertheless *necessary* for their persistence? Those whose philosophical teeth have been cut on heavy doses of science fiction may think not. They may see nothing worrisome at all in the idea of

[14] Van Inwagen, *Material Beings*, 92.

[15] The idea of "smooth" replicas or "immaculate" replacements can be credited either to Shoemaker "Identity, Properties, and Causality," in *Identity, Cause and Mind* (Cambridge: Cambridge University Press, 1984), 234–60, or David Armstrong, "Identity through Time," in *Time and Cause*, ed. Peter van Inwagen (Dordrecht: D. Reidel, 1980), 67–78.

spatiotemporally discontinuous existence. Consider an occupant of the starship *Enterprise* who enters the transporter. He or she disappears at one time and in one place only to reappear at a later time and in a different place. How are we to describe what happens in such cases? We could say that the person who enters the transporter travels into the future and traverses space, unlike others who may travel into the future to the same place. Others persist into the future one minute at a time and traverse space one meter at a time. Occupants of the starship *Enterprise*, on the other hand, are able, by means of the transporter, to skip over intervening times and places.

But those steeped in science fiction might claim that there is another equally plausible account of the space-time travel of our Trekkie. One could say that she goes out of existence at one time and in one place, only to reemerge at a later time and in a different place. After all, this is how we might plausibly describe the case of the persistence of physical objects of other sorts. Take the camera in our earlier example. Assuming the camera cannot exist as a widely scattered object, it seems plausible to say of the camera that it went out of existence at one time and then came back into existence at another.

Whatever your considered view on the possibility of spatiotemporally discontinuous existence, it is considerations such as these that have led some to maintain that spatiotemporal continuity is normally merely a consequence of persistence and not its ground.[16] What is absent in the simple spatiotemporal continuity criterion of persistence is any mention of the role of *causation*. Yet surely, if the tennis racquet in my hand has persisted into the present, then its existence in the immediate past must be causally relevant to its existence now. So too with human bodies. If the human body sitting across the table from me at 10:00 A.M. is not causally connected with the one across from me at 9:58 A.M., then it is plausible to think that the human body across the table from me at 10:00 A.M. is not a continuation of the body that was there at 9:58 A.M. but rather is a numerically distinct replacement.

Causal considerations, therefore, seem especially pertinent to the giving of persistence conditions for material objects of any sort. Of course the kinds of causal dependencies relating an object at earlier and later stages of its career will very likely differ according to the kind of object whose career we are tracing. Different kinds of persisting thing, in other words, have different persistence conditions. What it is in virtue of which a

[16] See, for example, Armstrong, "Identity through Time," 76.

human body persists is different from what it is in virtue of which a *table* persists. But even so, causal considerations are relevant to the persistence of each.[17]

Peter van Inwagen offers the following principle for the persistence of organisms.

> If the activity of the xs at t_1 constitutes a life, and the activity of the ys at t_2 constitutes a life, then the organism that the xs compose at t_1 is the organism that the ys compose at t_2 if and only if the life constituted by the activity of the xs at t_1 is the life constituted by the activity of the ys at t_2.[18]

It seems certain that the activities of the simples caught up in a life are *causal* activities, given that a life, as we've said, is a self-preserving event. Restating van Inwagen's principle so as to make explicit the causal element involved, and with a view to arriving at a necessary and sufficient condition for the persistence of an organism, we might say:

> If an organism O at t_2 is the same as an organism P that exists at t_1 (where $t_1 < t_2$), then the (set of) simples that compose P at t_1 must be causally related in the life-preserving way to the (set of) simples that compose O at t_2.

Let's call this condition the life-preserving condition, or LPC for short. LPC makes it a requirement on the persistence of an organism that immanent causal relations hold among the different stages of an organism's career.[19] And here we have what I think is both a necessary and sufficient condition for the persistence of a human body.

[17] See Chris Swoyer, "Causation and Identity," *Midwest Studies in Philosophy* 9 (1984): 593–622.

[18] Van Inwagen, *Material Beings*, 145.

[19] Such stages need not be thought of as temporal parts of the persisting organism; like the life lived by an organism, they need only be thought of as events. Thus, following Dean Zimmerman, we can define "temporal stage of an organism" as follows: "*s* is the temporal stage at *t* of an organism $O =^{df}$ there is a set *R* of all the intrinsic properties and internal relations O has at *t*, and s is the event of O's exemplifying *R* at *t*." See Zimmerman, "Immanent Causation," in *Mind, Causation, and the World*, Philosophical Perspectives, no. 11, ed. James Tomberlin (Malden, Mass.: Blackwell, 1997), 435–71; and also his "The Compatibility of Materialism and Survival," *Faith and Philosophy* 16 (1999): 194—212. Zimmerman offers the definition of "temporal-stage" for objects in general; I have taken the liberty to make the relevant substitutions so that the definition applies to organisms in particular.

A human body B that exists at t_2 is the same as a human body A that exists at t_1 just in case the temporal stages leading up to B at t_2 are immanent-causally connected to the temporal stage of A at t_1.[20]

IV. Resurrecting Bodies

It will no doubt be noticed that nothing in the condition for the persistence of bodies just suggested rules out the possibility of intermittent existence. If intermittent existence is possible on this view, however, then it also must be possible for causal relations to cross temporal gaps. Now for all I know such is possible, but for the sake of argument I want to suggest a view of resurrection that does not require that possibility.[21]

Given these metaphysical constraints here is a way resurrection could go. It seems possible that the causal paths traced by the simples caught up in the life of my body just before death can be made by God to fission such that the simples composing my body then are causally related to two different, spatially segregated sets of simples.[22] One of the two sets of simples would immediately cease to constitute a life and come instead to compose a corpse, while the other would either continue to constitute a body in heaven or continue to constitute a body in some intermediate state.[23] In other words, the set of simples along one of the branching paths at the instant after fission fails to perpetuate a life while the other set of simples along the other branch does continue to perpetuate a life. If this is at least possible, as it seems to be, then we have a view of survival compatible with the joint theses that human persons are essentially physical objects and that such objects cannot enjoy gappy existence.

Perhaps a picture will help to make clear the view I have in mind. Let the smaller circles below represent the physical simples propertied and

[20] Immanent causation, then, is supposed to contrast with so-called transeunt causation, in that in the latter the state of one continuant, A, brings about state-changes in a numerically distinct continuant, B. In the former type of causation, however, a state x of thing A brings about a consequent state y in A itself. For more on the notion of immanent causation see Zimmerman, "Immanent Causation." For a definition of "temporal-stage," see the preceding note.

[21] What follows builds on my "Persons and Bodies."

[22] Dean Zimmerman was the first to suggest this view in a paper presented at the 1994 meeting of the Pacific Division of the American Philosophical Association. I take up the view in my "Persons and Bodies," and Zimmerman develops it in exquisite detail in his "Compatibility of Materialism and Survival."

[23] We will assume not only that persons are essentially persons but that being alive or conscious is a necessary condition for human personhood. Therefore, there is after the fissioning only one possible candidate for a person-constituting object, since the surviving corpse is not a living organism and so not capable of subserving consciousness.

related in such a way that they are caught up in the life of my body. Let the larger circles represent the life into which the physical simples are caught up. Let the box represent a corpse. Broken lines will represent causal paths. This view of resurrection might be visually depicted thus:

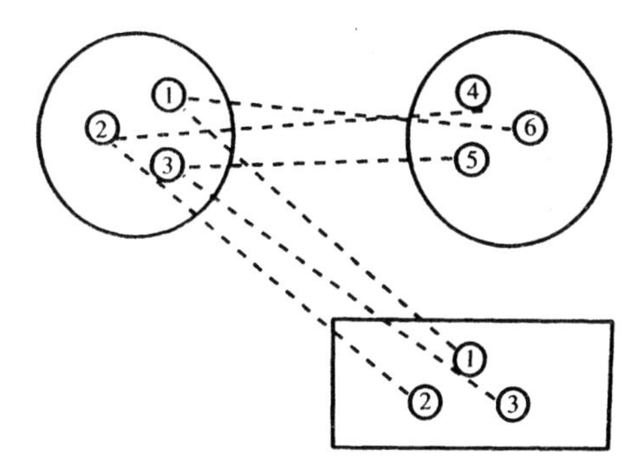

Notice on this view that the stuff left behind in the corpse at death really is the stuff that at one time did constitute me and is no simulacrum.[24] True, none of the simples that survives in the living body is identical with any of the ones left behind, but the life now associated with the simples that survive in the living body is identical to the life once associated with the simples left behind in the corpse—that is, they are immanent-causally connected with them in the relevant way, the life preserving way. Think of the fissioning as an all-at-once, rather than a gradual, sloughing off of the simples.

Several important questions come immediately to mind concerning the view of resurrection by fissioning of causal paths. First, how are we to understand the precise instant of fission, that instant such that at any later instant my body would no longer exist? How can we understand that instant in such a way that the all-at-once sloughing off of the simples is an event in the biography of the surviving body? I can conceive of at least two different ways for doing so.

On the first view, there would be a last temporal instant at which the simples now composing my body and caught up in its life would be so composed and caught up; and that temporal instant would be, simultaneously, the first temporal instant at which a whole new batch of simples come to be so caught up. For a temporal instant I would be constituted by

[24] Actually, on van Inwagen's view as well, the stuff left behind in the corpse really is the stuff that at one time did constitute the person. In fact, on his view, it still constitutes the person. What is not true on his view is that the corpse one grieves over really is the mass of cell-stuff that at one time did constitute the person. What is mourned over, according to van Inwagen, is a simulacrum. The corpse, remember, has been whisked away by God.

more simples than I was an instant earlier or would be an instant later, and the all-at-once sloughing off would be a sloughing off of all the simples that at the instant before wholly composed my body but now only partially compose my body. A picture of this view might be as follows.

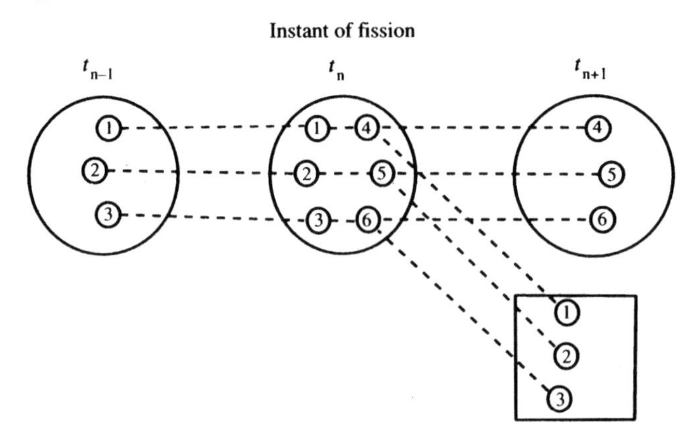

Notice that the sloughing off of the simples does figure in the biography of the surviving life insofar as the simples that wind up in the corpse were an instant earlier caught up in the same life as those that continue to be caught up in a life.

On the second view there would be an instant such that any instant prior to it the simples caught up in the life in question would be just those that came to be so caught up through the ordinary means of continuous, gradual replacement of those originating the life, and such that at any subsequent instant the simples caught up in that life would be a wholly new set of simples and those that get caught up through ordinary means of continuous, gradual replacement.[25] Here's a picture.

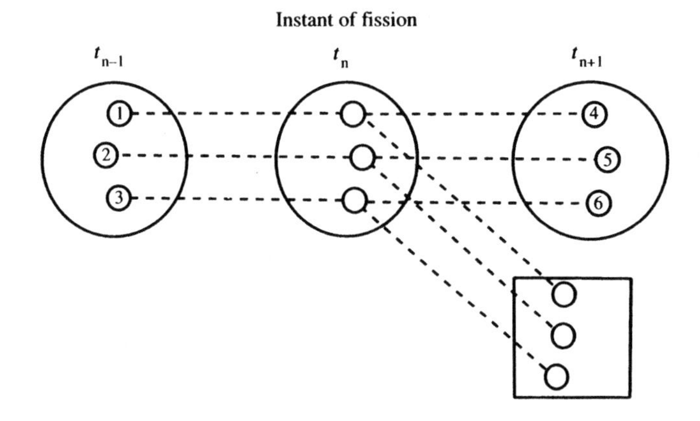

[25] I thank Bill Hasker for bringing this possibility to my attention and also for suggesting the analogy with geometry alluded to later in this section.

This view elicits an obvious question: What simples are caught up in the life of my body at the instant in question? One plausible answer is this: whatever simples compose the corpse at the next instant. It is those simples that are caught up in the life of my body at the instant of fission. But *at* the instant in question can we say what simples constitute its life? I think not. This should not worry us, however. After all, consider the case of the direction of a line at any given point on the line. Assuming the point is the vertex of an angle, there simply is no answer to the question, What is the direction of the line at *that* point? We can say what the direction of the line is before or after the point, but at the point the direction of the line is undefined. Just as this undefinedness creates no special problems in the latter case, neither does it create any special problems in the case under discussion.

These then are two ways things might look at the instant of fission. Of course, there may be other more elegant ways to capture just what happens at that instant. But the really important point is that if human persons are essentially physical objects and it is not possible for such objects to cross temporal gaps, then it is still possible for human persons to survive into an afterlife.

I suppose it could be objected that so far I have been working with a view of time according to which time is composed of discrete instants with very neat boundaries which bump smoothly up against one another. But suppose time is continuous and not discrete. What then? Well I think nothing much follows with respect to the view of resurrection here entertained. I think we must say something very much like this. At any time earlier than t_{n+1} (in the illustration) 1, 2, and 3 are caught up in the life of my body, and really there is no first instant when 4, 5, and 6 come to be caught up in its life. Or we could go the other way and say that 4, 5, and 6 compose my body at any time later than t_n, and really there is no last instant at which 1, 2, and 3 composed it. Either way, on a continuous or discrete view of time, the view of resurrection suggested here can be maintained.

V. The Metaphysical Cost

The view of survival I have been explicating, like most others in the neighborhood, comes with a metaphysical price tag. Part of the cost involves giving up the assumption that material continuity is necessary for the persistence of physical objects. Whereas we may be willing to allow physical organisms in particular to gradually replace some or all of the matter that constitutes them, we may not be willing to allow for an all-at-once replacement like that entailed by the view of resurrection under discussion. Since I believe that what ultimately matters for the persistence of organisms is the perpetuation of a life-preserving causal relation, this is a price I am willing to pay.

It has also been said that a steep price to be paid for this view of survival is that it entails what seems obviously false, namely, that no human being ever dies.[26] I have two points to make in reply. First, this consequence is not unique to my view. On a standard interpretation of Descartes, for example, *people* are immaterial substances, and as such do not die. Now one might say, Yes, but surely *something* dies on the Cartesian view, namely, a person's body. True, but something dies on my view too, namely the cellular tissues my body was once made of. Human beings do not die on the view of survival I have been entertaining, but that's because I am taking a human being to be (or to be essentially constituted by) a body that is distinct from the cell-stuff that constitutes it and am trying to work out a view of persistence into an afterlife that doesn't allow for temporal gaps in that body's existence. To criticize my view on the grounds that, according to it, human beings don't die is just to take issue with my attempt to provide an account of survival that satisfies the desiderata laid down at the beginning of the chapter, namely, that human persons are essentially physical objects and that physical objects cannot enjoy spatiotemporally discontinuous existence. A theist, however, may have reasons for believing each of those claims and metaphysic-independent reasons for believing in the resurrection. Such a theist may indeed be led to countenance such a view as I put forth despite the unusual consequence that, according to it, human beings do not really die.

There is a more serious problem with this view, however. The view seems to be committed to a closest continuer theory of personal identity. For it seems possible that both fission products survive the fission, even if only for an instant. If so, what becomes of their spatiotemporal ancestor? Since one thing cannot be two things, we must say that the original body ceases to exist and two new bodies come into existence, at least for an instant. Yet if one product *had* perished immediately upon fission, then the spatiotemporal ancestor would have persisted. But doesn't the mere possibility of an equal claimant to identity tell against the persistence of an organism insofar as it renders identity contingent?[27]

[26] Bill Hasker raised this objection.

[27] I set my self up for this problem in "Persons and Bodies" by claiming that after fission both fission products do *in fact* constitute lives, even if only for an instant. In the present paper I recant that claim and present the view in such a way that at no time do both fission

If Dean Zimmerman is correct, the possibility of fission is a problem for any physicalist who is also an endurantist. Says Zimmerman: "I am convinced that *any* materialism concerning human beings that eschews temporal parts can be driven in similar fashion toward a closest continuer account of human persistence conditions."[28]

If one is both a physicalist and an endurantist, and if Zimmerman is right, then I suppose one could bite the proverbial bullet and accept a closest continuer theory of personal identity. But I think Zimmerman is mistaken. For starters, if one is not only a physicalist and endurantist but also a theist (and theism is true), then one might quite plausibly appeal to God's ultimately good purposes for God's human creatures as a reason for believing that God would never allow both fission products to compose a life, even if only for an instant. Not only does the theist have a plausible reason for believing that God would never allow such a state of affairs, but the theist has plausible reasons for believing that God *could not* allow such a state of affairs. Here's why. If God is a necessary being and essentially wills the good for God's human creatures, then there is no world populated with human creatures at which God would will for their ultimate demise. But assuming temporally discontinuous existence is not possible, a doubly successful fission would forever terminate a human life. Therefore, it is plausible for the theist to believe that there is no world where each fission product composes a life. And this provides the theist who is both a physicalist and an endurantist with a reason to believe that it is *impossible* for both fission products to compose a life, even if only for an instant.[29]

Still, it might seem that invoking God's ultimately good intentions for God's human creatures under the specter of fission is simply ad hoc. Appealing to God's good intentions strikes me as no more ad hoc here than with respect to the doctrine of resurrection itself. For it seems that the doctrine of resurrection gets its theological purchase on the ultimately good

---

products constitute lives. Bill Hasker, however, believes my view is still open to criticism, since even if in fact both products do not constitute lives, they could. He raises this objection in his *Emergent Self*, chap. 8.

[28] See Zimmerman, "Compatibility of Materialism and Survival," 201.

[29] Ted Warfield and Steve Davis have wondered whether the argument just presented doesn't make resurrection necessary and unmiraculous; after all, on the view presented, God *cannot* allow for the ultimate demise of a human being. I am inclined to think that God's disallowance of ultimate demise makes resurrection no less miraculous. Suppose, for example, that God *had* to create. Is it clear that God's having to create would render creation any less miraculous? I don't see how.

intentions God has for God's human creatures. And it is plausible to believe that these intentions are not arbitrary but rather flow out of a stable disposition that is essential to God. So it seems to me that the appeal to God's ultimately good intentions for God's human creatures is no more ad hoc in this context than it is in the context of explicating the doctrine of the resurrection itself.

It might be argued, however, that the real problem with closest continuer theories is not that they are illogical but that they seem to violate a plausible principle of persistence, namely, what Harold Noonan calls the "only *x* and *y*" principle, that is, the claim that whether or not some objects *x* and *y* compose some concrete individual F should have nothing to do with events involving numerically distinct objects that are spatiotemporally segregated from F. This is what is at the heart of Zimmerman's charge. And this much seems right: whether or not the simples composing me compose *me*, and not some other thing, should have nothing to do with events occurring outside of the spatiotemporal path occupied by me. And this also seems to conflict with the materialist view of resurrection presented. However, I am not so sure that it does or has to. Since I believe that immanent causal connections are what secure identity across time for material objects, it must be the case (assuming the "only *x* and *y* principle" is true) that there is something in the nature of immanent causal connections that make cases of fission such that the immanent causal relation goes one way, the other, or neither. In other words, there must be something in the nature of immanent causal connections that prevents the relation from ever going both ways. I frankly admit that I cannot say what ingredient in immanent causation accounts for this. But neither have I claimed that a completely informative account of the relation is available. Perhaps the relation itself, or at the very least some ingredient in it, must be treated as primitive. It is that ingredient that accounts for the failure of both fission products ever to be immanent-causally connected to their spatiotemporal ancestor.[30] So far as I can see, this is all that is needed to avoid a closer continuer theory of personal identity.

My aim in this chapter has not been so much to defend a particular view of resurrection as to sketch a view that I believe is coherent and compatible with a materialist view of human persons. It might, for all I know, turn out to be true. If it should turn out that gappy existence is a

[30] I thank Trenton Merricks for suggesting this line of defense against closest continuer worries.

real possibility, then, on the view I have suggested, it must be possible for immanent-causal connections to cross those gaps. However things might turn out on that score, this much at least seems certain: If you and I should turn out to be wholly physical objects, nothing contained in any of the ecumenical creeds needs to be denied. We may still confess, with orthodox Christian believers the world over, *I believe in the resurrection of the body and the life of the world to come.*

JOHN COOPER

Biblical Anthropology and the Body-Soul Problem

The basic reason why most thinkers during the Christian centuries of our history embraced dualistic anthropology is probably less philosophical than religious and theological. They believed that the human soul or self can exist apart from the physical organism, not primarily because of proofs of the soul's immortality, but because the church taught this as biblical doctrine. Death temporarily separates soul and body until their reunification at the final resurrection.

In more recent times body-soul dualism has fallen out of fashion among philosophers, scientists, and the intellectual community in general. Many Christians are among those who have turned against it. They have not simply rejected Christian doctrine in favor of modern thought, however. They have reread the Bible and concluded that it has been misinterpreted by traditional Christianity. Theologians now claim that the traditional body-soul distinction is not really found in the Bible. Hebraic anthropology is actually monistic and holistic. Historians of doctrine explain the discrepancy by pointing to the influence of Greek dualism on the formation of the Christian doctrine of humanity. In view of these developments modern Christians do not feel that they have abandoned scriptural teaching in favor of contemporary antidualistic sentiments regarding the structure of human nature. In fact they find them nicely compatible.

Of course this move also obligates these Christians to abandon the traditional doctrine of the afterlife, which assumes a dualistic anthropology of some sort. The major alternative proposals are an immediate resurrection or a period of nonexistence between death and resurrection.

This chapter surveys the biblical representation of the body-soul relation in the light of its teaching about the afterlife. I defend traditional eschatology and anthropology while admitting that some of their formulations are overly Platonistic. I summarize a case for the claim that the best reading of Scripture still yields the teaching that human persons continue to exist, probably consciously, between death and the final resurrection.[1] This doctrine in turn entails that humans are so constituted that they can exist temporarily without physical organisms. Though expressed in a variety of nonphilosophical ways, this anthropology is consistently found in Scripture and its sources. I close by raising issues concerning the relevance of this conclusion for Christians who reflect on the body-soul or mind-body problem.

I. The Old Testament

Much of the theological case against traditional dualism is based on appeal to Old Testament or Hebrew anthropology. First it is charged that the Hebrew words for "body," "soul," and "spirit" simply do not have the Platonic meanings which Christian orthodoxy has ascribed to them. Then it is claimed that Hebrew anthropology is so thoroughly holistic or monistic that the separation of the soul and body would have been inconceivable.

There is some truth to the charge that Platonism has been read into Hebrew anthropological terms.[2] *Nephesh* and *ruach,* often translated "soul" and "spirit" respectively, have a variety of meanings—some organic, some psychological. Both may sometimes be translated as "person," "self," or by personal pronouns. But it is doubtful that either term is ever used in the Old Testament to mean an immaterial personal entity which survives death.

Further, instead of systematically categorizing and separating organic and psychological terms and functions, the Old Testament interchanges them. Just as *nephesh* and *ruach* have biological meanings, physiological terms such as "heart," "kidneys," and "bowels" can have psychological-personal

[1] I have made the case more fully in *Body, Soul and Life Everlasting: Biblical Anthropology and the Monism-Dualism Debate* (Grand Rapids, Mich.: Eerdmans, 2000).

[2] Excellent presentations of Hebrew anthropology are found in Walter Eichrodt, *Theology of the Old Testament*, vol. 2 (Philadelphia: Westminster, 1967), chap. 16, section 2; and Hans Walter Wolff, *Anthropology of the Old Testament* (Philadelphia: Fortress, 1974), chaps. 2–7.

meanings. The organs are the seat of desires, beliefs, and mental acts. In addition, synecdoche—the use of part terms to refer to a whole—is a common Hebrew figure of speech. The cumulative picture that emerges from all the above is not Platonic dualism. Rather it is an example of the undifferentiated psychosomatic anthropology common in the ancient Near East and among tribal peoples worldwide—holistic in the sense that the mental and physical are viewed as integrated and interdependent.

There are two reasons why Hebrew anthropology cannot be construed as pre-philosophical monism, however. The first has to do with the composition of a living human; the second with the human condition after death.

The children of Israel were no more monists than they were Platonists. For a human being is created when God conjoins two ingredients: the dust of the earth and the breath of life (*ruach* or *neshama*). The breath of life is the vital force and not a Platonic substantial soul; but it is clearly distinct from the dust in nature and origin. The human body is formed from the earth; but it does not live or function humanly until God adds *ruach* or *neshama* from the outside.[3] It is exceedingly difficult to see how this picture of dual-ingredient composition can be interpreted as a figurative, nontheoretical form of monism or materialism. It is somewhat more suggestive of a soft dualism such as Aristotelian hylomorphism.

The most compelling reason against conceding Old Testament anthropology to the monists is its picture of the afterlife. Just as the Israelite view of human life was similar to their neighbors' psychophysical holism, the Israelite view of death exemplifies a typical ancient Near Eastern form of animism. Death is not the end of existence. It is rather the entrance of the individual as a ghost—an ethereal quasi-bodily being, not a Platonic soul or Cartesian mind—into the dreary and lethargic, if not soporific, existence of the underworld, *Sheol, Abaddon,* or in the Septuagint, *Hades.*[4]

Surprising as it may seem in view of the currently popular mythology about Hebrew monism, this personal eschatology and the anthropology it involves are virtually undisputed among Old Testament scholars. Details about degrees of consciousness and activity are unclear. But there is little doubt that the Israelites believed in the actual existence of the dead.[5] Talk

[3] In Genesis 2.7 God breathes *neshema* into the humanly formed dust and a *nephesh chayah* (living being) results. In Ezekiel 37:10 *ruach* quickens the bodies formed from dry bones.

[4] Cooper, *Body, Soul and Life Everlasting,* chap. 3; Eichrodt, *Theology of the Old Testament,* 210–14; Nicholas Tromp, *Primitive Conceptions of Death and the Nether World in the Old Testament* (Rome: Pontifical Biblical Institute, 1969), pt. 2.

[5] Wolff, *Anthropology of the Old Testament,* 102–9; Otto Kaiser and Edward Lohse, *Death and Life* (Nashville, Tenn.: Abingdon, 1981), 34.

of *Sheol* is not merely a poetic way of speaking about extinction. The return of Samuel at Endor, though unusual, is perfectly possible in the Hebrew scheme of things. Animism such as this, though holistic with respect to life, must be considered a nonphilosophical form of dualistic anthropology. The ghost separates from flesh and bones.

The dead were typically referred to not by *nephesh* or *ruach* but by another term—*rephaim*. How are these terms related? It is clear that *ruach* (spirit, the vital power) departs at death, taken by God. But it is debated whether the individual in Sheol is still *nephesh* or what is left of the *nephesh* after it dies. If the former, then the Hebrews did use the word "soul" for those physical bodies, as tradition always claimed. In either case, individuals exist beyond death without flesh and bones.

Existence in *Sheol* is not ultimate, at least not for God's faithful. While some Psalms (for example Ps. 23, 49, 73) merely trust God for an unspecified salvation from *Sheol,* Isaiah 26:19 clearly promises that the *rephaim* will undergo bodily resurrection when God restores his kingdom.[6] For the first time, late in the Old Testament, we have the notion of an intermediate state—the *rephaim* in *Sheol*—between death and future resurrection.

II. Intertestamental Judaism

Jewish beliefs about life and death developed in several directions between the Old and New Testaments.[7] One line, found in Ben Sirach and the Sadducees, considers *Sheol* terminal. Another strand adopts Greek dualism and, like Plato, affirms an afterlife of everlasting disembodiment. In the main, however, Judaism followed the line of Isaiah and elaborated an eschatology which involves temporary separation from fleshly existence until the final resurrection. This is especially true in Palestinian Judaism, including the Pharisees and Rabbis, the background of Jesus and Paul.

Whatever the meanings of *nephesh* and *ruach* in the Old Testament, both terms and their Greek translations, *psyche* and *pneuma,* are now regularly used to refer to the discarnate dead awaiting resurrection, often consciously.[8] This practice is far wider than Hellenistic Judaism and flows

[6] Wolff, *Anthropology of the Old Testament,* 109–10. Cf. Ps. 16:10, 49:15, 73:26.

[7] Cooper, *Body, Soul and Life Everlasting,* chap. 4. H. C. C. Cavallin, *Life after Death: Paul's Argument for the Resurrection of the Dead in I Corinthians 15,* pt. 1, *An Inquiry into the Jewish Background* (Lund: Gleerup, 1974); George Nicklesburg, Jr., *Resurrection, Immortality, and Eternal Life in Intertestamental Judaism* (Cambridge: Harvard University Press, 1972); D. S. Russell, *Between the Testaments* (Philadelphia: Fortress, 1965), chap. 7.

[8] I En. 22 and II Esd. 7; cf. Cooper, *Body, Soul and Life Everlasting,* 89–94.

naturally from Old Testament anthropology. It is not necessarily a Greek import.[9]

It is interesting to note that the dead are sometimes said to be sleeping even when they are conscious during the intermediate state.[10] "Sleep" in reference to death, then, is not necessarily a euphemism for nonexistence or unconscious existence. Rather, it can suggest the bodily inactivity and dreamlike quality of consciousness during the intermediate state.

Most Jewish believers affirmed the resurrection of the body, but not all in the same way. For some it was the perfect restoration of the earthly body to its original nature. Others understood resurrection as the transformation of the natural body into a glorified body. Still others viewed it as the translation of the physically resurrected person into a mode of spiritual existence appropriate for dwelling in heaven. Crucial to notice is the fact that all these versions of resurrection presuppose the dichotomy of soul and body at death.[11]

The point of this survey of intertestamental accounts of the afterlife is to provide background for understanding the New Testament. It is fairly well established that the Pharisees and Rabbis, who debated with Jesus and educated Paul, embraced an intermediate state-final resurrection eschatology and the body-soul distinction which comes with it.[12] This is important in evaluating the philosophical debates over the anthropological texts of the New Testament.

III. The New Testament

The fact that Judaism and the New Testament continue to use many Old Testament anthropological terms and their meanings makes it difficult to settle the monism-dualism debate by general word studies. *Soma, sarx, kardia, nous, psyche,* and *pneuma* are used in various ways—sometimes in contrast, sometimes paired as synonyms, sometimes in synecdoche.

[9] Cf. Kaiser and Lohse, *Death and Life*: "it must be maintained that the conception of the intermediate state after death could develop organically on the basis of the Old Testament beliefs about death and the soul, whatever outside influences may have contributed to this development" (41); also 86–91.

[10] For example, I En. 100:5 with 102:4–5; II Esd. 7:32 with 78–80; II Bar. 36:11.

[11] Cooper, *Body, Soul and Life Everlasting,* 86–89.

[12] Lester Whitelock, "Pharisaic Ideas of Judgement, Resurrection, and the World to Come," in *The Development of Jewish Religious Thought in the Intertestamental Period* (New York: Vantage, 1976), 99–116.

Systematic conclusions are elusive. It is only in connection with death and the afterlife that the matter begins to clarify.

Three main types of personal eschatology compete for legitimation by the New Testament.[13] One is the intermediate state-final resurrection view of traditional orthodoxy. Another proposes an immediate resurrection. The third is the extinction-recreation view, which holds that persons cease to exist at death and are recreated at the resurrection. Of course it is possible that more than one view is found in the New Testament. But let's see how the survey turns out.

I shall argue that the intermediate state is the only definitely attested position. First, it is consistent with every relevant text, whereas both the immediate resurrection and extinction-recreation views conflict with some texts. Second, there is substantial positive evidence that New Testament writers embraced an intermediate state, whereas there is no such evidence favoring either of the other positions.

Let us first consider the problems afflicting the alternatives to the intermediate state. The major difficulty for the immediate resurrection theory is the fact that the New Testament repeatedly portrays the resurrection as a general future event which will occur at the return of Christ, not for each person at his or her death. This is so in the Gospels, for example in Luke, where the resurrection is "in the age to come" (20:35), and John where it is to occur "on the last day" (11:24).[14] Likewise in Revelation 20. Even more interesting are the writings of Paul, since II Corinthians 5:1–10 is the main appeal of the immediate resurrectionist.[15] I Thessalonians 4:16 and I Corinthians 15:52 unquestionably correlate the resurrection with the return of Christ's return. All the books which chronologically surround II Corinthians seem to teach a general future resurrection. A final consideration is the resurrection of Jesus himself, which occurred on the third day, not at the instant of his death. The major problem with the immediate resurrection theory, then, is that it must explain away the consistent New Testament witness that the resurrection is general event which will occur at the return of Christ.

The extinction-recreation theory founders on those texts which imply the continuing existence of the dead. As we saw, neither the Old Testament nor

[13] Cooper, *Body, Soul and Life Everlasting,* 116–19.

[14] Theologians can of course interpret these phrases to be consistent with several eschatologies. But most biblical scholars take the Gospel writers as placing salvation history on the same time line as general history. See, for example, A. J. Mattill, Jr., *Luke and the Last Things* (Dillsboro, N.C.: Western North Carolina, 1979).

[15]Cf. Murray Harris, *Raised Immortal: Resurrection and Immortality in the New Testament* (Grand Rapids, Mich.: Eerdmans, 1985), 98–101.

intertestamental Judaism affirms that the departed are nonexistent. Jesus' assertion against the Sadducees that the patriarchs "are alive to God" (Luke 20:38) and the availability of Moses and Elijah for this transfiguration do not suggest their extinction. In II Corinthians 5:6–10 and Philippians 1:20–24 Paul distinguishes between being "in the body" or "in the flesh" and "away from the body" "with Christ." Both options require his existence.

The only way extinction-recreationists can reconcile their theory with these texts (and others to be considered below) is to postulate that they express the viewpoint of first-person consciousness, not actual existence.[16] Because the departed are unaware of the existential gap between death and resurrection, the New Testament speaks as though there were unbroken continuity. The main difficulty here is that there is silence rather than positive evidence in the New Testament and its historical context to support this hypothesis.

A word about sleep metaphors is also in order. Extinctionists take the "sleep" of death as a euphemism for nonexistence. However, it could just as well be read, as Cullmann does, to imply that souls exist but are unconscious.[17] And we have mentioned instances where "sleep" refers to conscious, perhaps dreamlike existence during the intermediate state. The point is that allusions to death as "sleep" are no special support to the extinction-recreation theory.

Thus we see that both the immediate resurrection and extinction-recreation eschatologies are in prima facie conflict with significant New Testament data. How does the traditional view fare in comparison? First, it does not suffer from a prima facie conflict with any New Testament text. Second, the very data that trouble the other theories can in fact be used to generate a deduction of the intermediate state, which follows from the present existence and future resurrection of the dead. But third, there are several texts which provide positive support for the intermediate state and a dualistic anthropology. These positions are not merely argued from silence or inferred from data that do not explicitly contradict them.

Consider the following apparently dualistic texts. Most familiar is Matthew 10:28, where Jesus warns that although humans cannot kill the souls when they kill the body, God can destroy both in *Gehenna*. This is not the language of the Old Testament, for there to kill the body is to kill

[16] Cf. Bruce Reichenbach, *Is Man the Phoenix? A Study of Immortality* (Lanham, Md.: University Press of America, 1983), 185.

[17] Oscar Cullmann, "Immortality of the Soul or Resurrection of the Dead?" in *Immortality and Resurrection*, ed. K. Stendahl (New York: Macmillan, 1965), 57.

the *nephesh*. This statement reflects contemporary Jewish usage, which is demonstrably dualistic regarding *psyche* in connection with death and *Gehenna*.[18]

Consider also Luke 24:37–39, Jesus' appearance to his disciples on Easter. When he stood among them they were startled, supposing they saw a ghost or spirit (*pneuma*). But Jesus pointed out that spirits do not have flesh and bones as he had. It seems impossible to construe this exchange as anything but animistic dualism. This may also shed light on the meaning of Jesus giving up his "spirit" at his death (Luke 23:46). A third dualistic text is Paul's mystical experience in II Corinthians 12:2–4. Like Enoch in Jewish tradition, he was taken up into Paradise in the third heaven. But he is unsure whether, like Enoch, this was in the body or apart from the body. Both were thought possible in contemporary Judaism.[19] The mere fact that Paul entertains the dualistic possibility undermines the claim that he is a monist, if it does not prove his dualism.

Another dualistic text is Hebrews 12:23, where the spirits (*pneumata*) of just people made perfect are presently located in the heavenly Jerusalem with God and the angels. Since Hebrews 6:2 and 11:35 mention the resurrection, this appears to be the intermediate state.

Similar to other Jewish apocalyptic texts, Revelation envisions the souls (*psychai*) of the martyrs (6:9) and a great multitude of saints in heaven before the final resurrection (20:4–5). Whatever the doctrinal yield of this book for the church, an intermediate state is part of the vision given John by the Spirit on the Lord's day.

The parable of Dives and Lazarus (Luke 16:19–31) also clearly portrays how pious Jews imagined the intermediate state.[20] It parallels the scenario of Hades in I Enoch 22, including the great divide and the thirst of the damned. But it is a parable whose point is the love of money. Thus it illustrates eschatology but does not necessarily teach it.

How weighty is Jesus' promise that the repentant thief would be with him in Paradise that day (Luke 23:43)? The most obvious interpretation of this saying is still the one favored by most scholars.[21] And it is clear that Luke means for his readers to receive Jesus' promise for themselves as

[18] Cooper, *Body, Soul and Life Everlasting*, 129–31.

[19] C. K. Barret, *Commentary on II Corinthians* (San Francisco: Harper and Row, 1973), 308–9; F. F. Bruce, *I and II Corinthians* (London: Oliphants, 1971), 247.

[20] I. Howard Marshall, *Commentary on Luke* (Grand Rapids, Mich.: Eerdmans, 1978), 632–39.

[21] Cooper, *Body, Soul and Life Everlasting*, 139–41; Marshall, *Commentary on Luke*, 870–73.

well. This is doctrine. Jesus was neither extinct nor raised immediately. He was temporarily in Paradise in the realm of the dead.

Most hotly debated are the Pauline texts. It must be admitted that there is no knockdown proof text for the intermediate state in Paul. But it is the only option consistent with all his pronouncements. Texts which affirm a future resurrection rule out immediate resurrection but may be consistent with extinction-recreation. I Thessalonians 4, I Corinthians 15, Romans 8, and Galatians 3 are examples here. Texts which assert continuing existence squeeze out extinction-recreation but may leave room for immediate resurrection. II Corinthians 5, Philippians 1, and Romans 8:38–39 are cases in point. Continuing existence between death and future resurrection is the only major option compatible with all these texts. Interestingly, Paul's mode of expression does not contrast soul and body, but typically distinguishes himself and his body: "I" and "the body" or "my body."[22]

An important biographical factor must not be overlooked in interpreting Paul. He had been a Pharisee, educated by Gamaliel, the grandson of Hillel. The evidence is consistent that the Pharisees embraced a dualistic anthropology and affirmed an intermediate state between death and the resurrection at the Messiah's coming. In Acts 23:6–9 Paul explicitly aligns himself with the eschatology of the Pharisees against the Sadducees. As Luke explains, the Sadducees denied the resurrection as well as angels and spirits (*pneumata*), but the Pharisees affirmed them all. The events of Acts 23 took place after most of the relevant epistles were written, indicating that Paul's views on this matter had not changed since his youth.

Since the intermediate state-resurrection eschatology is the only option consistent with all the Pauline texts and well supported by their historical background, it is clearly the best reading. The same is true for the non-Pauline books. The New Testament does not present us with several incompatible views, but Christianizes the personal eschatology and holistic yet dualistic anthropology of first-century Judaism. Traditional orthodoxy, though sometimes too Platonistic, was on track all along.

IV. Biblical Anthropology and Christian Philosophy

How Christian philosophers appropriate this conclusion, assuming it is correct, will depend on our view of the reason-revelation issues and our biblical hermeneutics.

[22] II Cor. 5, 12; Phil. 1.

Regarding reason and revelation, some Christian philosophers believe that philosophy should be based on reason alone, using revelation where possible to evaluate how close it can get to the truth. Other Christian philosophers hold that truths of Scripture may or must be included within philosophical reflection. But all Christian philosophers confess the authority and truth of Scripture, desiring their philosophical theories of human nature to be in harmony with it. In one way or another, biblical anthropology is normative for all Christian philosophers.

This does not yet settle the body-soul question for Christian philosophers, however. Hermeneutical questions entangled in the reason-revelation problematics remain. For it is possible to recognize, as Bultmann does, the anthropological and eschatological teachings of the New Testament writers but deny that they are binding on modern Christians without proper philosophical reconstrual. The abiding truth of revelation can be identified only when what conflicts with science and the modern worldview is interpreted away. In that case the specific teachings of Jesus and Paul as such are not necessarily obligatory today. Someone might feel rationally convinced of a materialist ontology, for example, and thus would accept as the biblical teaching of anthropology and eschatology only what can be harmonized with materialism. How the Bible is normative in the modern world is thus a crucial issue.

But suppose Christian philosophers ought to believe the teachings of Scripture without major reprocessing. It must still be determined what precisely is being taught. If biblical doctrine includes specifics of anthropology, then Christian philosophers must seek to develop a view of human nature which philosophically comports with what Scripture means by "soul," "spirit," "heart," "mind," "life-breath," "flesh," and "body." If a more general picture of human nature is being taught, then the nontheoretical, holistic dualism of the biblical writers ought to function as a starting point or evaluative framework for the theories of human nature.

Suppose, however, that through the Bible the Holy Spirit intends to teach an intermediate state-resurrection, whereas the anthropological specifics are only the culturally relative means of expression. In that case Christian thinkers would have the freedom to adopt any philosophically tenable anthropology or mind-body theory which allows for an intermediate state. What is required is an account of persons as entities distinct enough from their bodies that God can maintain them in existence without their bodies. Various forms of dualism would obviously qualify—Augustinian, Thomistic, Cartesian, and perhaps Kantian, for example. But other metaphysical traditions might offer candidates as well. An idealist who held that the human body is a temporary manifestation of mind or spirit could account for disembodied personal experience. A materialist who claimed that the mind or even the person emerges from the physical organism as a distinct entity could likewise envision an intermediate state. And John Cobb has argued that Whitehead's process philosophy allows for personal existence after death. Perhaps a new approach will be discovered.

Although not all these philosophies are dualistic in the sense of positing two basic kinds of substance or principle, all are dualistic in that they distinguish person and bodily organism strongly enough to allow for the person, sustained by God, to survive their dichotomy at death. Since I am convinced that biblical doctrine remains normative and that Scripture teaches the intermediate state, I believe Christian theories of the human constitution must be dualistic at least in this general sense. And I prefer those which take seriously the entire biblical depiction of human nature.

STEPHEN T. DAVIS

Physicalism and Resurrection

A research program of certain contemporary Christian philosophers holds that a physicalist or materialist view of human beings is compatible with Christian theology and especially with Christian belief in the general resurrection. I once would have considered myself a participant in this research program, but no longer do so.[1] My problem is not the fit of physicalism—in at least some of its permutations—with Christian claims about resurrection. I continue to believe that the two can be consistent. My problem is physicalism itself. There is no doubt that this theory is the dominant position on the mind-body problem among contemporary philosophers. But my own view is that on purely philosophical grounds, physicalism is untenable.

This is not the occasion to explore the relevant difficulties;[2] suffice it to say that for me the most intractable problem is the area of consciousness, especially in explaining what it is like to have conscious experiences like being in pain or seeing the color blue or experiencing the taste of an orange. Philosophers use the term *qualia* for the felt, subjectively experienced character of experiences. It seems to me about as clear as anything could possibly be that people experience things like pain and blue and the

I thank Kevin Corcoran, William Hasker, Amy Kind, and Trenton Merricks for their helpful comments on an earlier draft of this essay.

[1] See my *Risen Indeed: Making Sense of the Resurrection* (Grand Rapids, Mich.: Eerdmans, 1993), xi, 85–146.

[2] They are spelled out with clarity in Richard Swinburne, *The Evolution of the Soul* (Oxford: Clarendon, 1986), 21–61. See also Lynne Rudder Baker, *Saving Belief* (Princeton: Princeton University Press, 1987).

taste of an orange, that qualia exist, and that accordingly there is in each case something it is like to have these experiences. But despite the heroic and unceasing efforts of physicalists, I do not see how the existence of qualia can be consistent with physicalism. Physicalists typically either argue that qualia do not exist at all[3] or else that they do exist but are physical (in this case, high-level neural) facts.[4] I am not able to explain why here, but I find none of these approaches convincing. That is why I am no longer a participant in the research program. I flirted for a time with functionalism, but qualia seem to constitute a problem for that theory as well; it seems clear to me that two mental states could be functionally identical and yet differ qualitatively. Property dualism provided a temporary stopping place, but (again for reasons I cannot explore here) I found this theory unsatisfactory too. I decided several years ago simply to swallow hard and call myself a substance dualist.[5]

But I am still interested in the research program and wish to comment on some relevant issues. If the question is whether physicalism as a theory in the metaphysics of substance can be consistent with Christian teachings about resurrection, I hold that the answer is yes. There are two distinct ways of understanding the general resurrection that might seem promising to physicalists. The first we can call *temporary nonexistence* and the second *immediate resurrection.*

Temporary nonexistence (sometimes misleadingly called "soul sleep")[6] says that at the point of death people (who on physicalism are identical to or at least are essentially constituted by their bodies) simply cease existing. Then, later, on the day of the general resurrection, God reassembles the bodily particles, revivifies the body, and thus reconstitutes the person. There are biblical texts that with some stretching can be interpreted as supporting this theory, but temporary nonexistence has almost always

[3] See, for example, Daniel C. Dennett, *Consciousness Explained* (Boston: Little, Brown, 1991), 372.

[4] See, for example, John Searle, *The Rediscovery of Mind* (Cambridge: MIT Press, 1992), and *The Mystery of Consciousness* (New York: New York Review of Books, 1997).

[5] I do not deny this: if it is difficult to see how a physical thing could be conscious, it is equally difficult to see how a nonphysical thing like a soul or immaterial mind could be conscious. Consciousness is a deep mystery. But the point is that I would claim to know on other grounds that at least one nonphysical object is conscious, viz., God. I also know that *I* am conscious, but I do *not* know that I am an entirely physical thing.

[6] The term is inaccurate several times over. The soul as the immaterial essence of the person plays no necessary role in the theory. The person does not sleep during the interim period; rather, the person simply doesn't exist. And "sleep"—essentially a bodily activity—is a misleading metaphor in any case.

been a minority teaching in Christian thought. Very few mainstream theologians or authoritative creeds have embraced it. But another, purely philosophical, difficulty plagues the theory as well: the presence of the temporal gap makes the problem of personal identity particularly difficult. On what basis can the two temporally separate persons be identified as two episodes in the life of one and the same person?

Immediate resurrection might then appeal. On this theory, people (who again on physicalism are identical to or are essentially constituted by their bodies) live and then die, but at the moment of death God raises the body and reconstitutes the person. Since there is no temporal gap to be dealt with, at first glance the problem of personal identity will seem less intractable. However, the continuing presence of the corpse (in the grave or in the form of ashes) presents a new problem, at least on some ways of understanding what I will call below the physics of immediate resurrection. If physicalism is true, then Jones is identical to or is essentially constituted by Jones's body; but when Jones dies, it then seems that Jones is simply Jones's corpse, and so any new Jones-like body that God might create will be (not Jones but) a duplicate. (We might be less inclined to insist on this point if corpses always simply disappeared at death, but they don't.) Furthermore, a biblical difficulty exists: although there are a few texts that can be interpreted as supporting immediate resurrection (e.g., Luke 23:43; II Cor. 5:1–10), the preponderance of New Testament testimony is that the general resurrection occurs in the future, at the eschaton.

What about the physics of immediate resurrection? There are at least three ways in which the event might occur. (1) At the point of death, God takes the simples of which one's body consists (let's say atoms) to the afterlife in the form of a resurrected heavenly body; simultaneously, God creates a simulacrum out of new atoms which then constitutes the corpse.[7] (2) At the point of death, God brings it about that the causal path traced by the atoms (or other simples) of one's body split into two qualitatively equal paths, one of which is then used by God to constitute the resurrection body in the afterlife and the other of which is used to constitute the corpse. (3) At the point of death, God reconstitutes the person out of atoms that were not previously parts of one's body; perhaps they were in the vicinity of one's body at death; and they exist as they do because they are immanently causally connected to the atoms of the premortem body in

[7] See Peter van Inwagen, "The Possibility of Resurrection," in *Immortality*, ed. Paul Edwards (New York: Macmillan, 1992), 242–46.

a life-preserving way; thus they constitute a continuation of the life of the original person.[8]

Let me now discuss five topics raised in the chapters by Merricks, Corcoran, and Cooper: the role of criteria in the debate, resurrection as reassembly, the "closest continuer" theory of personal identity, the possibility of duplication, and the relationship between Scripture and philosophy for Christian philosophers.

I. Criteria and Criterialism

One fascinating aspect of Trenton Merricks's chapter is his rejection of what he calls criterialism. Rightly or wrongly, most philosophers who discuss the problem of personal identity make use of criteria. Some proposed criteria of personal identity are spatiotemporal continuity, sameness of memory, sameness of body, immanent causal connectedness among the simples that constitute one's body, and uniqueness.[9] But Merricks holds that "there are no criteria of personal identity over time." So criterialism (the view that there are such criteria) is false. Merricks first argues that there are no good reasons to accept criterialism. Then in section 5 of his paper he briefly argues against it. His point is that given the sort of claim that criterialism is (it asserts that one state of affairs is a necessary and sufficient condition for a separate state of affairs), the fact that there is no reason to accept it is itself a reason to reject it. It follows, according to Merricks, that the identity relation (a primitive and unanalyzable relationship that holds between a person existing at one time and that same person existing later) can hold without any criterion or explanation at all. For if there were a true criterion of personal identity, it would serve as an explanation. The upshot is that even if we are unable to supply an informative criterion of personal identity that physicalist resurrection satisfies, physicalist resurrection may still be tenable.

Is this a good argument? Well, I have doubts. Let me ask: What exactly is a criterion? (Merricks, of course, explains clearly what he means by the term, but let me approach things in a slightly different way.) There are many ways in which this term is used in philosophy. Criteria have been

[8] The second and third models are suggested by Kevin Corcoran in his essay in this volume.

[9] In another essay, Merricks spells out in detail what a criterion of personal identity must be, and shows that some of the putative criteria that I have listed are not informative enough to count as criteria. See Trenton Merricks, "There Are No Criteria of Identity over Time," *Nous* 32, no. 1 (1988): 106–24.

suggested for (among many other things) meaningfulness, truth, validity, goodness, justice, virtue, and beauty. All of the following uses and more can be found in philosophical texts. A criterion is

a way of telling that ———,
compelling evidence for ———,
a test of ———,
a standard for ———,
a necessary condition for ———,
a sufficient condition for ———,
a necessary and sufficient condition for ———.

Notice that "criterion" can be used in an epistemological way, as in the first two uses (as ways in which *we can tell* what something consists in or that something is the case), or in a metaphysical way (as establishing what something *consists in*). Of course criteria are disputable, and philosophers often debate them. Even if we agree on what sort of thing a criterion must be, we may still dispute a particular proposed criterion. A criterion is useless in settling an issue between two disputants unless they agree on its adequacy. Indeed, people who propose criteria in the area of personal identity normally think of them as being either necessarily true or at least metaphysically necessary and sufficient conditions. Let's take a true criterion of personal identity to be: (1) metaphysical, and (2) a necessary and sufficient condition. A criterion of personal identity will thus establish what personal identity consists in, what it is for a given person A to be *the same person* as a later person B.[10]

Now the problem of personal identity is a particularly difficult and perplexing area of philosophy. Discussions of it in the philosophical literature often amount to arguing for and against competing modal intuitions. Thus the great prevalence of the "test case" method, in which a story is told which is made as plausible as possible and which the teller hopes will lead others to see things as the teller does.[11]

My problem with Merricks's argument is that I do not see how the abandonment of criterialism amounts to an advance in the debate. It is true that the critic can no longer use the absence of the satisfaction of a

[10] Merricks (ibid.) distances himself from the view that a criterion of personal identity tells us what personal identity consists in.

[11] Merricks grasps this point. He notes that "our fairly feeble faculties for discerning what is possible deliver no clear and justified judgments about the possibility of temporal gaps and resurrection" ("No Criteria of Identity," 108).

criterion as a club to beat over the head of the defender of physicalist resurrection. But what prevents that selfsame critic from presenting non-criteria-based arguments? Surely the same intuition that led the critic to propose (say) material continuity as a criterion of personal identity will still be there and needs to be answered. So I don't see how we are any better off than we were before. Although I agree with Merricks that temporal gaps do not rule out physicalist resurrection, temporal gaps still constitute a worry for many philosophers. And a successful defense of physicalist resurrection will have to include a way of assuaging that worry.

Presumably Merricks holds that once criterialism is rejected, (1) there is no explanation of identity holding between any *x* and any *y* (nothing *makes* the premortem person identical to the resurrected person); and (2) there are no remaining arguments that critics of physicalist resurrection can give except what amount to question-begging demands that one share their intuitions. But surely it is still open to such critics to raise the old criteria-based objections (for example, resurrection violates Reid's notion that things can come into existence no more than once; or, resurrection violates the spatiotemporal criterion of personal identity) in new, non-criteria-based ways.

Thus a critic might argue against resurrection as follows: (1) propose some statement S not as a criterion but simply as a *true* statement; and (2) show that resurrection is inconsistent with S. (Let's say that S is: "Things can come into existence no more than once.") Since we know that S is true and that resurrection is inconsistent with S (so it will be argued), we know that resurrection is false. Admittedly, this is not an argument to the effect that resurrection is *impossible;* but one suspects that the critic of resurrection will not mind the result that resurrection is *false.* (As a believer in resurrection, I reject this argument; but it *is* a non-criteria-based argument against resurrection.)

Now Merricks will doubtless reply that in affirming S such a critic is betraying an "overweening confidence" in her modal intuitions. And that may be correct. And if the critic responds that in denying S, Merricks is betraying an overweening confidence in *his* modal intuitions, Merricks will insist that he is neutral about the truth of S on purely philosophical grounds; he will only claim to know that S is false by revelation. So—he will say—it isn't a matter of his modal intuitions after all; it's a matter of confidence in Scripture. But surely scriptural teachings about resurrection only deny S if they are understood to presuppose *(a)* the truth of materialism, and *(b)* the falsity of immediate resurrection. Dualists who believe that the person exists during the interim period as an immaterial soul need not deny S. Accordingly, it seems that Merricks is going to have to argue against S, and it will not much matter whether he is arguing against a putative criterion of personal identity or a putative true statement—or indeed whether his rejection of S is philosophically or theologically motivated.

So, again, I don't see that defenders of physicalist resurrection are much better off than they were before the rejection of criterialism. Let me express the hope that we hear more from Merricks in the future on this score.

II. Resurrection as Reassembly

In the Patristic period, it was common for Christian writers to defend a reassembly model of resurrection. Resurrection after death simply meant that at the moment of resurrection God locates the atoms of which your body consisted at death, reassembles them, reanimates the whole, and thus reconstitutes you as a person. Merricks and Corcoran both hold this model to be untenable, and pretty much for the same reasons—the cannibalism problem and van Inwagen's counterexample (both to be explained below).

Now if reassembly is taken to mean that all my atoms at death will be reassembled in the correct way in the afterlife, and that thus it will be me in the afterlife (correct reassembly of all the old atoms is a sufficient condition of identity), Merricks and Corcoran are well within their rights in rejecting the theory; clearly, it *is* refuted by the cannibal case. But surely reassembly can be taken to be a more sophisticated theory than this (as it was by many of the Fathers). And the ways in which it needs to be made more sophisticated can easily been seen by attending to the two problems. So in this section of the paper I will defend reassembly, but in a slightly different version.

Suppose I die, a cannibal eats part of my corpse and then, the next day, he dies. Suppose then God wants to resurrect, via reassembly, both of us. But it seems that God cannot do so; some of the atoms of which my body consisted at the moment of my death are also atoms of which the cannibal's body consisted at the moment of his death. (Let's call them "shared atoms.") Who gets the shared atoms? Since there is no principled way of answering that question—so it is said—resurrection as reassembly is impossible.

But this is a premature conclusion. All that is required is that God consistently follow some sort of identity-preserving policy for what to do with the shared atoms. Augustine, for example, suggested that God award the shared atoms on the basis of who *first* possessed them (and will presumably use new atoms to fill in the empty spaces in the body of the one who *later* possessed the shared atoms).[12] Lots of other policies seem possible. I see nothing here that constitutes a serious threat to identity or to physicalist resurrection.

Peter van Inwagen objects to reassembly as follows: What if God here and now, in the presence of van Inwagen the adult philosopher, creates a replica of van Inwagen's ten-year-old self, using only atoms that were part of the ten-year-old's body but are not part of the adult philosopher's present body?[13] Which person would then be van Inwagen? Surely each could truthfully say, "I am van Inwagen." Now the intuitive answer to this question is to say that the adult philosopher is van Inwagen and that the ten-year-old is the impostor, being (as he would be) the result of a trick performed by God. But both Merricks and Corcoran think this reply is arbitrary on resurrection as reassembly, and that there is no principled reason for privileging the older van Inwagen with his later atoms.

But that is not so; there *is* such a principled reason—one that in my view applies to all versions of resurrection as reassembly. Surely resurrection always means the continuation of the bodily existence of the person who has died *at the psychological stage that that person had reached at death.* (By "psychological stage" I mean simply the overall beliefs, feelings, memories, intentions, and other personality characteristics that one has at a given point in time.) Nobody to my knowledge has ever seriously claimed that those who die at, say, age seventy are resurrected with the memories and personality that they had at, say, age ten (which would entail that sixty years of experience and memory are simply wiped out). And what is true of personality and experience is true of the body. The promise and model of the general resurrection for Christians is of course the resurrection of Jesus Christ (Rom. 8:11; I Cor. 15:20, 23; Phil. 3:20–21; I Thess. 4:14; I John 3:2). And notice that Jesus was not raised as a younger version of himself.[14] So resurrection also means the continuation of the bodily existence of the person who has died *at the physiological stage reached at death.*

[12] Augustine, *The Enchiridion on Faith, Hope, and Love* (Chicago: Henry Regnery, 1961), bk. 88. See also Augustine, *The City of God* (Garden City, N.Y.: Doubleday, 1958), 22.20.

[13] Van Inwagen, "Possibility of Resurrection," 120.

[14] Some church fathers toyed with the idea of elderly people being resurrected into much younger versions of their bodies. But this has never been a connected Christian teaching about resurrection, and so far as I know has never been applied to mental or personality characteristics.

Now in the general resurrection, perhaps God will change our bodies in certain ways in order to make them fit for the resurrection world; virtually all Christian writers about the resurrection have affirmed that God will do that. Still, what is resurrected is the seventy-year-old person, the body as it existed at death, not some earlier version.[15] Merricks is correct that having all the same atoms arranged in the same way is neither a necessary nor a sufficient condition for sameness of body. But it might be *part* of a sufficient condition, where another part is some sort of condition about the causal relationship between the body at its last living moment and its first resurrected moment.

In short, I see no serious problem for resurrection as reassembly (as I am understanding the theory) in either objection. Reassembly remains a viable method of resurrection that God can use.

III. Death and the "Closest Continuer" Theory

One main motivation for adopting some version of immediate resurrection is avoiding the philosophical problems that arise when there is said to be a temporal gap in someone's existence. But on the version of survival of death that Corcoran advocates, material continuity no longer counts as a necessary condition for the persistence of physical objects like human bodies; he stresses instead the need for a life-preserving causal relationship. And that, Corcoran continues, raises two problems: (1) it looks as if human beings don't truly die; and (2) it looks as if one is committed to some version of the "closest continuer" theory of personal identity. Corcoran himself, of course, holds that these points do not follow, and he argues against them. I agree with him but will oppose them in a different way.

The first objection is answered by a theological commitment incumbent upon all Christian views of resurrection: surviving death is not a natural attribute of human beings. The view is quite unlike, say, immortality of the soul, most defenders of which consider that immaterial souls quite naturally continue to exist after the death of the body—this is something that souls characteristically do. So it might be correct to say that human beings (who on this theory are identical to their immaterial souls) do not truly

[15] Merricks admits that neither objection to reassembly precludes the possibility of a resurrected person's body consisting of *some* of the atoms that his body consisted in at death. And I am suggesting that there can be cases where some will be enough to preserve identity.

die. Their bodies die, but *they* don't. But no Christian view of resurrection should say this. The point is rather that all human beings die and that death amounts to permanent annihilation of the person *apart from the miraculous intervention of God.* Just as the New Testament insists that "God raised Jesus from the dead," so every resurrected person lives on after death *only* because God acts to make it happen.[16]

Here indeed is my central difference with Corcoran at this point: I agree with him that "God essentially wills the good for God's human creatures." But I deny that this entails that God must resurrect them or in some other way provide for survival of death. I consider resurrection a free decision on God's part, a free gift of grace that is not required by God's goodness or righteousness. There are possible worlds in which humans are permanently annihilated at death.

The second objection is that if one accepts Corcoran's preferred model of physicalist resurrection, and if I am right in my above objection to Corcoran's argument about God's necessarily resurrecting us, then apparently one must give up on robust notions of identity and instead retire to a "closest continuer" analysis. On such a view, the best we can say is that someone in the afterlife is the closest available candidate for continuing the life of the deceased. And if that were true, physicalist resurrection would be in deep trouble. Indeed, I do not see how a Christian can hold this theory. Christian teachings entail that *we*—the very persons whom we are—will survive death. This is because we are to be rewarded or punished in the next life for what we are and do in this life, and it hardly seems fair to reward or punish someone in the afterlife for what a different person did in this life. So the question for Christians philosophers can never be, Under what conditions will some future person preserve what matters most to me? but rather, Under what conditions will some future person be the same person as me?

Why does it seem that closest continuer theories are the only ones available for those who hold Corcoran's version of resurrection (again, if I am right in what I argued against him above)? It is because of the possibility of duplication. On the two models of physicalist resurrection that he suggests, it is possible that *both* products of the fission of causal paths that occurs at death survive. (I am speaking here not of all cases of fission but only of cases where the fission produces two or more equally good claimants.) And if that were to happen, neither survivor (or no survivor)

[16] The same is true, in my opinion, of the continuation of the soul during the interim period between death and resurrection in dualist theories of Christian resurrection. The soul does not naturally survive death; it does so only because of divine intervention.

would be identical to the person who died; that person would not have survived; and the only available question is: Who is that person's closest surviving continuer? In other words, identity is now dependent upon the contingent fact that only one product of the fission of causal paths survives (the other is a corpse). And surely—so it will be said—this violates the principle of the necessity of identity (about which I will say more later).

Now one point to be made in response to this objection is that it is an objection to *all* theistic survival of death theories, and not just Corcoran's. If God exists and is omnipotent, it seems possible (in some strong sense of "possible") that God will bring it about that there are multiple Smiths in the afterlife who are equally strong claimants to Smithhood. (As we have seen, in his paper Corcoran argues against this point, but I remain unconvinced.) Indeed, God could perform that sort of trick quite apart from bodily death. God could bring it about, as I walk down the hall one fine day, that at a certain moment I disappear and two equally plausible Stephen Davises continue the walk down the hall, both created at the same instant by the same causal process, and thus proving (since identity is a transitive and symmetric relation, and since the two obviously are not numerically identical to each other) that Stephen Davis has perished. Doesn't this show, with the necessary changes, that the survival of any human being from any one moment to the next depends on something contingent, viz., God's not being in the mood to perform this particular trick?

IV. The Duplication Objection

Merricks, too, is worried about the possibility of duplication. He takes it as a prima facie objection to at least the most straightforward version of the psychological criterion of personal identity. So I had best say something about the duplication objection.[17] The point is not to claim that God actually *will* create (using in each case the same causal method with the appropriate causal connections to the premortem Smith) two, or two hundred, qualitatively similar Smiths in the afterlife, thus proving that the premortem Smith has not survived death. The defender of survival can always insist that God in fact will do no such thing. The point is that the *mere possibility* that

[17] To the best of my knowledge, it was introduced into the literature by Bernard Williams in his "Personal Identity and Individuation," *Proceedings of the Aristotelian Society* 57 (1956–57). It has since been discussed by many authors. My own more complete thoughts on it are found in *Risen Indeed,* chap. 7.

God *could* do such a thing renders identity with the premortem Smith and thus survival of death impossible. Or so it has seemed to many philosophers.

There are several moves that a defender of survival can make at this point. One move is to argue, as Corcoran does (noted above), that given God's aims and intentions it is in some important sense *impossible* for God to perform any such duplicative sleight-of-hand. But I have a theological concern with this move: in the light of traditional Christian insistence on the sovereignty of God, I believe it is important to preserve the freedom of God as much as possible. So although Corcoran may in the end be correct, I will explore his suggestion no further.

Another move is to introduce a new criterion of personal identity into the discussion, viz., uniqueness. And I do want to discuss this point. This criterion says that a necessary condition for a Smith-like person in the afterlife being identical to the premortem Smith is that the second Smith be unique. There must be no other exactly-as-qualified candidates for Smithhood in the afterlife. (A Smith-like person in the afterlife is *not* unique just in case there is another qualitatively similar and equally good candidate for Smithhood who was brought into existence in the afterlife through exactly the same causal process as was the first Smith-like person.)

This reply produces two objections. First, it is said, it absurdly makes the question of whether a given person in the afterlife really is the Smith who once lived depend in part on considerations that are wholly extraneous to Smith—for example, whether there are any competitors for Smithhood. Second, it is said, it absurdly makes identity to be contingent. Let me try to answer the two objections.

As to the first, it must be admitted that many philosophers see it as a powerful objection; they take it as a fixed requirement that (as Derek Parfit says) "Whether a future person will be me must depend only on the *intrinsic* features of the relationship between us. It cannot depend on what happens to other people."[18] And it is easy to see why they find this requirement plausible. John Perry points out that if uniqueness is allowed as a criterion of identity, God will have available a strange and (as we might say) nonviolent way of making sure that Smith does not survive death—not by permanently annihilating Smith (or by doing anything *to Smith*) but by making two or more duplicates of Smith, through the same causal process, at the point of death.[19] Parfit raises several entertaining

[18] Derek Parfit, *Reasons and Persons* (Oxford: Oxford University Press, 1986), 267.

[19] John Perry, *A Dialogue on Personal Identity and Immortality* (Indianapolis: Hackett, 1978), 32–33.

conundrums about teletransportation if uniqueness is allowed as a criterion of personal identity. For example, suppose Jones is teletransported from the earth to the moon, and that all is well and Jones is safely located on the moon. But now what if some clever scientists on Io have picked up the signal and, with their own teletransportation receiver, have brought it about that a duplicate Jones is simultaneously on Io? If so, Jones no longer exists.[20]

I hold that Parfit's requirement is false, that uniqueness *is* a criterion of personal identity, that identity *can* depend in part on matters that are extrinsic to the persons we are talking about, and that what results is odd but not incoherent. Let my try to establish these points.

Notice the following properties of persons:

being the shortest basketball player in the NBA
being the first person to climb K-2
being admired by the president of the United States
being a widow

These are properties such that whether a given person has them depends in part on properties of other persons. Whether you have the first property depends in part on whether any team in the NBA has signed a player who is shorter than you; whether you have the second depends in part on whether anybody climbed K-2 prior to your ascent; whether you have the third depends on the mental state or dispositions of (not you but) the president; whether you have the fourth depends in part on whether there is some person who is now dead and who was married to you at the time of his death.

Those who defend uniqueness as a criterion of personal identity can now simply suggest that properties like "having survived death" and "being identical to the Smith who died last year" are properties of this sort. Let me then distinguish between *nonrelational properties* and *relational properties*. The first sort are properties like "*x* is healthy," "*x* is a carpenter," and "*x* is forty years old." Intuitively they seem nonrelational because only one property bearer—viz., *x*—is mentioned in each statement. Relational properties would include "*x* is wearing a sweater," *x* "is taller than y," and "*x* loves y." In such cases, more than one property bearer is mentioned.

Let me suggest a way of determining whether a property is relational or nonrelational. It is more a rough-and-ready rule than a rigorous criterion.

[20] Parfit, *Reasons and Persons*, 199–200.

If a property F is relational, then if *x* is F, it follows directly that some *y* is G (where *y* is neither identical to nor a proper part of *x*; and where *y*'s having G is a contingent fact about *y*). Again, this rule gives us an intuitive feel for relationality more than an airtight criterion.

With relational properties, these sorts of things follow: it is logically impossible for you to have the property of wearing a sweater without the sweater having the property of being worn by you. It is logically impossible for me to have the property of being taller than my son without my son having the property of being shorter than I. It is logically impossible for you to have the property of loving your mother without your mother having the property of being loved by you. But this is not true of nonrelational properties. You can have the property of being healthy or being a carpenter or being forty years old without your having those properties directly entailing any contingent truth about the properties of any other thing.

Again, assuming that F is a relational property, then if *x* is F, it follows directly that some *y* is G. If *x* is in fact F, then some *y* is in fact G. That is, *x* cannot be F without *y* being G. So if *y* is not G, then *x* is not F. It follows, then, that so far as relational properties like F are concerned, one way of falsifying a claim that "*x* is F" is by discovering or showing that "*y* is G" is false.

This provides us with a rule-of-thumb test for determining whether some property F is relational or nonrelational. The test is epistemological rather than metaphysical: a property F is relational if it is possible directly to falsify any such claim as "*x* is F" by showing that the other relevant thing fails (or other relevant things fail) to have the relevant property G (or, in some cases, *have* the relevant property G). What the relevant property bearer *y* is, and whether it is one thing or several, and what the relevant property G is (the property that *y* either must have or fail to have if *x* is to be F) will normally be quite clear in the context. One can falsify the claim that you love your mother by showing that your mother does not have the property of being loved by you. One can falsify the claim that Sally is a widow by showing that Sam, the only husband Sally has ever had, is alive. But there is no direct way to falsify the claim that Jones is a carpenter by discovering or showing that some other thing fails (or some other things fail) to have some other property.

Armed with this rule, we can see that properties like "being the shortest basketball player in the NBA" (and the others listed in that group) are all relational. One can falsify the claim that *x* is the NBA's shortest player by showing or discovering that not all other NBA players have the property of being taller than *x* (or fail to have the property of being shorter than *x*). It follows that some properties are such that whether a given property bearer has them is in part a function of whether certain other property bearers have (or do not have) certain other properties. In short, whether x is the NBA's shortest player does not depend entirely on x's own intrinsic properties.

What then about properties like "x is identical to y" or "x has survived death"? We can now see that they are, contrary to what we might have expected, relational properties. It is possible to falsify claims like "Jones has survived death" by showing that two or more afterlife persons share a certain property, viz., "being completely plausible afterlife candidates for Joneshood." Whether Jones has survived death does not depend merely on the intrinsic properties of Jones.

I have been answering the first objection to the use of the uniqueness criterion as a solution to the possibility of duplication. The objection is that it is absurd to allow that considerations wholly extrinsic to Smith help determine whether the Smith in the afterlife is the same person as the Smith who once lived. My reply is that this result is odd but not absurd, that uniqueness is a criterion of personal identity, that properties such as "survives death" and "is identical to Smith" are relational properties (which is the cause of the oddness noted above), and that the duplication objection to survival of death accordingly fails.

The second objection is that the introduction of the uniqueness criterion absurdly makes identity to be contingent, when as a matter of fact any such statement as "$x = y$" is, if true, necessarily true. Let me now turn to that objection.

I quite agree that if Smith is identical to Smith, then, necessarily, Smith is identical to Smith (that is, $S = S \supset \Box [S = S]$). Identity is a relation that, if it holds, must hold necessarily. And it seems that the introduction of the uniqueness requirement renders identity contingent by making the question whether the Smith who exists in the afterlife is identical to the Smith who once lived depend on contingent facts like whether there are any equally good competitors to Smithhood in the afterlife. It will be said, then, that the introduction of the uniqueness criterion makes necessary truths into contingent truths because Smith's being identical to Smith is made to depend on various contingencies. And that, it will be said, is absurd.

But surely something has gone wrong here. Suppose that the Stephen Davis who writes these lines in 1999 (call him SD_2) is identical to the Stephen Davis (call him SD_1) who saw Claremont for the first time in 1965. Now if "$SD_1 = SD_2$," then by the necessity of identity, it follows that "$\Box\, SD_1 = SD_2$." But if that statement is true, doesn't it follow that the statement "God permanently and completely annihilates Stephen Davis in

December 1975" is not only false but necessarily false? But that seems false, no? Didn't God have it within God's power, in December 1975, to annihilate me permanently and completely? The lesson that I draw from this argument is that the identity of one person with a later person, necessary though it is, depends on certain contingencies (like God not deciding to annihilate me in December 1975).

Notice that SD_1 is numerically identical to both SD_1 and SD_2 but is only qualitatively identical to SD_1. (SD_1 and SD_2 will obviously have different properties, such as their ages.) Now SD_1's numerical identity to SD_1 does not depend on anything contingent. It is either a brute fact or (if this in the end is different) a substitution-instance of one of the laws of logic, the Law of Identity. So I am not saying that all cases of *x* being numerically identical to something depend on certain contingencies. I make this claim only about the identity that obtains between two different temporal episodes of one and the same person, like SD_1's numerical identity with SD_2.[21]

V. Scripture and Christian Philosophy

John Cooper's essay raises in a striking way an issue that is of concern to all Christian philosophers: What is the proper relationship between the teachings of Scripture and the work of philosophy? This is a complex and much discussed question. I can only make a few remarks about it.

Like all other human beings, Christian philosophers want to know what to believe. And on some issues about which we are curious, both philosophy and Scripture are possible sources of information. This is surely true of resurrection and the afterlife. Most Christian philosophers see themselves as living under a methodological obligation to make all their beliefs that are relevant to matters on which the Bible speaks consistent with Scripture. I would hold that the Bible is trustworthy and reliable on all matters on which it speaks; Scripture is the source of religious truth above all other sources and the norm or guide to religious truth above all other norms or guides.[22]

If God wants to redeem fallen human beings, it seems sensible to believe that God will communicate God's method of salvation to those human

[21] This identity also depends on other sorts of (what I take to be) contingencies that I have not discussed, e.g., contingent facts about the nature of time and the persistence of objects.

[22] For further discussion of this point, see my "Tradition, Scripture, and Theological Authority," in *Philosophy and Theological Discourse*, ed. Stephen T. Davis (London: Macmillan, 1997).

beings so that they can know it and take advantage of it. Christians hold that this is precisely what God has done. They say that in Scripture *God speaks to us.* Accordingly, the Bible is unlike all other books; it is revelatory. Our received tradition is that all proposals on any subject that is relevant to Christian thought and practice are to be judged preeminently in the light of Scripture.[23]

The Bible says nothing about many issues that are of concern to philosophers. And on other such issues, the Bible says some things that might be relevant, but the problem is that the Bible is not a work of philosophy or even philosophy of religion. The concerns and questions of the biblical writers are different from those of contemporary philosophers.

Here are three questions that Merricks, Corcoran, Cooper, and I have been discussing and that seem to be addressed, more or less, in Scripture:

1. What is a human being?
2. When does resurrection occur?
3. How does resurrection occur?

Question 1 includes issues like dualism versus physicalism. Are human beings identical to or do they at least essentially consist in their bodies? Or do human being consist of physical bodies and immaterial souls, where the soul is the essence of the person? Or what? Here I wish to associate myself fully with John Cooper's conclusions on this matter. Question 2 addresses the question whether resurrection occurs immediately at death or in the eschaton. Here too I believe Cooper has sensitively surveyed the teachings of the Bible. I too am of the opinion that Scripture teaches that the general resurrection will not occur until the end of history. As to question 3, there is only a little in Scripture that is relevant to it. Philosophers are pretty much free, so far as I can see, to speculate about the physics of resurrection and the relationship between one's earthly body and one's resurrected body in the eschaton. Paul's simile—he likens this relationship to that between a plant and the seed that it came from (I Cor. 15:35–49)—is about all that I can think of that might be relevant.

Now it would be taken as the height of absurdity by secular philosophers if anyone were to suggest—as I am suggesting—that the teachings of the Bible and philosophical conclusions can be relevant to each other. But I believe that it is acceptable for Christian philosophers in certain instances to

[23] Obviously, like any text, the Bible needs to be interpreted. Sadly, I have no space to speak to that problem on this occasion.

allow their philosophical opinions to influence how they approach the Bible. They will be poor exegetes, however, if their philosophical views constrain the Bible, if the Scriptures are not free to speak as the Holy Spirit would have them speak. And on other occasions it is acceptable for them to allow what they take to be the teachings of Scripture to influence them as philosophers.

Let me say a word about each point. Given what the Fathers of the church called "the rule of faith," that is, the received and accepted way of interpreting the macro-message of Scripture (which was for them synonymous with the Christian message itself), I believe Christian philosophers are allowed to approach the Bible with certain controversial philosophical theses intact. Sound Christian exegesis and theology, in my view, even require them. Let me mention a few. (This will be very sketchy; each point—I know well—cries out for discussion.) First, *metaphysical monism is false.* This is the view that there is but one reality, and all differentiation is illusory; Christian theology requires at least that God is one thing and the world is a different thing. Second, *metaphysical materialism is false.* This is the view that the physical universe exhausts reality; there are no nonphysical objects; Christian theology requires that God (at least) is incorporeal. (This leaves open, of course, whether physicalism is true of human beings.) Third, *circular views of time are false.* This is the view that time and history endlessly repeat themselves; there is no novelty, and thus no one temporal event can have eternal significance; Christian theology requires that time is linear—it is moving in a certain direction, toward the Kingdom of God. (This leaves open, of course, whether the A Theory or the B Theory of time is true.)

Fourth, *moral relativism is false.* This is the view that all moral judgments and claims are relative to the person who makes them or the society she comes from; there are no transpersonal or transsocietal truths in morality; Christian theology requires that certain moral claims are true (ultimately coming, as they do, from God) quite apart from what any human being may think about them. Fifth, *hard determinism is false* (along with any view that similarly denies human moral responsibility). This is the view that because every human thought, motivation, decision, and action is wholly determined by antecedent conditions, no human beings are ever morally responsible; they can be rewarded or punished for prudential or utilitarian reasons, but they never "deserve" reward or punishment; Christian theology requires that human beings can legitimately be rewarded or punished for what they do for reasons of desert. Sixth, *epistemological skepticism is false.* This is the view (and there are many versions of it) that no knowledge-claim can ever be justified; that nothing (or very little) can be known; Christian theology requires that knowledge is possible precisely because God created us with the capacity to know; human cognitive capacities are uniquely designed by God for this purpose.

And it is also acceptable for Christian philosophers to allow the teachings of Scripture to influence their philosophical views. Indeed, I think Christian philosophers are to be encouraged not to fear doing that. It is true that it is part of the official view of philosophy's methodology that philosophers accept nothing "on authority," just because the Bible says so or just because Plato said so. (Whether philosophers actually follow that rule is another matter.) Still, in my opinion, Christian philosophers must not follow the procedure that was apparently followed by a Christian biology professor whom I once met and who told me, "I keep my faith in one pocket and my science in another." We are instead required to integrate all that we know, our faith and our learning, the teachings of Scripture and our research. One of the things that this means concretely is (as Alvin Plantinga has argued in recent years): don't give up too quickly on a given teaching from the Bible or theology just because it seems to conflict with current academic orthodoxy.

Physicalist resurrection is a legitimate option for Christian philosophers. Although I no longer see myself as a member of the team, I wish its defenders well. For scriptural reasons, temporary nonexistence seems to me a better model than immediate resurrection, despite the presence of the temporal gap. There are texts that can be interpreted along the lines of immediate resurrection, but I agree with John Cooper that the preponderance of scriptural teaching is that the resurrection occurs not at death but in the eschaton. But if this scriptural problem can be overcome, then I think either of the two models discussed by Corcoran seems promising; Peter van Inwagen's model is philosophically defensible, possibly impregnable, but it does seem to entail God fooling us in a massive way, which some might take to be theologically questionable.[24]

I want to stress my own hope that Christian philosophers not give up too quickly on reassembly (the model of resurrection preferred by the Fathers of the church). It seems to me that this theory can be successfully defended. Some philosophers find ridiculous the idea that God must some day cast about, locate, and reassemble the atoms of which a person's body consisted at death. But I do not. And one slight consideration in

[24] It is not dissimilar to the role of God in occasionalism, where God's tireless actions are said to give us the quite mistaken impression that physical events can cause mental events, and vice versa.

favor of reassembly (as opposed to no material continuity at all) is that it is, I think, the most natural reading of I Corinthians 15. Paul seems to be suggesting there that the earthly body *becomes* or *changes into* (rather than *is replaced by*) the resurrection body, just as a seed becomes or changes into a plant. But I do not want to be interpreted as saying that Christian views of resurrection *require* reassembly. As I have argued elsewhere,[25] it seems perfectly possible for God to use entirely new atoms in constructing our resurrection bodies as long as the atoms are configured in the right way, the causal path is correct, and the memory and uniqueness criteria are satisfied.

If philosophy were all that we had, if God—like the God of eighteenth-century and contemporary Deism—never spoke to human beings or otherwise intervened in human affairs, we would doubtless reason our way to hell. But God has graciously spoken to us—so Christianity declares—and has promised, among other things, that we will be raised from the dead. Merricks is quite right that for physicalists, all hope of the resurrection rests on the promise of God. My only caveat is that this is true for all Christians philosophers, dualists as well as physicalists.

[25] Davis, *Risen Indeed*, 107–9.

Contributors

LYNNE BAKER is Professor of Philosophy at the University of Massachusetts at Amherst. She is the author of numerous articles and three books: *Saving Belief: A Critique of Physicalism*; *Explaining Attitudes: A Practical Approach to the Mind;* and *Persons and Bodies: A Constitution View.*

JOHN COOPER is Professor of Philosophical Theology at Calvin Theological Seminary. He is the author of *Body, Soul and Life Everlasting: Biblical Theology and the Monism-Dualism Debate.*

KEVIN CORCORAN is Assistant Professor of Philosophy at Calvin College. He works primarily in metaphysics, philosophy of mind, and philosophy of religion and has published articles in these areas.

STEPHEN T. DAVIS is Professor of Philosophy and Religious Studies at Claremont McKenna College. He has written over fifty articles and has written or edited some thirteen books, including *Encountering Evil: Live Options in Theodicy*; *Risen Indeed: Making Sense of the Resurrection*; and *God, Reason, and Theistic Proofs.*

JOHN FOSTER is Lecturer in Philosophy at the University of Oxford and Fellow of Brasenose College. He is the author of *The Case for Idealism*; *Ayer*; and *The Immaterial Self: A Defence of the Cartesian Dualist Conception of the Mind.* His main interests are in epistemology, philosophy of mind, and philosophical logic.

STEWART GOETZ is Professor of Philosophy at Ursinus College. He works primarily in action theory and the philosophy of mind. He has published articles in the *American Philosophical Quarterly*, *Faith and*

Philosophy, Mind, Philosophical Studies, and *Philosophy and Phenomenological Research.*

WILLIAM HASKER is Distinguished Professor of Philosophy at Huntington College. He is author of *God, Time and Knowledge* and *The Emergent Self* and has published many articles in the areas of metaphysics and philosophy of religion.

JAEGWON KIM is currently William Perry Faunce Professor of Philosophy at Brown University. He has taught at University of Michigan, Cornell University, and Johns Hopkins University and is the author of *Supervenience and Mind*; *Philosophy of Mind*; and *Mind in a Physical World.*

E. J. LOWE is Professor of Philosophy at the University of Durham, U.K., specializing in metaphysics, philosophy of mind, philosophy of logic, and early modern philosophy. He is the author of *Kinds of Being*; *Locke on Human Understanding*; *Subjects of Experience*; *The Possibility of Metaphysics*; and *An Introduction to the Philosophy of Mind.* He is currently working on a book titled *A Survey of Metaphysics.*

BRIAN LEFTOW is currently Professor of Philosophy at Fordham University. He is the author of *Time and Eternity*; *Divine Ideas* (forthcoming); *Aquinas on Metaphysics* (forthcoming); and over forty articles in medieval philosophy, metaphysics, and philosophy of religion.

TRENTON MERRICKS is Associate Professor of Philosophy at Virginia Commonwealth University. He has published over twenty papers, many of which deal with personal identity or the nature of persistence.

TIMOTHY O'CONNOR is Associate Professor of Philosophy at Indiana University. He is the author of *Persons and Causes: The Metaphysics of Free Will*; *Agents, Causes, and Events*; and various articles in metaphysics, philosophy of mind, and philosophy of religion.

ERIC OLSON is Lecturer in Philosophy at the University of Cambridge. He is the author of *The Human Animal: Personal Identity without Psychology* and many articles on metaphysics and personal identity.

CHARLES TALIAFERRO is Professor of Philosophy at St. Olaf College. He is the author of *Consciousness and the Mind of God* and *Contemporary Philosophy of Religion* and the coeditor of *The Companion to Philosophy of Religion.* He has published in the *Philosophical Quarterly, Philosophy, Philosophy and Phenomenological Research,* and elsewhere.

INDEX